PENGUIN BOO

The GI Bride

Iris Jones Simantel grew up in Dagenham and South Oxhey, before moving to the US with her GI husband Bob at the tender age of sixteen. She now resides in Devon where she enjoys writing as a pastime. Her first memoir about her childhood, *Far from the East End*, beat several thousand other entries to win the Saga Life Stories Competition.

The GI Bride

IRIS JONES SIMANTEL

PENGUIN BOOKS

PENGUIN BOOKS

Published by the Penguin Group
Penguin Books Ltd, 80 Strand, London WC2R ORL, England
Penguin Group (USA) Inc., 375 Hudson Street, New York, New York 10014, USA
Penguin Group (Canada), 90 Eglinton Avenue East, Suite 700, Toronto, Ontario, Canada M4P 2Y3
(a division of Pearson Penguin Canada Inc.)
Penguin Ireland, 25 St Stephen's Green, Dublin 2, Ireland
(a division of Penguin Books Ltd)
Penguin Group (Australia), 707 Collins Street, Melbourne, Victoria 3008, Australia
(a division of Pearson Australia Group Pty Ltd)
Penguin Books India Pvt Ltd, 11 Community Centre,
Panchsheel Park, New Delhi – 110 017, India
Penguin Group (NZ), 67 Apollo Drive, Rosedale, Auckland 0632, New Zealand
(a division of Pearson New Zealand Ltd)
Penguin Books (South Africa) (Pty) Ltd, Block D, Rosebank Office Park, 181 Jan Smuts Avenue,
Parktown North, Gauteng 2193, South Africa

Penguin Books Ltd, Registered Offices: 80 Strand, London WC2R ORL, England

www.penguin.com

First published 2013
001

Typeset in Garamond by Palimpsest Book Production Ltd, Falkirk, Stirlingshire
Printed in Great Britain by Clays Ltd, St Ives plc

ISBN: 978-1-405-91264-8

www.greenpenguin.co.uk

MIX
Paper from
responsible sources
FSC
www.fsc.org FSC® C018179

Penguin Books is committed to a sustainable
future for our business, our readers and our planet.
This book is made from Forest Stewardship
Council™ certified paper.

ALWAYS LEARNING   **PEARSON**

To the more than 100,000 GI brides who left their homes and families to follow their hearts, but especially to those brave young women who fought loneliness, discrimination and disillusionment.

To the parents and families left behind, who didn't know if they would ever see their daughters again. Some never did.

To the Transatlantic Brides and Parents Association (TBPA), founded by the families of GI brides to support each other in their longing for daughters who lived across a vast ocean. The TBPA also championed affordable travel between America and Britain by sponsoring charter flights between the two countries. It subsequently formed American chapters to enable previously isolated GI brides to form a supportive sisterhood. The organization remains strong and continues to support many British ex-pats.

Together Again is the title of the TBPA magazine, and that was what we daughters and our parents hoped and prayed we would be: together again.

Contents

Foreword

It is 16 February 1955 and I find myself, at the age of sixteen, one of hundreds of British and German 'GI brides', about to embark on the journey of our lives. We have all said goodbye to our families, homes and countries, to travel halfway around the world to begin a new life with our American husbands in a country we have only seen or heard of in movies or on television. Is everyone as frightened and excited as I am? What can we expect in this strange new world? Will we be welcomed? Will I ever see my family again? What if I've just made the biggest mistake of my life – or are all of my dreams about to come true?

All of these questions, and more, crowd my mind as the USS *General R. E. Callan* begins its long voyage across the Atlantic Ocean. There is no turning back now: in a matter of days, I, with all the other apprehensive GI brides, will set foot on American soil. Our new lives will begin. How had I, a mere child, many thought, arrived in this place, at this time? How had this journey begun? And how will it end?

1: Looking Back

Life had not been easy for me in England. It had begun when my mother almost gave birth to me in the toilet and, in some ways, it didn't improve a great deal after that.

I was born into poverty on 5 July 1938, in the East End of London. My parents were living temporarily with my grandparents in Station House on Blackwall Pier, where my grandfather was the stationmaster. The pier, Brunswick Wharf and the railway station were part of the East India Docks on the banks of the River Thames in Poplar, which is situated within the sound of the famous Bow Bells, at the St Mary-le-Bow Church. According to *The Victorian Dictionary*, 'Only those born within the sound of Bow Bells are properly called Cockneys.' I was not always proud of my Cockney label and heritage: to the upper classes, the term suggested indolence, dishonesty, illiteracy, lack of manners and absence of personal hygiene. That label, and the tell-tale accent, defined a Cockney's station in life and served to trap them in an often cruel, discriminating world.

My older brother, Peter, and I were born in peacetime Britain, but that peace was soon shattered when war was declared against Germany in 1939. My earliest memories are of air-raid sirens, anti-aircraft guns and bombs exploding; worst of all was the sound of my mother crying. In my fright and confusion, I would crouch in a corner, to hide my own tears. At night, we hunkered down in our air-raid shelters, feeling the earth shudder beneath us as bombs landed nearby. Afterwards, we often had to wipe away the dust and dirt that filtered through the cracks in the corrugated-iron roof. Filled with terror and wishing my mother would hold me close to her, I often cried myself to sleep, wondering what it would feel like to be blown to pieces by a bomb.

My mother suffered a series of nervous breakdowns during those years, and my father was a physical wreck from working at the Woolwich Arsenal, which was bombed almost nightly, and from continuous nights on fire-watch duty. I have no doubt that the physical and psychological illnesses people experienced at that time were greatly exacerbated by sleep deprivation and inadequate nutrition.

Peter was one of the first children to be evacuated out of London in what the government called 'Operation Pied Piper', the scheme to keep Britain's children safe. Because I was younger, I wasn't evacuated until much later: Germany had developed unmanned missiles, the V1 and V2, that were about to be deployed in a new nightmare of attacks.

My family spent the war years wondering if we would survive, or if we would ever see each other again. We could only wait and hang on to hope. My brother and I had different experiences at our wartime billets: Peter's was not happy but I was lucky enough to be taken in by a kind family in South Wales. The local children ignored me when I first arrived in the coal-mining town of Maerdy, but although I was lonely, I made happy times for myself, playing on the beautiful mountainsides of the Rhondda Valley. Luckier than many other evacuees, I had plenty to eat and was well cared for. It broke my heart when I had to leave my Welsh family to return to the family I had begun to forget.

My family all survived the war, but I believe we came out of it with scars, not necessarily physical – although my father had many from his work at the arsenal – but emotional. They stayed with us throughout our lives. When Peter and I returned to our parents after the war ended, we found it hard to readjust to each other. For a while, we were like strangers in our own home, and I know my mother had a difficult time dealing with us. We were not the same children who had left years earlier when we were just five or six years old. Our parents were different too: the war had changed them. There seemed to be an invisible wall between my mother and we children, which seemed to strengthen when, in late 1946, she gave birth to a third child, our brother Robert. As soon as he arrived, he demanded almost all of Mum's attention, and she slipped once more into depression. Perhaps it was what we now call post-natal depression, but I learned that it had much to do with my father's habitual philandering.

Approximately two years later, as the memories of war faded, London's poor were encouraged to move out of the city, to enable the clearing and rebuilding of the slums and bomb-damaged areas. The government offered brand new houses on newly built London County Council (LCC) housing estates, located mostly in rural areas. Many Londoners refused to leave the city, but when we were offered the opportunity, Dad seized it. He decided we would have a better quality of life if we moved away.

On 1 May 1948, the Jones family trundled off in a borrowed truck, loaded with all our worldly possessions, and headed for the South Oxhey estate, which was near to Watford in Hertfordshire. We were met with a troubling situation: the houses were new, modern and inviting, but with little of the infrastructure of the new town in place, we all wondered how we would survive. The houses sat in a sea of mud and building detritus; there were few roads and no pavements, schools or shops. We looked at one another, each of us thinking, What's Dad got us into now? Our new life was about to begin, and at that moment, we all dreaded it, none more so than poor Mum. I can still hear her saying to Dad, 'And they call this progress?'

For us children, life in the countryside, in spite of the mud and lack of amenities, was exciting. There were fields and woods to explore, berries and bluebells to pick, trees to climb and camps to build. Even Mum seemed to relax a little. She made us all laugh one morning when we awakened to find that cows from a nearby field had trampled down our flimsy fence and were wallowing in the garden. 'Blimey, them's big sparrows,' she said. It was wonderful to hear her make a joke because it didn't happen often, especially in those early post-war days.

It was fun taking the bus to school in Watford, even though we were not welcome there. The local people didn't want us so-called 'dirty Londoners', and we suffered a great deal of derision and discrimination. That changed when we were provided with our own schools and the rest of the amenities we needed to be independent of their

4

precious resources. I felt much happier when I discovered that my best friend, Sheila McDonald, had also moved with her family to the new estate – neither of us could believe our luck.

Mum had never seemed happy. She battled constantly with depression and was never able to show me the affection I craved. As a family, we were always trying to make her laugh but she'd usually tell us to stop mucking about. When I tried to get close to her, she pushed me away, telling me to stop bothering her. It was worse after she gave birth to my youngest brother, Christopher, and once again fell into a deep depression. This time it was so bad that she went away with the baby to convalesce, leaving me, at the age of twelve, to take care of the family. I loved being woman-of-the-house. For the first time ever, I felt wanted and needed, but when Mum came home, I was invisible again.

In my early teens, I began to spend time with some fun-loving young neighbours. From them, I received an extremely colourful sex education; my mother never talked about sex, and certainly not to me. She was too embarrassed to buy sanitary towels; she simply used pieces of old rags, which she laundered and reused. Of course, I knew nothing of this: she was good at hiding the things she didn't want anyone to know about.

During our early years in South Oxhey, my father worked at Odhams, the printing company, in Watford. He was instrumental in starting the estate's first Sunday school, perhaps trying to mend his philandering ways. When that affiliation ended, he joined the Watford Spiritualist Church and was soon involved in healing and clairvoyance. He became increasingly popular and respected in the world of spiritualism, and was eventually president of the church. He spent more and more time away from home, while Mum became increasingly withdrawn. She wanted nothing to do with the church and wouldn't join in when Dad wanted to talk about it so I became Dad's audience at home. I loved listening to him: at last, someone was paying attention to me. He and I drew closer, but that, I believe, drove a bigger wedge between my mother and me. She was jealous, and if I'd thought she didn't like me before, I was sure of it now.

When I reached fourteen or fifteen, I began dating. According to Mum, I was boy crazy, and she told me off endlessly. I talked back to her now, telling her that at least someone was paying me some attention because she certainly wasn't. 'What do you want from me?' she'd shout. I'd tell her that a few kind words would be nice. She would turn her back and walk away, shaking her head as though I'd asked for the impossible.

Yes, I went out with lots of boys, and sometimes young men who were far too old for me, even though I was soon tired of fighting off their demands for sex. I was also fed up with insults about my virginity. But just when I'd decided that my mother and grandmother were right when they claimed that men were after only one thing, I met my Mr Wonderful. Not only did he prove them wrong, he brought a ray of sunshine into my life, which began to change.

I'd been to the cinema with a girlfriend and we were on our way to catch the train home when we heard someone call out to us. Two American soldiers asked us for directions. Neither of us wanted anything to do with American servicemen because girls seen with them were called 'Yanks' meat'. No one with any self-respect wanted that label attached to her. We tried to ignore them but we were finally convinced that their intentions were honourable: they really needed directions. Well, one thing led to another: they ended up taking the same train as us and then they walked us part of the way home. We talked until the street lights went out, leaving us in the pitch dark, and we still hadn't given them directions back to their base. It was after midnight by now and my friend and I knew we'd be in big trouble if we didn't get home soon. We scribbled directions on a piece of paper and off they went.

At that time I was just fifteen, had recently left school and was working in a dress shop in Watford. There was no way I wanted to get involved with American soldiers and I didn't think they'd be interested in me. I assumed they were after the older girl I was with, but she was less interested even than I was because her father was an abusive brute – he would have killed her if he'd found out she'd been talking to them. As it happened, he gave her a black eye for being out late, then threw her and her clothes out into the street.

The only thing my mother worried about was what the neighbours would think about me coming home late. She would have been mortified if someone had seen me talking to Americans.

The next week I was putting new stock away in the shop when the manageress called me into her office and told me there was a telephone call for me. I was shocked and thought it must be a mistake, especially since I didn't know anyone who had a phone. I was even more shocked when the caller turned out to be the good-looking American soldier I had met the previous weekend; he wanted to take me out on a date. I was almost speechless. He explained that he had remembered where I'd said I worked and had looked it up in the phonebook. My God, I thought, he's either desperate or actually interested in me. I knew I couldn't talk to him for long on the phone so I agreed to see him the following Saturday. Until then, I had to keep it secret from my parents and control the butterflies and palpitations that stayed with me for the rest of that week.

At last Saturday arrived and I wondered if he would turn up. He did. He was waiting for me outside the shop when I finished work. We grinned like Cheshire cats, and although we had planned to go to the movies, we never did. We had dinner at a little café and talked until it was time to catch the last train home. His name was Bob Irvine, and not only was he a perfect gentleman, he was funny and kind. Above all, he treated me like a real lady. He asked if he could see me again and I told him I'd have to think about it because I knew my parents wouldn't approve. I asked him to phone me the following week. I also explained that we had no phone at home and that he would have to ring me at work. He was shocked that anyone could still be without a telephone, but he hadn't been in England long enough to learn of the many differences between our two countries.

After one or two more dates with Bob, I mustered the courage to ask my parents how they would feel if I invited a young American soldier home for Sunday tea. Eyebrows shot up, mouths flew open, and I thought that the house and my parents might explode. The inquisition began. How did I know an American soldier? What was I thinking? Was I insane? And, of course, an unspoken question hung in the air: what would the neighbours think?

Where we lived, it was almost impossible to avoid meeting Americans. Their military bases surrounded Watford. There were air force bases at Bovingdon and Ruislip, and an army base at Bushey. I believe there were then as many as twenty-four US bases in southern England, and most of the young men and women stationed there were serving their mandatory two years' national service; they were almost all single and undoubtedly 'feeling their oats'. The Second World War might have been over for seven or eight years but the American presence in Europe was still strong.

In the 1950s the attitude to American service personnel in England had changed: during the war years, I don't believe young women who went out with 'Yanks' had been stigmatized as they were now because most eligible young British men were away fighting. The war had brought new priorities: civilians as well as the military were at risk of losing their lives and everyone seemed to grab what joy they could. When peace came, young British men resented the American presence and their perceived domination in the area of dating; they didn't think they stood a chance against the Yanks with all their money, charm and confidence. Most young Englishmen were serving or had just completed their own mandatory national service; they had far less money to spend on girls. 'Yanks' meat' implied that those girls were selling themselves to the higher bidder. I hated the thought of acquiring that label, but what can you do when Fate steps in?

9

I knew how my family would react to my friendship with an American soldier, but how must Mum's friend, Mrs Gradley, have felt when all three of her daughters married Americans and left England?

After I'd convinced my parents that Bob was just a lonely boy away from home for the first time, they agreed I could bring him home occasionally for Sunday tea.

Well, it wasn't long before my family and I had fallen in love with the handsome young American soldier, and our courtship began. It quickly became apparent that our relationship was not just a passing fancy and soon Bob asked me to marry him. When I told him I couldn't because I was only fifteen, he was angry and let me know it. About a week later, he came back to the house and said he was willing to wait for me for as long as was necessary: he loved me and would do whatever he could to ensure that we ended up together.

The original plan was for him to return to the United States and for me to join him when I was eighteen. However, knowing how miserable we would both be if we were separated, my parents reluctantly allowed us to be married. We became engaged on 5 July 1954, my sixteenth birthday, and were married on 16 October.

Within a few months of our wedding, I sailed away from England, away from my history and all I had known. Now, with the love I had always lacked, and my heart full of hope, I looked forward to a new and better life in America.

2: Voyage to America

'Seasickness: at first, you are so sick you are afraid
you will die and then you are so sick you are afraid
you won't die.' Mark Twain

Oh, my God, if anyone had told me how ill I would be on that voyage, I might still have been an unmarried, virginal teenager. But, there I was, sixteen years old, the child-bride of an American soldier, about to sail across the Atlantic Ocean on a troop ship to a new life and an uncertain future in the United States of America.

The USS *General R. E. Callan* was a converted battleship. Its voyage had originated in Bremerhaven, Germany, and it was transporting GIs and their families back to the United States after their tours of duty. The lumbering vessel had none of the luxuries found on large commercial liners and, of course, everything was painted the regulation battleship grey. The gangways leading to the cabins were narrow, barely allowing room for passing. The four-berth cabins were tiny, and when I first saw where I would be living for the coming days, I could almost hear my mother saying, 'Crikey, you can't swing a cat in 'ere,' and she would have been right. Dependants, and perhaps officers, were assigned to those cabins, while lower-ranking servicemen travelled, slept and ate separately, on a lower deck referred to as the hold. My cabin was equipped with two double-tiered bunks, four narrow lockers and two small washbasins set into a vanity-type counter. I shared this small space with three other women, all of them older than I was, of course.

We shoved our suitcases under the bunks, then introduced ourselves. First, there was Barbara McCarthy, who sounded posh and was very attractive; she was from Leeds.

'How do you do?' she said. 'Nice to meet you.'

Blimey, I thought, she's not going to be much fun.

Next, there was Gladys, I don't recall her last name, but she was from the north of England and had a broad northern accent. "Ow do? 'Ow are ye?' she said, pumping my hand. Gladys was short and chubby, and had served in the British Army, which perhaps explained the manly handshake.

Last, there was an American. 'Hi, girls,' she drawled, in what I later learned was a Southern accent: she was from Atlanta, Georgia. I can't remember her name but I do remember that she was pregnant and had little to do with us three English girls since she had a number of American friends on board.

We flipped a coin to see who would get which bunk. I got a lower bunk but later gave it to the American girl who, because of her pregnancy, had morning sickness.

Soon after I'd stowed away my few belongings, Bob came to find me. 'Come on, honey, let's check out this lovely hotel,' he said, and hand in hand we explored the ship. First, and most important, we found the showers and toilets.

'Good thing I brought a dressing-gown,' I said. 'I

wouldn't fancy walkin' all this way in me nightie, not with all these men around.' Next, we discovered the dining rooms, the movie theatre, then walked around the different decks. Knowing that the ship was about to set sail, we stayed on the main deck, standing at the rail, arms wrapped around each other, until my uncle, who had come to see us off, disappeared into the distance, and darkness swallowed England's coastline. There was no going back now, and I felt a dull ache in my heart as we went below for a meal.

Our first day at sea was not too bad, but as the water became choppier, I began to feel queasy. I'd been told that seasickness usually passed in a day or two but, oh, how wrong that turned out to be – at least for me. The Atlantic became increasingly rough, making it more and more difficult to navigate the corridors and stairwells. People were being sick everywhere and on one occasion, as I attempted to make my way up a spiral stairway, someone vomited on me from two decks above.

'Shit!' I heard someone mutter, and I couldn't have agreed more. I would struggle to one of the water fountains in the corridor for sips of ice-cold water, which I thought might make me feel better, only to find that it, too, had become a repository for vomit.

'I'll bring you some saltine crackers,' offered Barbara. 'They're supposed to help when you feel sick.' I already knew that was what our pregnant cabin mate was surviving on, so I tried some. It might have helped some people but I was an exception. I remember going into a toilet cubicle on a day when the sea was particularly rough and being unable to sit on the commode because of the pitching and lurching of the ship. I kept flying head first into the door, each time almost knocking myself out. Eventually I grabbed at the toilet-paper holder, trying to save myself from further injury, but it came away in my hand and I crashed to the urine-soaked floor. There I sat, bawling my eyes out.

During the second day of the voyage, we were called for lifeboat practice: a nightmare. Those of us who were seasick had a dreadful time getting ourselves into the life-jackets and finding our allotted mustering points. It must have been far worse for the mothers: they had to hold their children while both were wearing those cumbersome jackets – it looked almost impossible. Many of those women were German and could speak no English. I supposed they were asking questions about what to do and where to go, but no one seemed able to communicate with them. Where were their husbands? I wondered. Surely they had to take part in the exercise too. I saw one young woman, with a baby in her arms, fall down some stairs. She sat sobbing into the strangling life-jacket until someone finally came to help her. I vowed then that if there was another lifeboat practice on this voyage, I wouldn't participate.

With seasickness still making my life a misery, I discovered that if I dressed early in the morning and made my way up to the highest deck, where it was freezing cold and windy, I could stave off the nausea, at least while I was in that semi-frozen state. Every muscle in my body, but especially my abdomen, ached from heaving and vomiting. Up there, I would find a deck-chair and wedge it in such a way that it wouldn't slide around. Then, bundled up in my winter coat and a blanket, I'd stay huddled for as long as possible, breathing in the frigid air. As soon as I went back below, the gut-wrenching nausea began again, and I remember thinking what a blessed relief it would be if someone tossed me into the churning sea – anything to escape the agony.

Bob joined me when he could. 'Come here, sweetheart, let me hold you,' he'd say, as he wrapped me in his arms and tried to comfort me, but nothing took the nausea away. At night, I would swallow a double or triple dose of Dramamine, curl into a ball on my bunk, and eventually drift off into dreams of the nights I'd spent on a similar bunk in an air-raid shelter during the war, while bombs fell all around us.

It was on the seventh day of the voyage that the weather improved: the sun came out and the sea calmed. I could walk about without fear of being flung against walls or down stairwells or, worse, swept overboard. Life aboard ship became bearable. Our Atlantic crossing took ten days and I felt fairly well for the last few and even managed to enjoy the experience. My three cabin-mates were pleasant girls. Barbara McCarthy, who insisted we call her Bobby, and I became close friends, and remained so for many years, in spite of my early reservations about her being too posh for me. I was thrilled to learn that she, too, was heading for Chicago. Throughout our friendship, Barbara and I were glad to have each other; we shared many good times and were always there for one another, offering comfort and support through the many traumatic events that were to occur in our lives.

Bobby and I had many bouts of the giggles over our roommate Gladys: her size and shape meant she could hardly get herself up onto her bunk.

'Give ooz a boonk oop, will ye?' she'd say, and of course, we did, all the time laughing until we cried. Gladys's husband, Arthur, was also short. He reminded me of a leprechaun and was probably the minimum size accepted into US military service. When we spotted him on guard duty, it was all we could do to stop ourselves laughing aloud: all you could see under his helmet were his enormous horn-rimmed glasses and two big ears sticking straight out. Poor lad, he reminded us of a chamber pot.

The four girls in our cabin were assigned to one of the ship's officers' tables in the dining room. It was far too nice to be called the mess – we even had fresh flowers on our table each day. The food was superb and I was sorry to have missed the first seven days of such fine fare. The men at our table were great fun; they teased us unmercifully, mostly about our accents but particularly about certain terminology. In my scrapbook, I have a paper table napkin, often called a serviette in Britain, and the captain had written on it in large letters 'THIS IS A NAPKIN', then everyone at the table had autographed it. That was just one example of how the differences between American and British English caused confusion.

We saw little of our husbands during the Atlantic crossing. They were still officially in uniform and had duties to perform, including guard duty. We usually saw them for two or three hours each day and on one or two evenings if they weren't working. With so many newly married couples on board, a great deal of hanky-panky went on in remote corners of the decks and corridors. It was not unusual to turn a corner and run smack-dab into someone's moment of passion; I often wondered how people could do 'it' standing up. The small cinema on the ship showed films until the wee hours each night, and when the lights dimmed, there was more lovemaking in those seats than appeared on the silver screen. Perhaps limiting contact between couples was supposed to rein them in. It didn't work. I wasn't interested in making a public spectacle of myself, but then, I was just a baby in that department. I was happy enough with a cuddle and remembering what had happened between us during our honeymoon in London. I could hardly wait to get back to the warmth and closeness we'd enjoyed then, and afterwards in our room at Mum and Dad's house.

As our voyage neared its end, our excitement grew. We newcomers to America could hardly wait to see the famous skyline of New York and its welcoming Statue of Liberty. It was as though the whole ship was holding its breath, just waiting for someone to announce the sighting of land. Unfortunately, we all missed it: it happened while we slept on that last night at sea and the announcement came over the loudspeaker at dawn.

Rising at that ungodly hour, I dressed with trembling hands, knowing we had docked in New York's harbour. I knew that Bob must be as excited as I was but I had no idea when he'd be able to join me on deck.

As I stepped out into the frigid late February air, I thought, This is it. I'm in the land of the Doris Day and

Fred Astaire movies and my new Technicolor life is about to begin. I just knew it was going to be full of vibrant colour, unlike the drab grey England I'd left behind.

I pushed my way through the animated crowd and wriggled into a spot at the ship's railing, which I grabbed with both hands. Squinting against the bright winter sunlight, I scanned the harbour and skyline for something that would tell me I wasn't dreaming; that we had in fact arrived in America. Then I saw it, the Statue of Liberty, recognized throughout the world as the symbol of all that this great country represented. Many of my fellow passengers cheered but I stared at her in silence, my heart beating wildly. I had seen black and white pictures of Lady Liberty before, in magazines and newsreels, but now I discovered she was green, and so much more beautiful than I had expected.

As I wiped away a tear, I thought of the oceans of tears the Lady must have seen since she'd become the sentinel at the gateway to the United States, as she watched the ships and their 'huddled masses' pass through the portal and into the arms of America, their Promised Land. She was silhouetted against the clear blue sky and the towering skyline of New York City, a breathtaking scene.

I must have looked a complete idiot, gazing in awe at the panorama before me. Until someone pushed in close behind me and rudely poked a finger into my gaping mouth. I bit down, hard.

'Ouch!' I heard, followed by my husband's familiar chuckle.

'I should have known it was you,' I said. 'Serves you right.' He never could resist teasing me. If Mum had been there, she might have done the same thing: she often made fun of me when I daydreamed, mouth agape, 'Catching flies,' she'd say, and called me Dilly Daydream. Suddenly, I missed her and my heart lurched, but there was no time for that now.

'Come on, honey, you can't stand there all day. It's time to make sure we have everything packed and get ready to go ashore.'

This is it, I thought. This is really it.

3: New York

We said our goodbyes to the USS *General R. E. Callan* and its crew, waving at them as we disembarked. Then, herded aboard ferryboats, we crossed the bay to a different pier. On the way, we passed close to the Statue of Liberty. She was enormous and, quite simply, magnificent.

At our next landing place, we entered a huge building, which I believe might have been part of Ellis Island. Still on wobbly sea legs, my heart pounding and my stomach in a knot, I stood in line with the others, waiting for clearance through Immigration and Customs. A girl behind me began cow-like 'mooing', and then another joined in. Soon we were all laughing, which helped to ease the tension.

Once that tedious process was completed, military personnel ushered us towards waiting buses, which transported us to a hotel in the city where we were to stay while our husbands were processed out of the army and back into the United States. Hooray, I thought. I get to sleep with Bob again. I was like a wide-eyed child at Christmas as we rode across town, seeing all the huge cars in so many different shapes and colours. I craned my neck to glimpse the tops of the skyscrapers and then there it was, just as I'd seen it in movies and magazines, the Empire State Building, just as spectacular as I'd expected, even without *King Kong*'s giant gorilla climbing up it. I mentally planned a trip to the top before leaving New York.

When we arrived at our hotel, someone showed us to our rooms. Compared to the cramped quarters we'd endured on board ship for the past ten days, this was pure luxury. Bob turned up a few minutes later. We slammed and locked the door, grabbed each other's hands, jumped up and down with excitement (well, I did), then melted into each other's arms.

'At last,' he gasped. 'I don't think I could have waited much longer.'

'Me neither,' I croaked, and he held me tightly to him. It was our honeymoon all over again.

Later that evening, I discovered that an American friend, Mary Lou Loy, whose husband was in the same unit as Bob, was in the same hotel. I had forgotten they were on the ship with us, perhaps because I had been ill for most of the voyage. I was delighted when she offered to take me under her wing while we were in New York and our husbands dealt with their army obligations.

The next day I was ready to see the sights. The men had to check in at the army base early that morning, so we girls had a late breakfast, then went off to explore the Big Apple. Fortunately, the hotel was within walking distance of almost everything we wanted to see, including the Empire State Building, Times Square, Radio City and all the department stores. We had two or three days in New York and I wanted to squeeze in as much as possible.

As Mary Lou and I strolled around the streets, I felt as though I had somehow landed on a movie set. I didn't know where to look first. If I had been an electrical circuit board, I would have gone into overload and blown a fuse.

I had to keep reminding myself that it was not a dream and I really was in one of the most famous cities in the world. Little Iris Jones, the council-house kid, was in New York City, USA. Wow!

Besides sightseeing, shopping was high on my list of priorities and that was where I got into the first of several embarrassing situations. Before leaving England, I had purchased a traditional English tweed skirt, one that would go with everything, of course.

'Would a nice dark brown jumper go well with this skirt, Mary Lou?' I asked. She laughed. 'You mean sweater,' she replied.

'Yeah, whatever you call it.' I chuckled.

'I'll take you to Macy's. You should be able to find what you're looking for there,' she said, and off we went.

We found the less-expensive sweater department in the basement of what I now knew was one of New York's most famous shops. I hadn't expected to find merchandise down there but Mary Lou explained that most department stores had 'bargain basements'. We soon found the sweater department and I stepped up to the counter where a young black woman was working. She smiled sweetly. 'Good morning, ma'am, welcome to Macy's. How may I help you today?'

I smiled back at her. 'Could you show me a nigger-brown jumper, please?' I asked shyly.

Immediately, I heard a loud choking sound from Mary Lou. At the same time, I noticed that the assistant was no longer smiling. Instead she looked shocked and visibly recoiled.

I don't know who was more aghast, the poor sales

assistant or Mary Lou, as they both stood there, caught in a moment of disbelief at what they had just heard.

'Let's go,' whispered Mary Lou, once she had gathered her senses. She grabbed me by the arm and dragged me away.

'What's wrong? What happened?' I protested, but her lips were sealed and she was shaking her head.

Once we were safely outside the store, I learned what a terrible faux pas I had made. I had had no idea that the word 'nigger' was a derogatory term in America and was mortified. Tears of embarrassment stung my eyes. The thought had entered my mind that I should have said 'sweater' instead of 'jumper', but I was completely unaware of the magnitude of my linguistic error.

That incident was the first of many, especially during the first months of my life in America. In the 1950s, there were no such taboo words in England, or not that I was aware of, and I had never experienced the racial sensitivity that was so much a part of American life. There were then no such issues at home, as far as I knew, and I was in for a rude awakening: I was upset to learn that in many places African Americans did not have equal rights and were often segregated from white people.

When we had recovered, we set off for the next item on our agenda: a trip to the top of the Empire State Building. The lift went up 102 floors, but we got out at the eighty-sixth for the viewing area. It was awesome, if a little scary, especially when I learned that the tower actually swayed in the wind, but it was exhilarating and I was breathless with wonder at the panorama before me. I squeezed Mary Lou's hand until she yelped. Poor girl, I'd done the same thing to her when we were riding up in the lift, which she kept reminding me was an 'elevator'.

The following day we visited Radio City. We had received free tickets to attend a live show called *Beat the Clock*, hosted by the famous Bud Collyer. During the show, he announced that a group of GI brides from England was in the audience and we received a welcoming round of applause. Then he came out into the audience to chat with a few of the girls, and wanted to know what an English girl might have bought on her first visit to America.

'What does this young lady have in her big shopping bag?' he said, into the microphone. 'Welcome to New York. Now, would you mind showing us what you've bought?' he asked.

She had purchased a silk scarf with a picture of New York on it. 'It's for me mum, back in England,' she told him.

'Very nice too,' he said, and went on to another girl.

'Hi, honey, and what do you have in your bag?' he enquired.

'I bought a pink jumper,' she told him.

'A pink jumper,' he echoed. 'That's a strange colour for a kangaroo.' The poor girl sank into her chair as the audience roared with laughter. Then, just when I thought I was safe, he stopped next to me.

'And what American treasure does this young lady have?' he asked, and thrust the microphone into my face.

For a moment, I stared blankly into his eyes and my mouth became an arid wasteland. After swallowing hard and blushing ninety shades of red, I managed to conjure a squeak. 'It's nothing interesting, sir,' I said, but he persisted and I had to let him peer into the bag. It was then his turn to blush. He faked a laugh and said something about English girls carrying their lunch around with them. In fact I had a large box of Kotex sanitary pads.

When I told Bob about it that evening, I thought he was going to bust a gut laughing. 'It's not funny,' I said. 'I thought I was going to die, or at least faint.'

'I'd better get you out of New York before you get into any more trouble,' he said, having heard about the incident in the department store.

I spent most of my time in New York oohing and aahing at the shop windows. At that time, pink, black and grey were in fashion, even in men's clothing, which was a bit of a shock, considering the conservative black, grey, brown and tweed worn by most Englishmen. I was even more surprised to see several pink cars.

One thing that had always been high on my list of 'important things to do when I get to America' was to have a banana split. I'd heard of them and seen them in movies and they looked like works of art. Mary Lou located a Walgreen's drugstore with a soda fountain, and in we went. My eyes must have been as big as saucers – I had never seen anything like it, except in the movies. You certainly would never have found food served in an English chemist's or pharmacy. I could hardly wait to write and tell the family about all these weird and wonderful things.

When the 'soda jerk' placed the banana split in front of me, all I could do was stare in disbelief. It was huge, enough for several people. I dug into that dish of decadence and did my best to finish it. After what seemed like an hour, it looked as though I had just rearranged it. Mary Lou was having a whale of a time watching me and laughing.

'What?' I said.

'You're just so funny,' she replied, trying to get serious.

At the end of our stay in New York, we were on the move again. This time a bus took us to a small airport where those of us going on to Chicago boarded a military plane for the onward flight. I had never flown before and I'm so glad that all planes are not like that one.

There were no passenger seats: we had to sit on benches that ran lengthwise down the sides of the aircraft.

'Blimey,' I said to Bob. 'I hope they give us all a parachute. This thing don't look very safe to me.'

'Don't worry, honey. I'm sure the pilot wouldn't fly it if it wasn't safe. Just relax, we'll soon be there.'

Easy for him to say, I thought, and had to remind myself that this, after all, was military transport and not a commercial airline. The flight to Chicago was bumpy. If we hadn't been strapped to our seats, I'm sure we would have been injured. However, we survived, and I was relieved to arrive in one dishevelled piece.

4: Chicago and the In-laws

We arrived at Chicago's Midway Airport in the small hours. It was freezing cold so we were glad that Bob's parents were there, waiting to take us home to the suburb of Elmwood Park. We would stay with them until we could find our own apartment.

I'd been excited about seeing Bob's mother again – we had met briefly when she was in England for our wedding. She had stayed only five days, during two of which Bob and I were away on our brief honeymoon in London. We'd had a longer honeymoon planned but had to cancel it because of Mother Irvine's visit. Afraid of flying, she'd had to take the long journey from Chicago to New York by train to board the ship. After the wedding she'd had to get back to America for the birth of her first grandchild. Lucky her, I thought. Her voyage on the *Queen Mary* had taken five days, compared to our ten.

There was an emotional reunion between the Irvines – well, between mother and son. All his father did was grunt and shake hands. I was to learn later that he never had much to say unless he was complaining: he was a miserable, cigar-smoking curmudgeon and I was already intimidated by his abrupt manner.

'Welcome home, son,' Mother Irvine said, through squalls of tears. Then she turned to me. 'Welcome to America, dear.' She gave me a quick hug. 'Oh, my, you look awful.'

Thanks a lot, I thought. You don't look too good yourself. Could this be the same gushing woman who had come to England for our wedding only months before? The first thing she said when she met me was how much prettier I was than I appeared in photographs, which had endeared me to her. She had hugged me and my parents and told us how happy she was to be there, meeting her son's new family. She almost froze to death while she was with us, but she got on well with everyone she met and had nothing but praise for all that she experienced. She had even laughed at the craziness of the traditional dances at our wedding reception, especially 'Knees Up, Mother Brown' and 'The Lambeth Walk', although she wouldn't join in. We had all thought she was warm and fun-loving, just like us. I saw nothing of that now. Perhaps she's as tired as we are, I thought, giving her the benefit of the doubt. After all, it was the middle of the night.

'Yeah, hi, Robert,' grunted his dad, then grunted something else at me and shook my hand with just the tips of his cold, bony fingers.

I'll always remember my first impressions on the journey from Midway Airport to the Irvines' house. First, we drove down Cicero Avenue, one of the city's main thoroughfares, which still had streetcars running on overhead electric lines. They reminded me of the old British trolley buses, except they were not double-deckers. The streets were strewn with litter, which I hadn't expected, and the apartment buildings were dreary, all with open, grey-painted back stairways. So far, what I had seen was ugly and disappointing. Also, the street lighting was dim, which added to my impression of a city that was old and tired.

We were in an industrial area on the south side of the city, heavily populated by working-class people, but I was shocked to see so many people living on top of one another. I wondered where all the lovely white clapboard homes were, with their rolling lawns and white picket fences. I had expected congestion in New York but, for some reason, not in Chicago.

Bob and his mother chatted on the drive home but his father clutched the steering wheel as though his life depended on it; he reminded me of a vulture, his head, atop a scrawny neck, thrust forward in grim determination as he pulled towards the kerb at each corner. I later learned that he had developed the habit during his years of driving buses and pulling over at the stops.

Bob burst out laughing.

'What's so funny?' his dad grunted.

'Aw, nothin',' replied Bob, stifling his laughter. He told me later that his mom had elbowed him in the ribs. Her husband had a nasty temper when provoked.

I felt relieved when we left Chicago's inner city behind and entered the suburb of Elmwood Park. It was still drab and, although it was not yet full daylight, it was clear that these monotone neighbourhoods were unlike Hollywood movie suburbs. Here, the small square brick bungalows huddled together in row upon row of sameness. The garages, at the rear of each property, were accessed by way of alleyways that ran behind the properties; they'd been planned that way, I supposed, so that they could be built close together on the narrow plots of land. We had lived like that in England but in rented council housing. Somehow I'd thought it would be different in America,

29

where people owned their own homes, and my heart sank a little. This place was definitely not in Technicolor.

When at last we turned on to the street where the Irvines lived, and I saw their house, I gasped in delight: they had left the Christmas lights up to welcome us home – even more of a surprise in that it was now early March.

'It's beautiful,' I said.

'Holy cow,' added Bob. 'I sure didn't think it would still be Christmas here.' He looked happy.

'We thought you'd like some brightness in your life after all that . . .' She glanced across at me. I wondered what she would have said if I hadn't been there, probably something about the lack of central heating and a telephone in my home, the British rain, and our rather low standard of living.

'It's wonderful,' I murmured. 'Thank you.'

I had never seen the outside of a house decorated with lights before; back at home, we had never had any Christmas lights. In fact, last Christmas was the first time ever that we'd had a tree. Bob had bought us a tiny one and we'd sat it on top of the television, decorating it with homemade paper chains. Here, multicoloured lights outlined the windows, doors and roof. It was magical.

Mr Irvine pulled up in front of the house, a bungalow, and parked there temporarily while we unloaded the luggage. I started towards the back of the car to help with the suitcases but Mrs Irvine elbowed me out of the way. 'Go wait by the front door. Daddy will let you in while I help Robert with the bags,' she said, somewhat dismissively. I did as I was told. My father-in-law lumbered up the front steps, fished around in his coat pocket and produced an enormous ring of keys. After some mumbling, he unlocked the door and let me in.

'Just go on in, Ira,' he said. Jeez, I thought. He doesn't even know my name.

Bob and his mother, who were both breathing heavily from lugging the cases up the steps, soon joined us.

'Well, here we are at last,' said Mrs Irvine. 'I thought today would never come.' Great tears began to cascade down her face, but she was smiling.

'Yeah, you'll be in your grandmother's old room,' grunted 'Daddy'.

'I did tell you Grandma's gone to stay with Aunt Freda, didn't I, Robert?'

'Yes, you did, Mom. Hope she wasn't upset that she had to move out.'

'No. It was Freda's turn to have her for a while anyway, but she'll be down for a visit with the others soon. They'll all want to see you, Robert.'

'And meet my wife,' Bob interjected.

'Oh, yes, of course,' stuttered his mother.

Inside the Irvines' house, which reeked of cigar smoke, all the Christmas decorations were still up and an artificial tree was loaded with baubles and twinkling lights. There were piles of presents beneath it, and we were told they were all for us, but they would have to wait. I was exhausted and desperately needed sleep, and so, hoping the outside world would look less dreary and frightening in the daylight, I asked if I might be excused. At long last, I collapsed into bed.

The following day, I slept until mid-afternoon, at which

time Bob woke me. 'Come on, sleepyhead, everyone's waiting to talk to you,' he said.

'Everyone?' I groaned. 'Who's everyone?' I felt as though I was about to be put on display, and I suppose, in a way, I was.

'Just Mom and Dad so far, but I'm sure my sister and her family will be here soon.' I scrambled to prepare for the inquisition, my stomach clenched. I was nervous to the point of nausea again.

Bob showed me to the bathroom. He gently pushed me inside and followed me, closing the door behind us. He took me in his arms and held me close, whispering in my ear, 'Remember, you're my beautiful girl and I'm proud of you. Don't be nervous about meeting the family, I'll be holding your hand all the way. Try to remember that they're probably nervous too. They've never had a daughter-in-law before.' He chuckled, the way he always did, and, as always, it made me feel just that little bit better.

I felt safe wrapped in his strong comforting arms, and at that moment, I almost cried tears of happiness. His caring and closeness reminded me of the love that had brought me to this strange land of contrasts. His people were different from my own. I had to get used to that, and I hoped that my disappointment in them and their world would relax into familiarity, that I would soon feel at home with them.

'Thank you for loving me, Bob. I just hope I'm not a disappointment to you or your family,' I whispered into his neck, as I breathed in the familiar warm smell of his body. The scent of his Old Spice aftershave suddenly reminded me of my mother and I smiled on the inside;

she had liked the smell so much she had started using Bob's bottle as perfume and he had surprised her by buying her one of her own. We had all laughed about that, and about her blush when she realized she had been found out.

'You'll never be a disappointment to me, honey. I just hope you're not disappointed with us.' He gave me a reassuring hug. 'Come out when you're ready. I'll be waiting for you.' He smiled the smile that had drawn me to him in my other life, the life I had left behind for him. Now I was ready for anything.

'Would you like something to eat, honey?' asked my mother-in-law, when I came into the kitchen. 'Waffles, eggs, bacon?' I didn't know what waffles were, and I certainly didn't have the stomach for eggs and bacon at that time.

'No thanks, Mrs Irvine, I'm not hungry, but could I have a cup of tea, please?' I was desperate for a cup of tea. I *needed* a cup of tea.

'Oh, my dear [it sounded like 'deeyurr'], I've just made you a whole pot of coffee,' she said. 'I'll have to see if I have any tea bags – oh, and you can call me "Mom", if you like.' Tea bags, I thought. Ugh.

And so began my introduction to a completely new world of food and drink. It wasn't something I had expected to cause problems, but it did – and for a long time too.

My mother-in-law did eventually produce some ancient tea bags but I would have killed for a 'real' cup of tea. She seemed quite distressed when I put two into my cup instead of the customary one, but it was the only way to get any flavour into the tea, and even then it left a lot to be desired. 'When I have tea, usually if I'm ill, I use the same tea bag all day,' she mumbled.

Later that first day, Bob's sister, Roberta, came over with her husband, Mike, who was Ukrainian, and their baby, Clarice. They sat around us while we opened our presents. Their generosity was overwhelming and I didn't know what to say. Between them, they had bought us everything – and I do mean everything – we needed to start our home. It felt a little odd to be opening Christmas presents in March, with the sound of carols playing in the background. I must have sounded like a broken record, saying, 'Thank you,' over and over again.

When Roberta and family left, we piled all of our presents around the edge of our small bedroom, then crawled onto the bed.

'Well, honey, what do you think?' asked Bob.

'I'm in a state of shock. I've never seen so much stuff – it's embarrassing. I don't know what to say to them – it's just too much, Bob.'

'You'll get used to it. In this family, if one person gets something new, everyone gets the same. Relax and enjoy it.' But how could I enjoy it when I knew how little my own family had?

The following weekend, the Irvines threw a big welcome-home party for us. Relatives and neighbours poured in to meet me and greet Bob. The house was crowded with people chattering, laughing, asking me questions and feasting from a table laden with food, most of which was unidentifiable, at least to me. My senses were already being assaulted by the stink of cigar smoke but add to that the smells that went with all that 'foreign' food, and I felt queasy. I wasn't used to the scent of German and Polish sausage, sauerkraut, pickled herrings and cheese. Little did I know that marrying into a German family, some of whom were Wisconsin dairy farmers and who had brought the stinky cheeses, meant I needed to develop a much stronger stomach than the one I had.

Again, family and friends showered us with gifts and I felt welcomed by their many kindnesses, although I was annoyed and embarrassed to overhear a conversation Bob's mother had with another woman.

'She's quite pretty,' said my mother-in-law, 'but so frail-looking.'

'She doesn't look as if she's ever had a decent meal,' said another.

'Yes, she's pathetically thin,' my mother-in-law replied, and I wondered how they would feel if they heard me saying, 'Ooh, she's pathetically fat.'

'She comes from a very poor family,' came yet another comment.

'Stupid cows,' I mumbled, under my breath.

'What was that you said, honey?' someone asked, but I just shook my head and walked away. Then someone tapped my arm and pulled me towards a small group of visitors.

'Say something in English, honey,' she said.

For a second, I didn't know how to respond. I wasn't sure what she meant. 'I'm talking English,' I replied. 'English people speak English.'

'Isn't that just the cutest thing?' she remarked to the group, who laughed, but I still didn't know what the silly cow meant.

'Has she had much schooling?' I heard another old biddy ask my mother-in-law. 'It doesn't sound as though she has.' I didn't hear the response, but by then I'd heard enough from behind their cupped hands and I went outside, wondering if there was anything right about me or the way I spoke. 'Just going to get some fresh air,' I told Bob, but I was seething and fighting back tears of hurt and anger.

Some of what they were saying was true, but I certainly didn't need to be constantly reminded of it. I'd thought I'd left all that behind.

Linguistic differences often made people laugh or ask for explanations. I could understand that, and didn't mind being teased or corrected, but I didn't need to hear whispered criticism of myself – it was as if I had the plague.

In my early days in America, simply telling someone the time often brought laughter and teasing. For example, I would say it was five and twenty past ten, or five and twenty to ten; Americans would say twenty-five *of* ten, or twenty-five *after* ten. There were many similar examples of the differences in our supposed same language. Parts of cars had different names: the British 'bonnet' for the American 'hood', 'boot' for 'trunk', 'petrol' for 'gas' and 'wings' for 'fenders', to name a few. Most people know and understand those differences now because of television and other media, but back then, those little differences were new and even somewhat entertaining. In America, 'fanny' referred to someone's bottom, while in Britain it meant 'vagina'. I had to be vigilant while I was learning to speak American-English. I just hoped that in the company of the Irvines or their friends I wouldn't make a complete fool of myself by inadvertently saying something dreadful.

My in-laws, who were first-generation German immigrants, obviously thought that their new European daughter-in-law would fit their preconceived notion of *Hausfrau* because among the gifts I received were several 'housedresses' in size sixteen! They were unbelievably ugly. In large pastel plaids and floral designs, they zipped up the front and had two large patch pockets. I weighed just over six stone and wore size six, so those dresses would have gone around me twice, if I had ever worn them. I modelled one for Bob, and fortunately, he saw the funny side of it and we had a good laugh about them.

'That's what you get for marrying into a German family,' he said. I soon discovered it was just the tip of the iceberg.

5: A World of Contrasts

During the next few weeks, things went reasonably well. The Irvines took me out in the car to see some of the sights and familiarize me with the area. On the first trip I was introduced to supermarket grocery shopping. I had never seen such huge stores or such a variety of goods. There was aisle after aisle of shelves and refrigerated units containing merchandise stacked almost to the ceiling. I was used to little British shops in which everything was lined up on shelves behind the counter and the assistant handed you what you wanted. Alternatively you could give them your shopping list. Then they would gather the items on your list for you and place them on the counter. American supermarkets also sold meat, vegetables and fruit; in the UK, those items came from separate shops, such as the greengrocery or the butcher's. I wondered what my mother would have thought of such a 'super' shop – she'd probably have got lost and had a nervous breakdown trying to find what she wanted. Oh, and the shock of having someone actually pack your purchases in large brown paper bags, then offer to carry them to the car for you! Mum always shopped at the customer-owned Co-op shops because you got points for what you bought. I can still remember her Co-op number because it was important: it paid dividends.

Still on the subject of groceries, I was amazed by the

Irvines' vast stockpile of food and household necessities. When shown around their house, I saw shelves in the basement laden with canned goods, paper goods, laundry and cleaning products. Stacked up the edge of the attic stairway were staples such as sugar, flour and boxes of cereal. In the attic itself, which used to be Bob's bedroom (his desk and bed were still there), there were still more household supplies. Did they think there might be another depression or war? Struck by the extreme contrast to home life in England, I pictured Mum's pantry in which you would usually find a small bag each of flour and sugar, perhaps a tin of corned beef for emergencies, a bag of soda crystals for use in the bath and laundry, salt and pepper, a sack of potatoes and little else. Mum went to the shops every day, to buy the food for that day's meal. There was no money for extras and, of course, you could only buy what you could carry home in your shopping bag or basket since hardly anyone we knew had a car. My goodness, I thought, life is certainly different here in America, and it was going to take some getting used to.

The next important visit was to the family burial plots. At first I thought the Irvines took us there for Bob to pay his respects to his deceased relatives because he'd been away for two years but, no, it was for a far more (pardon the pun) cryptic reason. They went to check the 'grave blankets', which were rectangles of woven pine branches – to keep the graves warm in the winter, I supposed. To me, that was just plain weird. I couldn't conjure the image of a dead person or ghost shivering with cold and reaching out for a blanket. Later, when I researched the strange custom, I discovered that grave blankets were also available to celebrate a variety of occasions. You could (and apparently still can) buy birthday blankets, Christmas blankets, Valentine's Day blankets, and more. I still have no idea how the custom originated but I had to give credit to the good old American entrepreneurial spirit. They certainly knew how to make money, even out of their dead.

Driving around in the suburbs was a strange, almost surreal experience. It bothered me that nothing looked permanent. All of the shopping areas, or strip malls, as they were called, were single storey and strung out along concrete parking strips. Little of the construction was in bricks and mortar and most buildings reminded me of the prefabricated houses built in Britain after the war. I remember wondering why they didn't construct multi-storey buildings, as they did in Europe and in the larger American cities, where shops usually had apartments or other businesses above them. Bob said it was because there was more land to build on in America. Everything reminded me of what I'd seen in movies about the old Wild West, except that there were proper roads and the shops had modern frontages. I hoped that I wouldn't have to live in that wasteland: I needed to be somewhere that felt more lived in, where I didn't feel so unattached, so disconnected, like an untethered balloon blowing about in the wind. Those wide-open places, which looked barely used, didn't seem very different from ghost towns. Years later, watching the American television series *The Twilight Zone*, I was reminded of my early impressions of Chicago's newer suburbs; there had been something eerie about them back then.

The most important visit of all, as far as the Irvines were

concerned, was to the church that the family attended. They were Lutheran, a denomination I had never heard of before. Mrs Irvine worked as housekeeper to the minister and his wife, which surprised me: every vicar or minister I had known in England, not that I had known many, was poor. They could not have afforded a housekeeper, and certainly wouldn't have been driving a brand new Cadillac or spending their winters in Florida, as this minister did. I was also shocked that members of the church had to sign a pledge as to how much they would give it each week or year since the church's budget was based on projected income. Apparently, the pledge could be as binding as any other contract. I remember thinking how mercenary it sounded. It was definitely not my idea of religion. American churches seemed to operate like businesses and I hated the idea.

I was amazed again when I saw how Bob's mother and sister dressed for church on cold days. Along with their Sunday dresses, full-length fur coats and high-heeled shoes, they wore white ankle socks over their nylon stockings. I found that most unattractive and peculiar and hoped they wouldn't expect me to follow suit. I'd rather have died than wear socks over my nylons.

Every Sunday after church, the family would gather at the Irvines' house for midday dinner, and then at Roberta's for the evening meal, or supper, as they called it. I would mentally hold my nose against whatever strong food smells prevailed and pray for something I could eat without gagging.

At first I thought it was nice that the family spent so much time together, but soon the obligation became a nuisance. They expected us every Sunday, which gave us no freedom to do anything else at weekends, especially if Bob was working overtime on Saturdays. Those Sunday meals, always served on the best china, crystal and silver, meant lots of washing-up afterwards: every piece had to be cleaned individually, by hand, never allowing one to bang against another. Then, each item wrapped in its special protective cloth, it all went back into storage until the next Sunday. The process took hours and, believe me, I dreaded the routine; there were times when I would have given anything for our old Sunday dinners back home, when Mum dished up the food in the kitchen to make sure each person got the appropriate quantity, according to their place in the family, and we shared one glass.

I was soon experiencing problems after I'd eaten some of the rich food, especially the heavy German dishes prepared by my mother-in-law. I had to refuse some, asking if I might just have some toast, and she would be offended, often bursting into tears.

'No one's ever insulted the food I prepared for them,' she would choke out between sobs. I felt awful about it, but what could I do? I didn't mean to hurt her feelings and certainly couldn't control my physical reactions. 'Please, Bob,' I said, 'could you explain to her about the simple diet I've always been used to? I can't just change overnight. Please try to make her understand.'

'I'll try,' he said, 'but my mother's a stubborn German and I doubt she'll be willing or able to change either.'

Poor Bob. I remember how frustrated he became with both of us. He and I had little private time together and even our lovemaking was strained: we were always concerned that his parents might hear and know what we were doing; I mean, did we really think they didn't know? Occasionally we ended up laughing at our fumbling efforts to be quiet under the covers.

'Is everything all right in there?' we'd hear from next door. It wasn't easy to sleep in the bedroom adjoining theirs, knowing how thin the walls were. It had been different when we were with Mum and Dad: we joked about it through the wall and had some good laughs. I was beginning to think that those people never laughed. They seemed devoid of any sense of humour.

'Do you think they've ever done it?' I asked Bob. I tried to imagine it and ended up giggling.

'Nah, I musta been adopted,' he said. 'There's no way I coulda come out of those two.' I was glad he was different from the rest of his family.

Bob had told me his sister had learning difficulties and had attended a special school. He also claimed that his mother had been instrumental in Roberta and Mike getting together. Apparently Mrs Irvine had worked with Mike and had arranged the whole thing, even their marriage. I didn't intend to allow our lives to be dictated, as theirs obviously had been.

It soon became apparent that our living with Bob's parents wasn't going to work. I was terribly homesick, which no one seemed to understand or have the slightest sympathy for, and I began to feel quite ill. I was constantly hurting my mother-in-law's feelings by not eating the food she'd prepared or staying in my room to write letters or read, sometimes just to cry. The situation worsened when, just a few weeks after our arrival, I received word that my

43

granddad had died. I was devastated and inconsolable for days. My poor husband was at a loss to know what to do. There was no one to share my grief with so I buried my head under the bed covers and wept.

At about that time, and perhaps to take my mind off my grandfather's death, Bob announced that he was taking me away for a few days. He had realized that I needed a break from all the stress and we really did need some time alone together.

He didn't tell me where we were going. It was a surprise, he told me, and it certainly was.

'I need to give my car a good workout,' he said. 'Dad did drive it occasionally while I was away, just to keep it in order, but it needs a real road-trip to get it in good shape.' I'd been thrilled to learn that Bob had a car and felt as though I had taken a giant step up in the world. I don't remember what make it was, but it was huge compared to British cars.

We drove to the neighbouring state of Wisconsin. First, we stopped to see some relatives who were dairy farmers. There, I helped gather eggs and learned how to size them and place them in cartons. Although Bob's aunt Freda was his mother's sister, the two women were as different as chalk and cheese, just like my mother and her sister, Iris. Mum was blonde and chubby, still had a Cockney accent and was a messy housekeeper, while her sister was dark-haired and slender, her speech was refined and she kept an immaculate home. Here on the farm, the family worked side by side, seemingly enjoying each other's company, but best of all, laughter echoed throughout that old farm-house. Why couldn't Freda and her husband have been my parents-in-law? I thought. They were much more like my own family. I was sad when we left, but soon cheered up when I discovered the next of Bob's surprises.

We left the flat farmlands and soon the terrain became a little more rugged and hilly.

'Where are we going?' I asked.

'Wait and see,' replied a grinning Bob. 'It's a special surprise and I think you'll really like it.'

We drove into a town called Wisconsin Dells and I loved it as soon as I saw all the old, mostly white clapboard houses, many surrounded by white picket fences. This is more like it, I thought. None of the buildings was new, like the California houses in movies. They were old and had real character.

The main street through the town displayed numerous advertising signs for local attractions. Among those I remember was the Tommy Bartlett Water Show, Duck Rides on the Wisconsin River, and the Authentic Indian Ceremonial. The latter caught my attention and made my heart somersault.

'Can we really see Indians here? Are they real Indians? Can we go to the Ceremonial?' The questions tumbled out, one after another. I was as excited as a child at Christmas.

'Of course we can go. We're going to see everything, if you want to, and yes, they are real American Indians,' he assured me.

We pulled into the driveway of a large old house. The sign in front said 'The White House'. It was a guesthouse and there were vacancies.

'Good,' said Bob. 'I was hoping we could stay here.

This is where my parents and my sister spent their honeymoons. It's cheap but comfortable.'

Oh dear, I thought. Something else that everyone in the family has to do the same. Honeymoons. I didn't really mind, though, because it was nice, and cost only three dollars a night.

I don't remember much about the other attractions we saw but the Indian Pow-Wow was amazing. That evening, we boarded a boat that took us down the Wisconsin River. It ran between high craggy cliffs, and on the way, a guide pointed out various unusual rock formations. There was the high, chimney-shaped Stand Rock, separated from the cliff behind it by just a couple of yards or so. We learned that you could pay to see a dog jump from one to the other. It sounded dangerous, and one woman asked the guide if there was a safety net in case the dog didn't make it. I don't recall the guide's answer, except that he ended up laughing and saying, 'Well, they can always get another dog,' which I thought was disgusting.

The boat tied up at a wooden landing, and we all filed off. It was now dusk and a guide led us down a dimly lit pathway between rocks and scrubby trees. Soon we entered a clearing and a new scene opened before us. We were in, I believe, a naturally formed, vaguely circular arena. In the centre, on a slightly raised area, the tepees were arranged in a semi-circle, with a blazing bonfire in the middle. Rows of benches for the audience circled the space. We crowded onto the seats and soon the show began. I'd always been a dreamer and was immediately drawn into this exhibition of America's true history, its living history; it was not only colourful, but also beautiful and moving. Tears pricked my eyes as I listened to Indian folklore and learned what their dances and songs meant. I felt privileged to have come halfway around the world to witness this re-enactment of an old way of life. At that time, I was unaware of the other part of their history in which they had been slaughtered in their hundreds of thousands for the white man's greed, but that is another story.

The next day, as we wandered around town, I recognized one of the Indians from the previous night's show; he had been the narrator. He was now in ordinary clothes but accompanied by an older man in full Indian garb. We watched the first man get into what looked like a brand new Cadillac.

'Do you think it's his?' I asked Bob.

'I can't think why not,' he replied.

'Where do you think he keeps it? I didn't see anywhere to park cars at their camp last night.'

Bob laughed. 'You don't seriously think they live in those tents, do you? They all live in suburban houses now. They make tons of money entertaining people like us.'

'Oh,' I said. 'I thought it was real.'

The older man in his regalia, with an enormous feathered headdress, now stood alone close to where we had parked our car.

'Do you think he'd let me have my picture taken with him?' I asked Bob.

'Well, there's no harm in asking,' he replied, and I surprised myself by going up to the man and asking his permission. The man nodded but said nothing. I stood as close to him as I dared and smiled, while Bob focused and took the picture. As I stepped away and started to thank

47

him, he stuck out his hand for payment. My jaw dropped but Bob took a dollar bill out of his pocket and handed it to the Indian 'chief'. 'It was worth the dollar just to see your face,' he said to me.

'I'm such a gullible idiot,' I said, and we laughed as my flushed red face began to fade back to normal.

Initially disappointed that I had not visited a real Indian encampment, I was still happy to have seen the show. At last I had seen a little of the America of the Technicolor movies, and I loved it.

After our few days alone, it was time to return to our own reality. I wasn't looking forward to going back, but now, with renewed strength, I was ready to try again.

Once we were home, Bob and I began looking for an affordable apartment – and what a nightmare that turned out to be. The only inexpensive places we found were in the run-down and slum areas of the city. I certainly didn't fancy living like that. We finally settled on a two-room, third-floor walk-up apartment on Division Street on Chicago's west side. It wasn't the best neighbourhood in the world, but it wasn't the worst either. The apartment was like something out of a B movie. It had a bed-sitting room complete with a pull-down Murphy bed concealed behind mirrored double doors, a small kitchen and a bathroom. When I wrote home, I told my parents that, besides the kitchen and bathroom, the apartment had a living room, dining room and library but unfortunately they were all in one room. They found that very funny, especially the Murphy bed, which they'd never heard of. I had to send them pictures of it both behind the door and pulled down, ready for business. That crazy bed turned out to be a source of great fun for my usually sensible husband: he was always folding me up in it to wake me in the mornings.

'You bugger!' I'd shout at him, and he'd laugh his head off. I tried to do the same to him, but he was too heavy for me to lift, worse luck. 'If I ever get you up in that bloody bed,' I told him, 'I'm going to close the doors on you and leave you there until you beg for mercy.'

The apartment was on a busy main road, above shops that included a Jewish restaurant and a Polish delicatessen; the smells that drifted up from below made me feel more nauseous than ever. Next to those shops was the Adelphi Cinema, which added an even more B-movie atmosphere, with its marquee lights flashing on and off outside our window all night. I'd lie in bed, trying to get to sleep, but even though we pulled the window shades down, those flashing lights still crept in around the edges. Yes, I thought, I'm living in an American film now, but it was not the Technicolor one of my dreams. The good news was that this area felt far more European than the sprawling strip malls in the suburbs, or what I now thought of as 'the wasteland'. I often wondered what all those other GI brides thought of America and if they were as disappointed in it as I was; I suppose it depended on where you went. Many years later, my old friend June Gradley (now Armstrong), who went to live in Vermont, said she loved it there because it was so green and mountainous; it sounded a lot different from Chicago.

Before we'd moved into the apartment, we'd had to scrub down all the walls from top to bottom: they were filthy with black soot. On the advice of Bob's mother, we cleaned the torn and faded wallpaper with damp bread.

'Hooray! At last I've found something worthwhile to do with your horrible American sliced bread,' I told Bob.

'We'll probably be able to get some fresh baked in this neighbourhood. They're bound to sell it at the bakery or the Jewish deli but maybe only pumpernickel or rye bread,' he replied.

'What the heck are they?' I asked.

'Oh, God, something else you probably won't like.' He laughed. 'You might have to bake your own.'

That was a joke: I didn't know how to fry an egg. Poor Bob, it would be his turn to eat things he couldn't recognize once I started cooking.

We continued to scrub and scrape for days, but our sad little apartment hardly looked any different when we'd finished. The windows had been caked with dirt and we'd had to use razor blades to scrape off the encrusted grime.

'Jeez, I thought I was moving up in the world but, so far, this is definitely a move down,' I commented, to my poor husband. I immediately regretted what I'd said because he lost his usual smile.

'I'm sorry,' he said.

'Don't be. I was only joking,' I told him, but I wasn't.

At the time, we couldn't afford to buy paint so, other than a coat of cheap whitewash in the closet where we were to hang our clothes, we were stuck with the ancient wallpaper and scuffed, peeling paint.

'Too bad we can't take off this wallpaper,' I told Bob. 'It might be worth something on the antiques market.'

We unpacked our bounty of wedding gifts and set up housekeeping. It was exciting to have my own home for the first time ever, even though it was a bit seedy. We no longer had to worry about upsetting anyone and could even invite people to visit.

I'll never forget the first time the Irvines came for a meal.

'I've asked the folks to supper next Sunday,' Bob announced.

'Oh, God, what am I going to feed them?' I asked.

'Don't worry about it. I'm sure they'll enjoy whatever you prepare. Just relax, and it'll be fine.'

Hmm, I thought. Easy for him to say. At least they were coming for supper and not dinner: that meant I wouldn't have to cook a big meal.

After much agonizing, I remembered the big fancy salads my posh aunt used to serve and thought I could manage something like that. I covered a large platter with fancy foil doilies, arranged lettuce leaves artistically around the edge, then layered all the other salad vegetables in decreasing circles, ending up with a vase of celery sticks in the middle, surrounded by radish rosettes. It looked beautiful. To go with the salad, there was a plate of sliced ham and cheese, and bread and butter. The family said how pretty it looked and then we dug in. After they'd finished with the salad, they all just sat there. I thought they were waiting for dessert and went to get the pie I had bought.

'What's the main course?' enquired Bob, who had not had any input before and hadn't seen what I was preparing.

'What do you mean?' I said.

'You know, silly, the meat and potatoes.'

I stood there, stunned, looking from face to face.

'Haven't you cooked anything, honey?' he asked.

'No, of course I haven't. You can't have cooked meat and veg as well as salad. You have ham and cheese and bread with it.'

'Don't worry, Robert,' said his mother. 'We'll just eat when we get home.'

What?

I disappeared into the bathroom, where I stayed until my embarrassment and nerves had settled down. When I came back, the family was on their way out of the door.

'I'm sorry,' I called after them, hoping they didn't think I was a complete moron. How was I to know that Americans didn't consider salad a proper Sunday-evening meal? It took me for ever to recover from that soul-destroying incident. All I could think was how my family would have laughed at what had happened; it was just another example of the Irvines' lack of humour.

While we lived in that apartment, I had to take our washing to the laundromat down the street. I'd carry the heavy bag of wet clothes home, then hang them out on a line to dry. Attached to the railings on our open back porch, it ran across to the porch of another building. I'd have to lean over the railing, peg an article to the line, then carefully move it along by means of a pulley so that I could add the next item. The first time I saw lines of washing fluttering outside between old, soot-grimed buildings, I was reminded of the tenement blocks of flats I'd seen in the London slums. I'd always been glad that I'd never had to live like that in Britain. Now I wondered how I'd ended up living in just such conditions in bountiful America.

I used to swear when I dropped a clothes peg down all

three floors of the building to the ground: I wasn't about to go down all those stairs just to retrieve a peg. It was a different matter if I dropped an article of wet washing, though. I'd watch it sail down into the grimy courtyard, then reluctantly go down to rescue and rewash it. I almost cried if I dropped a sheet.

No, this was *not* the America I'd had in mind. It was no better than my home in England – in fact, it was decidedly worse. I was determined to get a job so that we could afford a better place to live.

6: American Firsts – Apartments, Job and Pregnancy

While we were still living with the Irvines, and before we found our own place, I had begun checking the newspapers in search of a job. I knew it would be difficult to find something suitable as I had only worked in shops, and I couldn't do that in America because I didn't understand the money well enough. I also needed a situation that would be no more than an easy bus ride away. Finally, I called an advertiser who was looking for someone to help care for her three children and made an appointment for an interview.

I took the short bus ride to their house. Mrs Joan Morris, the mother, and I hit it off right away. The Morrises were Jewish and, to me, appeared well off. I remember how impressed I was by their living-room sofa and armchairs: they were in white brocade trimmed with a heavy silk-bullion fringe. They were also sealed in clear plastic. I was fascinated. Were they new and still wrapped, or was the plastic intended to keep them clean? I do remember that they were uncomfortable to sit on and made rude noises when you sat down or stood up.

Mrs Morris was loud, animated and glamorous. She talked so fast my ears had a hard time keeping up with her mouth. We chatted over coffee for quite some time and then she told me I could have the job if I wanted it. I accepted and told her I could start the following week, just a few days away; I couldn't begin immediately because we were moving into the apartment that weekend and she assured me that would be fine. However, that evening, at the Irvines, I took a telephone call from her, which scared me to death: I thought she'd changed her mind. Instead she told me that her husband might have a more suitable job for me and would like to talk to me as soon as possible. I was intrigued.

Mr Morris owned a business that sent salesmen out with hand-pushed or bicycle-propelled carts to sell ice cream in the parks and streets of Chicago. He needed help in the office and was willing to train me. I would earn more money and work more regular hours than I would if I worked for his wife. I couldn't believe my luck when he hired me on the spot. 'Glad to have you aboard, kid,' he said, and from that day forward, he always called me 'kid' or referred to me as 'the kid', like John Wayne or Humphrey Bogart. The icing on the cake was that Happy Harry's Ice Cream Company was based around the corner from our new apartment so I'd be able to walk to work. Who says there's no such thing as miracles?

One of my jobs, at the end of each day, was to check the salesmen in, tally up the unsold products against sales and collect the money they had taken. Sometimes someone would not show up with his day's takings and I soon learned that men with drinking problems often took these jobs. They would abandon the ice-cream cart, make off with the money and find the nearest bar. On those occasions, Happy Harry became Unhappy Harry. It would take hours to find the abandoned vehicle and its now ruined contents, to say nothing of the lost income.

I kept records of the amount of money taken on each vending route, especially the parks. It seemed that Happy Harry's had the sole concession to sell ice cream in Chicago's city parks, which apparently was a very big deal. There were much larger ice-cream companies, such as Good Humor, which might have expected to be granted the park concessions, but in those days, it was definitely whom you knew that determined how contracts were handed out. Apparently, Harry was a good friend of the parks commissioner and money changed hands regularly between them. I had to work out the percentage of income from all park sales, of which ten per cent went directly to the parks commissioner. In fact I kept two sets of books: we did not report the correct gross amount to him, thereby cheating the cheat out of some of his kickback.

Later, after I'd left that job, Mr Morris phoned me. He instructed me that if anyone ever contacted me to ask how I had kept his records, I should tell them that I had never altered any of the figures, that we did not keep two sets of books, and that we always reported honestly and accurately. Who knows what might have happened had my employer or I been found out? Fortunately, no one ever approached me for information. I learned that, in those days, most things were run that way in Chicago's political 'Machine'. In later years I was to learn how different Chicago politics were. On Election Day, or on the days leading up to it, people would come to your door and offer money, bottles of whiskey or boxes of chocolates to swing your vote their way. They would drive you to the polls too. The Machine was powerful.

While I worked for the Morrises, who now insisted that I call them by their first names, Harry would often say, 'How about some lunch, kid?' Sometimes I went with him. Occasionally the parks commissioner joined us and I listened to their conversations. I'm sure they thought I was too naive to understand their business relationship, but I had my suspicions. I knew the commissioner was receiving kickbacks from the ice-cream business, but when he and Harry whispered behind their hands, I wondered if more shady deals might be going on. I once overheard something about a shipment of condoms that had come into the commissioner's possession – the pair discussed how much they could make selling them by the gross. Weird.

Harry and Joan treated me with great kindness, and Joan and I became friends, which was a good thing because I had realized I was pregnant and had no idea what to do about it. Joan, who was expecting her fourth child – I can't remember ever seeing her when she wasn't pregnant – insisted on taking me to her obstetrician.

My first visit to him was traumatic. I had never had a pelvic examination before and found it embarrassing and uncomfortable. I couldn't believe that I had to lie on an examination table, skirt up, panties off, so that this stranger could insert his rubber-gloved fingers inside me. I couldn't stop shaking: with my feet in stirrups and legs apart, my knees flapped up and down, like a bird's broken wings. I couldn't control them.

'Just take deep breaths and try to relax,' the doctor kept telling me. I wondered how he'd feel if he'd had to get himself into this weird position. I felt like a turkey or

57

chicken, waiting to be stuffed. How could I ever look him in the eye again after he'd had a good prod at my naughty bits, as Mum used to call them? Anyway, I survived the ordeal and the soft-spoken man did his best to put me at ease and to make the examination tolerable.

His name was Edward Crown, and he was the brother of the famous Chicago industrialist Colonel Henry Crown. The Crown family, who were among the city's most prominent citizens, at that time owned the Empire State Building, the Material Service Corporation and General Dynamics to name but a few. Dr Crown, who certainly didn't need to continue as a doctor, was still involved in the family business but took care of the obstetric needs of a few select society women and only because he loved his work. He agreed to be my doctor as a favour to Joan Morris, and perhaps because he felt a bit sorry for the skinny little sixteen-year-old immigrant girl.

My in-laws were pleased to hear that their son was to be a father, but they took little interest in my well-being. They had no sympathy for my debilitating morning sickness, which turned out to be twenty-four-hours-a-day sickness and lasted for more than six months. My own parents were excited to hear that they were to be grandparents but they were understandably worried. My mother started knitting baby clothes and repeatedly reminded me that I was now eating for two. She also sent me some second-hand maternity smocks that were so ugly they went straight to Goodwill Charities. Besides, I'd had enough of wearing other people's cast-offs.

Shortly after we moved into our apartment, something miraculous happened. An English woman and her

Ukrainian husband moved into the apartment next door. The first time I heard that English accent in the hallway, I thought I was dreaming but, thank God, I wasn't. The Hawryluks, Alice and Bill, had no children and were quite a bit older than we were, but we immediately became good friends. How wonderful it was to have someone nearby who not only spoke my language but ate the same food. In the meantime, I had also heard from Barbara McCarthy, the girl I had met on the ship, and although she lived on the other side of Chicago we could see one another now that we knew how to use the buses. Barbara was also pregnant so we always had lots to discuss.

As soon as Bob had finished with the army, he'd gone back to his old job as a carpenter for Western Electric Corporation. He worked all the overtime hours he could get so that we could prepare for the baby and be able to afford a larger, nicer apartment. Because of his hours, I spent a great deal of time alone so it was wonderful having an English neighbour, who provided proper cups of tea, baked beans on toast and regular doses of sympathy.

By then, summer was upon us and the temperature was rising. I had never been so miserable in my life. Our apartment had a flat, tarred roof so our rooms were like an oven. My pregnancy was taking its toll on my energy, I felt nauseated most of the time and, no matter what I did, I could never get cool enough to have a good night's sleep. We borrowed an ancient oscillating fan from Bob's parents but it didn't help much.

There was no breeze for weeks on end and our few windows, the ones that were not painted shut, were positioned in such a way that we couldn't create a cross-breeze.

One day at lunchtime, Harry said, 'Come on, kid. Let's take you somewhere cool. You look ready to cave in at any minute.' He took me to a small air-conditioned restaurant where, for an hour or so, I was able to relax. When we left, he told me he was taking me for a ride to give me some more cool air. We drove to the Lake Michigan shore, where we parked the car and sat on a bench in the shade, chatting for a while. Then he went and spoiled it all.

'Ya know, kid, I've become very attracted to you. I'd like to make love to you.'

What? Oh, no, I thought. What in the world is he talking about? By now, I was visibly pregnant: how could he possibly be attracted to me, and what was I supposed to say? So, I did the only thing I could. I laughed right in his face. 'You really had me going there for a minute, Harry. I thought you were serious,' I said.

'I'm dead serious, kid. I think I'm falling in love with you.'

I couldn't stop laughing, but the look on his face told me I'd hurt him. Did he think I was interested in him, or was he trying to take advantage of me? I didn't know. Then, stifling my laughter, I suddenly knew what to say. 'Harry,' I began, 'you know what your problem is? You have a thing for pregnant women. Now, let's get back to work before someone thinks there really is something going on between us.' Neither of us ever mentioned the incident again, but every time I looked at him, I wanted to slap him for being so stupid.

With the record heat of that summer, I would go into the ice-cream storage rooms at work and sit on top of the chest freezers, or I would ask Harry to place a huge block of dry ice in front of a fan to blow a bit of cool air on me. At home, I would strip off and sit in a bath of cool water, and at night I slept naked on the cool marble bathroom floor. Sometimes, in the evening, when I was tearful and desperate, we would take a blanket down to North Avenue Beach on Lake Michigan and lie on the sand for hours. Occasionally, finances permitting, we would find a cinema with air-conditioning and sit there until closing time. I had been miserable before, but now I was sure that the summer heat was going to finish me off. All I wanted was to go home to England but, of course, I couldn't tell anyone that.

When I was six or seven months pregnant, Bob surprised me with a day out at the Indiana sand dunes. It was a beautiful place, crowded on that hot sunny day. Once we were on the beach it seemed cooler and I settled in for the first comfortable day I'd had for weeks. A non-swimmer, I waded in the cool water while Bob swam and floated, enjoying every minute of it. We had a simple picnic lunch and afterwards I settled back for a snooze. I must have slept for a long time because Bob had to wake me to get ready for the long drive home. When I tried to stand up, I couldn't bend my legs. In fact, I felt stiff all over.

Eventually, Bob got me back to the car and we realized I had been in the sun far too long and was severely burned. I became so ill that he had to take me to a hospital emergency room. We also called Dr Crown, who was furious that we had allowed it to happen, but also worried. He told us there wasn't much we could do because of my pregnancy, which was exactly what the emergency-room staff had told us. We should just keep applying cold compresses and lotion. I certainly couldn't take anything for the pain and, believe me, there was plenty of it: the blistering was severe and took for ever to heal. I swore then that I would never again lie in the sun.

It wasn't just the record high temperatures that made the summer of 1955 nightmarish: it was also the year of the cicada invasion, and what a freaky experience that was. I had heard of locusts laying waste to places in Africa, but I hadn't expected such a thing to occur in Chicago. I had never heard of cicadas before, but now swarms of them filled the air and covered the trees, and the sound they made was deafening. It was most unpleasant going outside in the morning and having to walk on a carpet of dead ones – or maybe it was their empty shells: the crunching sounded as if I was treading on broken glass. It still gives me the shivers to think of it.

At weekends, we made the obligatory visits to the in-laws and, oh, how I dreaded those Sundays, especially since Grandma Neuhaus had moved back in. It drove me crazy listening to her and my mother-in-law chattering away in German. They seemed to forget that I was there, which made me feel even more excluded. True, Grandma spoke little English, but my mother-in-law, Clara, could have explained what they were discussing. I was always afraid they were talking about me. I suppose Bob was used to it. He wasn't much of a conversationalist himself, which often left me with the old familiar sensation that I was invisible, as I had so often felt during my childhood: my mother had been preoccupied with concerns about my father and had little time or patience for her children.

I still had to help wash all the dishes in the hotter-than-hell kitchen, with my feet swelling until they looked like great water-filled balloons. All I wanted was a cool, quiet spot in which to have a nap. The Irvines were not happy when we took some Sundays off to go apartment hunting. I knew they thought it was my fault and that I was being selfish, but Sunday was usually the only time we had together, since Bob worked on most Saturdays, and we simply had to find different accommodation before the baby arrived.

Soon after we had missed a Sunday at the Irvines', Bob received a phone call from his mother. In the course of the conversation she told him that their dog had died. I had never paid much attention to it because they always kept it tied up on their back porch. Once, on a particularly cold day, I'd asked if I could bring the dog inside but the Irvines had informed me that he was not a house dog. I never understood why people had a dog if they kept it outside. Anyway, on our next visit, I expressed my sympathy at their loss and asked what had happened.

'Well, sometimes he just went crazy,' said my mother-in-law, 'usually if he got overexcited, like if he saw a squirrel or something. He'd go mad trying to get at it.' It didn't sound crazy to me. That was what all dogs did. 'Anyway,' she continued, 'he tried to jump over the railing of the back porch and he hanged himself on his leash. We found him there when we got home from shopping. We thought it was strange that he didn't bark when we came in.'

'How awful for him,' I said, then added, 'and for you, too, of course.'

On our way home that evening, I couldn't hold back my laughter.

'What's so funny?' Bob asked.

'Well, I know how miserable I was living with your family. Maybe the dog was too. I was just wondering if maybe he committed suicide,' I replied, laughing so hard I could hardly get the words out.

'It's not funny,' he said, looking very serious, but then he saw the funny side and joined in. 'Yeah, if we think those Sundays are painful for us, that poor dog didn't even get to come in for dinner.'

'Yeah, but he didn't have to wash all those flippin' dishes either,' I said. Poor dog, I thought, but at least he doesn't have to put up with them any more. Bob was right, though: it wasn't funny, poor little guy, tied up on the porch no matter what the weather. He'd earned his place in dog heaven.

We finally found an apartment, still on Chicago's west side but in a far nicer neighbourhood: it was quieter and more residential. After much deliberation, Bob decided we might just about be able to afford to go from fifty-five dollars a month in rent to seventy-five, even though it would be hard when I had to give up my job.

The apartment was on the second floor, had much larger rooms, a separate bedroom and a 'sun-porch'. It also had laundry facilities in the basement, which meant I would no longer have to go to the Laundromat. It was more convenient to do the washing down there, but I still hated it. The basement was dark, dirty and draped with enormous cobwebs. Bob's parents gave us their old washing machine, an ancient top-loader with a wringer on the side. You had to fill it using hoses, which you attached to the taps, one for cold water and the other for hot. At least a dozen lines were strung across the basement for the building's occupants to hang their washing to dry.

Worse than doing the laundry, though, was the ironing. At work, Bob wore what he called wash-pants and wash-shirts. In those days, they were made of heavy 100 per cent cotton twill and were almost impossible to iron. My mother-in-law told me I needed 'pants stretchers', which was what she used for Daddy's bus-driver uniforms – she always called him 'Daddy' when speaking to or about him – so Bob and I duly bought some. They were metal frames in the shape of a trouser leg that you inserted into each leg while they were wet. The frames were expandable and once you had them inside the legs, you stretched them as far as they would go. This stopped the trousers shrinking and supposedly made them easier to iron. Ha, I thought, easy for them to say. But I digress.

The new apartment was directly across the street from Our Lady Help of Christians Catholic Church on Iowa Street, which turned out to be a source of free entertainment as there were always weddings to watch on Saturdays from the glassed-in sun-porch. We moved in when I was seven and a half months pregnant, which was also the right time for me to stop working. I hated to leave my job with Happy Harry's, but since the season was slowing down anyway, it seemed perfect timing. Besides, I knew the Morrises and I would remain friends, and that I could rely on Joan if I needed advice or help, but I hated leaving my British friend Alice Hawryluk and all those lovely cups of tea.

Bob and I enjoyed shopping for our new home. We'd had to do it quickly because we had no furniture, except the kitchen table and chairs, which had been a gift. We bought a suite of living-room furniture, including curtains, table lamps, rugs for the floor and a TV set. We also bought a bedroom set, complete with cut-glass dressing-table lamps, and put it in the dining room, leaving the bedroom as a nursery for the baby. Everything we bought was the latest fashion. The couch and chair were covered with turquoise bouclé fabric, which had silver thread running through it. The curtains were bark cloth, with huge country scenes, in pink, turquoise and grey. The bedroom furniture and living-room tables were in blond wood. I thought it was all very posh, and although it would take a long time to pay it off, the whole lot had cost only about three hundred dollars. The entire apartment had recently had a fresh coat of paint – heaven compared to our previous, rather grim home. There were plenty of windows, too, making the rooms light and cheerful, and we could open them and enjoy refreshing cross-breezes. Summer had finally ended and the weather began to cool. I could now see a strong possibility that I might survive in this strange country, after all.

Shortly after we moved into our lovely new apartment, I received some bad news. Alice had had a freak accident about two weeks after we'd moved out of our old place. She had fainted in the bathroom one day when no one else was at home and had lain unconscious, her face wedged against the radiator's hot-water pipe where it came out of the floor. It had burned her flesh to the bone and left her terribly disfigured. I wanted to visit her but she wouldn't let me. 'I don't want you to see me like this while you're pregnant,' she said. 'It might not be good for you or the baby.' I didn't understand at the time but someone later told me that, according to old wives' tales, your baby could be disfigured if you looked at someone's deformity. I was surprised that Alice still believed such nonsense but I appreciated her concern for our unborn child.

7: Our Baby, Motherhood and My First Visit Home

We walked into Bob's parents' house one Sunday – and I almost had a heart attack. About forty people were crowded into the living and dining rooms and they all shouted, '*Surprise!*' I hadn't a clue what was going on so I just stood there, shocked, and gaped at everyone.

'What's going on?' I asked Bob. I knew it wasn't a birth-day party and it was the wrong time of year for any other celebration.

'It's a shower,' he said, with a huge grin. 'Presents for the baby. It's what people do here.' Oh, Lord, I thought. These Americans are so weird! Fancy making all these people who hardly know me buy gifts for a baby who isn't even here yet.

Bob's family certainly had surprised me. I was almost knocked off my feet – which wouldn't have been easy to achieve, given the size, shape and weight of me. Even my usually sensible husband had begun teasing me about my pregnant self.

Until that moment, I'd had no idea what a shower was. We didn't have them in the UK back in those days – well, not that kind anyway. The only showers in England were more like torrential downpours.

I couldn't believe my eyes when I saw so many people gathered, and with all those gifts too. Even people who were unable to attend had sent something. All we had left to buy was a pram. I still hadn't felt much warmth from Bob's family – in fact, mostly what I felt was disapproval, impatience or resentment – but when it came to gifts, they were tops.

By now, I had given up my job and was trying to enjoy our new apartment, but it wasn't easy. I had no friends nearby, and Bob was still working long hours, including most Saturdays. He would come home from work exhausted, eat his dinner and fall asleep before we had any chance to engage in conversation. I was desperately lonely. My only activities were the now more frequent visits to my obstetrician, talking on the phone to my friend Barbara McCarthy, or Bobby, as I now called her, taking short walks, cooking and cleaning, and re-organizing the baby's room, which I did every other day.

I loved putting the tiny baby clothes in the drawers and arranging the stuffed toys and other paraphernalia. I often took all the little things out to look at them – if the truth be known, it was like playing house. But this was no game because I was about to become a mother, and soon. Oh, how I wished my own mother could have been there to help me, not that she ever had in the past but I knew she loved babies and I was sure this would have brought us closer. It would have helped to talk to her on the phone, but that was impossible too: Mum and Dad still didn't have one.

I was supposed to be due before Christmas of 1955 and everyone thought that, since I was now enormous – and, believe me, I was – it might be sooner rather than later, but Christmas came and went with only slight twinges that we thought might be labour pains but were not. Then we hoped the baby would at least have the decency to arrive before midnight on New Year's Eve so that we would have the benefit of the 1955 tax deduction. With this in mind, dear Dr Crown sent me to hospital to have labour induced. The contractions started, but then they stopped again and the doctor sent me home, feeling very disappointed. New Year's Eve came and went, and by now I was so uncomfortable I had to sleep sitting up. I had gained at least fifty pounds, perhaps partly because my mother kept telling me to remember I was eating for two. After six months' morning sickness, I had really begun to enjoy my food, especially ice cream, and looked as though I'd been eating for four.

By 4 January I was still showing no sign of going into labour, so the next day Dr Crown sent me back to Columbus Hospital (on Lake Shore Drive in Chicago) to be induced again. This time it worked. Oh, boy, it certainly did. I thought it would never end. A strange thing happened while I was in the labour room: a man – I guessed he was medical staff – came in to examine me. All he did was fondle my breasts, and when he heard someone coming, he covered me and left. I was sure he had touched me inappropriately – he might have been housekeeping staff even – but I was in too much pain to think any more of it. When I mentioned it to Bob, he told me I was crazy.

When I was taken into the delivery room, Dr Crown hadn't arrived, so they gave me some kind of gas to slow things down. I could hear myself singing, apparently quite loudly, between contractions, and the nurses imploring me to be quiet. My doctor had asked them to slow the contractions because he didn't want to miss the big event, and he did not. I later learned that he had been concerned about the birth because of the size of the baby and my apparently immature pelvic measurement. It was a difficult delivery and I was sure I was going to die. What a relief it was, at last, to hear one of the nurses announce, 'You have a healthy baby boy.'

'You call that ox a baby!' was Dr Crown's response.

Phew! I'd done it. I had a son and he was perfect . . . If only my family was with me to share my joy and if only I felt less lonely . . .

Bob sent Mum and Dad a telegram announcing the birth of our baby and we received one back, congratulating us and telling us they were overjoyed. Later, when Mum heard that I'd had an episiotomy, she was horrified. Apparently, they were only performed in England when the life of the mother or baby was in danger. In some small way, I was pleased to hear that my mum was worried about me, but it made me miss her more than ever.

That dear Dr Crown: several months later, we realized we had never received a bill from him, and when I called his office to ask about it, I was told there was nothing to pay. I was reduced to tears by his kindness.

Bob was ecstatic that we had produced a boy; he cried as he thanked me for giving him a son. However, we did not give in to family pressure to name him Robert Henry Irvine III. Bob was a 'junior' but we thought that was as far as it should go. We named our son Wayne Robert: Wayne because it was an all-American name and Robert after his daddy, his paternal grandfather and my younger brother. They'd just have to get used to our break with tradition.

Foolishly, I was anxious to leave the hospital and get home to take care of the baby myself. I was still uncomfortable after the episiotomy, and shuffled along like an old woman. My friend Joan Morris lectured when she visited me in the hospital: 'Don't be in such a hurry! It'll be the last rest you have for years, believe me.'

Later I wished I'd listened to her. She was so right, and why wouldn't she be? She had recently given birth to her fourth child.

We left the comfort of the hospital three days after Wayne's birth, and then another nightmare began. I tried desperately to nurse him but it just didn't work. My breasts and nipples were extremely painful and he was not getting enough to eat. Consequently we were both crying a lot. In fact, the baby was screaming blue murder. By now, Bob was at his wit's end, frustrated because he didn't know what to do for either of us and short-tempered from lack of sleep.

'Maybe your mom could come over to help,' I suggested.

'I hinted about it last time I talked to her but she didn't offer. I don't think she can get away from Dad and Roberta – or she thinks they can't manage without her,' he said.

I kept my mouth shut. I was sure she didn't care enough, but that was nothing new to me.

I felt inadequate as a mother. Each day I wished my mother was with me, to give advice and support. She and I had never been close, but I knew that now she would have taken care of the baby and me, without hesitation.

The next blow to my confidence came when the baby's

paediatrician told me I must stop trying to breastfeed Wayne and give him a bottle. I followed his orders but was terribly disappointed at my perceived failure. However, Wayne was at last a happy baby and we all began to get some sleep.

Our respite was short-lived. A new problem arose. I developed mastitis. I was in agony with inflamed, engorged breasts, and bleeding, cracked nipples. I also had a raging fever and was delirious at times. I knew that I looked like an ugly, bloated cow, which made me feel even worse; I just wanted to die. Bob had been able to take only a few days off after we came home from the hospital and was already back at work, leaving me alone and in a dreadful state. Again, we thought Bob's mother might come to help when she heard how ill I was, but we were wrong. She came by bus, just once, and that was to drop off some homemade soup for Bob. For me, there was no one, and once again, I felt utterly alone and worthless. Yes, I was extremely sorry for myself.

I'm ashamed to say that, in those days, I was not a very good mother or wife. I just didn't know how to cope. What a blessing it was that Wayne had settled and was now such a contented child. He was a joy, but I still had great difficulty in keeping up with the housekeeping and other 'wifely duties'. Bob had insisted on having sex before I had completely healed down below and intercourse was excruciating. I later learned that a couple of the episiotomy stitches had torn loose; no wonder it had been painful. Saying no to my once gentle, patient husband was out of the question.

For a long time, I didn't want to get out of bed in the

mornings, often staying there until midday. I would get up to feed and change the baby but then would take him into bed with me and we would go back to sleep. I was realizing that I was very much alone and that I couldn't expect Bob's family to replace my own, and perhaps I was experiencing what is now recognized as post-natal depression. My depression deepened, and it was as much as I could do to function from day to day. Bob offered little comfort or support because, basically, he didn't know how. We were both frightened and I'm sure I wasn't alone in praying for an answer, and the answer came.

When we heard that my brother Peter was to be married in August 1956, Bob decided that perhaps it would be good for me to go home to show off our son and attend the wedding. To finance the trip, and against his parents' advice and wishes, he cashed in some of the savings bonds they had bought for him. Now, with me having new hope and energy, we made plans. In my secret heart I wasn't sure if I would come back to America but I desperately needed to go, and soon. At that time, plane fares cost a small fortune, but we decided that if I didn't go, the consequences might be far more costly.

Wayne was about seven months old and I had been away for almost eighteen when we made that first trip back to the UK. I felt as though I had lived another entire lifetime since Valentine's Day of the previous year. Now, buoyed by excitement, I had nothing but overwhelming gratitude to Bob for having found a way to make the journey possible. I believe he knew how much it meant to me and how much it might help me to be with my family for a while. Even as we prepared for the trip, my depression had begun to lift.

The journey was torturous. Carrying a heavy baby plus all his equipment was difficult enough, but back then there was no such thing as a direct flight from Chicago to London: we had to change planes in New York, where there was a long layover. It was difficult changing and feeding the baby, as well as taking care of luggage at the airport terminal. When we began our journey, we looked very smart, but by the time we got on that second plane, we were a sodden mess.

For the overnight segment of our journey, I had arranged to have a portable crib for Wayne to sleep in, but I had not counted on having to hold it on my lap; it made it almost impossible for me to move, especially when I had to use the toilet. The whole journey took twenty-four hours, whereas today it takes seven or eight. What a difference!

Dawn was breaking as our plane began its descent over England, and I wept uncontrollably to see the patchwork quilt of fields below. The sun was shining on my beloved homeland; it looked like heaven to me. All I could think was that I would soon see the faces of my own dear family, the family I had missed so much, and I could hardly wait. I was bursting with excitement.

An eternity seemed to pass before we staggered through the final gate after retrieving our baggage and clearing Customs. I scanned the waiting crowds. Then I saw them. My whole family was standing there, beaming from ear to ear. We fell into each other's arms, Mum took her grandson from me, and we wept with joy. I was home.

After the initial torrent of tears and repeated hugs, Dad was most anxious to tell me about the transport he had borrowed from friends to take us home.

'Come on, Iris, just wait till you see the lovely carriage that awaits you,' he said.

'Yeah, you won't half feel posh,' chimed in Mum.

Mum and Dad still had no car and, of course, I hadn't even thought of that small detail. What a laugh I had when I saw that they'd come to meet us in Knight's the greengrocer's van, which was used for fetching produce from the London market to the shop in South Oxhey; it was the only vehicle large enough to hold all of us and the luggage. We piled happily, if not stylishly, into the back of the grubby van; we had to sit on produce boxes, and baby Wayne travelled comfortably inside an orange crate, as we headed for home. It was not exactly a triumphal entry, but definitely far more fun.

When I walked into Mum's kitchen and she put the kettle on for a cup of tea, it was as if I had never left. I walked around the house just looking at and touching everything. It was wonderful to be home and I couldn't get enough of it. Mum took over with Wayne, and after I'd had 'a lovely cup of tea', I crawled into bed for a nap that lasted about sixteen hours. I was completely exhausted.

My first few days in England were filled with eating all the foods I had missed, talking for hours on end about my experiences in America and what was happening in my life, visits to family and friends, plus preparing for Peter's wedding. The greatest gift of all was the laughter. Oh, how I had missed it. Stupid jokes, my brothers and I teasing Mum to get her laughing and hearing her old refrain,

'Stop muckin' about, you lot,' and recalling funny incidents. My life in America had been devoid of such shared humour and lightheartedness, and I decided I had to find a way to bring it into my life there. I didn't know how I'd do it, but I knew it was what I needed.

A feature story appeared in the local newspaper, the *Watford Observer*, announcing, 'So Iris Will Be Home for the Wedding'. When Bob and I had got married two years earlier, it had published an article about our own wedding, probably because I was only sixteen. Now that I had returned home after just a year and half, I was newsworthy again: not many of the local girls who had married Americans had made return visits – or none that had received any publicity. I never did learn who had told the newspaper about my visit. It might have been Peter and Brenda when they were giving the details of their wedding to one of its journalists, as was usual back then, but it might also have been my father, who loved being in the limelight.

I felt quite the celebrity, and certainly all the attention and affection I was getting from family and friends was just what I needed to pull me out of the deep depression I had been experiencing.

The wedding was beautiful, and my reunion with our entire extended family and so many friends was wonderful. There are no words to describe how it felt to be back with my own people and to feel somehow reconnected with the world. All the time I'd been away, I had felt *dis*connected, like a piece in a jigsaw puzzle that doesn't seem to fit anywhere.

While Wayne and I were away, Bob wrote to me regularly, telling me how much he was missing us. He tugged at my heartstrings, but as the date of our departure neared, I began having panic attacks. Repeatedly, through torrents of uncontrollable tears, I told Mum and Dad that I was terrified to go back, that I didn't think I could do it again. Dad would also cry, but they both kept telling me that I had to return to America and try to make my life work there. They stressed that Wayne and I could have a much better life in America with Bob than we could ever hope to have in England, and that I owed it to my son to accept responsibility for the decision I had made when I'd married his father. Talking to Mum one afternoon, I heard things I didn't want to hear.

'You wouldn't want to end up here living in a council flat,' she said.

'Why would I have to live in a council flat?' I asked. 'I want to come home, Mum.'

'Where would everyone sleep? There isn't room now that you have the baby, Iris. You'd have to have the bigger bedroom and the two boys [my younger brothers] would be stuck in the box room.'

I didn't want to hear any more. I didn't want to accept that there was no longer room for me in what I still considered my home. In my heart, I knew she was right but the thought of leaving home and family again was tearing me apart and I was scared to death about the future.

After six weeks of nourishment to both body and soul, and after painful goodbyes, my little son and I flew back to Bob and another attempt at making a good marriage and a success of my life in America.

8: Back in the USA – Family, Friends and Independence

Arriving in Chicago, to an anxious, excited husband, I found that Bob had arranged for Wayne to stay with his parents so that he and I could go away by ourselves for a long weekend, a kind of second honeymoon. As I looked at him and saw the love in his eyes for both Wayne and me, I knew I had to give our relationship, and America, another chance, but this time I'd have to make an even greater effort.

Going home to England had been both a gift and a curse. I had loved being in familiar surroundings with my own people. The first time I'd left home and family I'd been filled with excitement and dreams, but this time I knew what awaited me. Now I had to face the harsh reality of the life I had chosen in spite of everyone's warnings.

'I can't wait to have you all to myself for a little while,' he said, as he drew our son and me into his arms.

'Uh-oh! Does that mean I don't need to pack anything for the trip except my nightie?' I laughed nervously.

'Well, who knows? Maybe you won't even need that,' he said, which was a bit bold for my usually shy husband. 'But I might give you time off for good behaviour,' he added. I wasn't quite sure what that meant, but we laughed at our own slightly naughty thoughts.

I'm sure we must have gone home to our own apartment

first, but I honestly don't remember much about it, perhaps because I was tired after the long flight from England. All I recall is the unpacking and repacking, first to get Wayne ready and dropped off with his grandparents, and then to organize ourselves. We were going to get to know each other again. I think we were both a little apprehensive: it was almost like going on a first date.

We stayed in a beautiful rustic lodge in Starved Rock State Park, which is near North Utica, Illinois, and is a very romantic setting. Holding hands, we took long walks along the river and through rocky canyons; we saw waterfalls, rode horses, slept late and generally enjoyed our time together. At first, we were a little shy and nervous, just as we had been on our honeymoon, but we whispered our love and slept in each other's arms. It was wonderful and I wanted our holiday never to end.

We were shy with each other throughout our marriage, perhaps because of our age, lack of worldliness, or because we had grown up in households in which outward displays of affection were rare. I was always amused that even as adults we could not call our sex organs by their anatomical names. Bob always referred to mine as 'Janey and her sisters', and even that sounded rude to me back then.

When we returned to our apartment, life was a little easier for me and I found myself better able to cope. I was healthier, physically and mentally, and couldn't have wished for a more perfect or contented child.

One of the first things I did after I'd got back was to call my British friend Bobby McCarthy. 'I'm back,' I said, 'ready to face the music again. I wish you lived closer, though. I need you to keep me sane.'

She laughed. 'Don't worry, Iris, I've found something that you'll love. It's a sort of club for British women and they meet once a month, downtown in Chicago. Most of the women were GI brides and they've all been through the same things that we have. I've only been to one meeting but it was great fun. We even had tea and English biscuits.'

'Sounds great! When do we go?' I said. I could hardly wait to see Bobby, and was thrilled at the prospect of meeting more fellow British women.

The organization was called Daughters of the British Empire (DBE), and Bobby had been right. The women I met there were amazing, but best of all was that each one had a great sense of humour. What a relief to find this haven, which made me a little less homesick. The members all seemed to love throwing parties and having get-togethers; there was usually a party every month at someone's home. It was comforting to be with people who enjoyed the same things and spoke the same language. Most of the women had been married during the war and were considerably older than I was, so I was the baby of the group and they all took care of me. At one of my early meetings, a wonderful woman named Joan Murphy, who was Regent of our DBE chapter, the House of Windsor, asked, 'How old were you, Iris, when the Second World War started?'

'One or two,' I replied, whereupon she choked, spraying tea from her nose.

When at last she composed herself, still with tears of laughter rolling down her face, she explained, to our puzzled group, 'That's how old I was when the *First* World War started.' We had a good laugh over that.

The British consul general and his wife attended one of Joan's parties. As always, after dinner, we played silly games. In one, the men stood behind a sheet with just their legs from the knees down showing, and the wives had to pick out their own husband's knees. Then it was the women's turn. Well, my poor Bob marched right up to the sheet, bent down and grabbed a leg. 'I'd know this skinny old sausage anywhere!' he shouted.

It belonged to the consul general's wife, and I honestly don't know who was more mortified, poor shy Bob or her. We teased him about that for a long time and my British friends nicknamed me Sausage Legs, which was nothing new since my brother Robert had once told me that my legs were like sausages. I don't think the consul general and his wife came to any more of our parties. They did invite us all to cocktails at their swish apartment once, but after one of our girls threw up over their bed, we never saw them again.

The DBE's annual fête was fun too. It was held at the British Old People's Home in Brookfield, Illinois, and was modelled on English village fêtes, with stalls, maypole dancing, games and races. They even served cream teas in the food tent, and it always ended with a performance by Chicago's Stockyard Kiltie Band. Hearing the bagpipes and watching the swirl of the kilts always made me emotional; it was hard not to cry. The old people's home, though, had been built next door to Brookfield Zoo, which provided material for many jokes.

Bob was usually reluctant to go to parties or events like the fête.

'We've been invited to a party this weekend,' I'd tell him.

'We're not going,' he'd say. 'You know I don't like parties.'

'Please, Bob, I've been stuck in the house for weeks and I need to get out.'

At first he made the effort to take me, and I think he managed to enjoy himself once he was there, especially after he'd had a few drinks, but later he began refusing to go. I didn't know why the fun had gone out of him, and decided to ask if it would be okay for me to go without him.

'Will you take care of the baby, then, if I can get someone to take me?' I'd plead. Sometimes he said yes, at others he said no; when he said no, I was devastated. When he agreed to baby-sit, I would arrange for someone to pick me up and take me, then bring me home. I didn't want to miss time with my English friends: I needed them. In addition, when I visited the neighbours I'd met in the apartment building, he usually chose to stay at home watching TV. For the most part, all Bob wanted was for dinner to be ready when he came home from work, then to sit in an armchair, where he usually dozed off until it was time to go to bed. My once fun-loving husband had disappeared and been replaced by an old stick-in-the-mud. When we were with people, the old Bob reappeared, his cute smile, his lovable chuckle, it was all there, so why couldn't he show it at home to me?

More and more frequently, after putting the baby to bed, I'd leave Bob snoozing in his chair and wander downstairs to my neighbours, the Ballmaiers, where at least I had someone to talk to. I'm sure Bob wasn't very sociable because of his upbringing. The Ballmaiers, Cindy and Phil, were true social animals. They always seemed to have company, always had the coffee pot on and always cooked huge amounts of food to feed whoever turned up. They were a blessing to me in those days.

Cindy and I still laugh about the time she came up to our apartment to have coffee with me and to let our two little ones play together. The boys, who were the same age, having been born just a week apart, were playing on the newly carpeted floor of our living room, while Cindy and I were in the kitchen, chatting over coffee and cake. Suddenly, an awful stench drifted into the kitchen, overpowering the aroma of the gorgeous, freshly baked cake we'd been enjoying.

'What's that smell?' I said.

'Smell?' she replied, almost choking on her cake. 'It smells like shit to me.'

We dashed down the hallway to investigate and, to my horror, found that one of the little angels had messed his pants. The result had fallen out onto the carpet and they were now happily bulldozing it everywhere with their toy trucks. No wonder they'd been so quiet.

One day when Cindy and Phil's child, Little Phil, came running through the living room he tripped over his toy Mickey Mouse guitar. As he started to cry, we heard him mutter, 'Fucking Mickey Mouse!' Of course, his parents claimed they had no idea where he had heard such language. That little boy, whose mouth was washed out with soap, is now a minister . . .

As I think about the Ballmaiers, I'm reminded of another entertaining event that they shared with me. I'm sure it wasn't funny to them when it happened, but I still grin when I think about it. Apparently, Cindy was in the living room talking to an insurance man. Phil was elsewhere in the house so was unaware that Cindy wasn't alone. Suddenly, he called out to her: 'Hey, Cin, come see the size of this turd I just did. I've never seen such a long one.' Poor Cindy, I can only imagine how she felt, and God knows what the insurance man thought. She said he left in rather a hurry.

I had never before met anyone quite like the Ballmaiers, nor have I since, but Phil claimed a special place in my heart because of something he did for me soon after we first met. He and Cindy invited Bob and me for dinner one evening, and when we got there, I had the shock of my life – well, almost. Besides cooking platters full of his famous fried chicken, he had baked a birthday cake for me, complete with eighteen candles. 'Cindy told me you'd never had a birthday cake,' he explained, 'and when she told me it was your birthday in a couple of days, I thought I'd better remedy that. I can't believe you've never had a birthday cake before.' Well, I cried like a baby. His thoughtfulness bowled me over.

I don't know when I began to get restless but I knew I needed to do more with my life. The problem was that I lacked the confidence and skills to go out and get a decent job, and I felt decidedly frumpy.

One day as I was browsing through the newspaper for inspiration, I saw an advertisement for Sabie's Modelling School. It offered evening classes and promised to 'give you the confidence you need to do something worthwhile with your life'. It was as though the ad was there just for me. I knew I was not model material but felt that if I went through their training I might gain the confidence I needed to make something of myself. I rang to ask for more information.

'Are you crazy?' shouted Bob.

'How selfish,' commented his parents, who somehow became involved in the debate.

'You go for it,' encouraged Cindy and Phil.

I begged and pleaded, promising I would find a way to pay back the money it would cost. One of my arguments was that I'd be able to get a decent job so that we could save to buy a house. That idea seemed to appeal to Bob, who said he'd think about it.

Of course, Bob and his family thought I was crazy, and I'd known they would, but I signed up anyway. I don't remember what it cost but it wasn't much. I managed to stretch the housekeeping money and was able to make small weekly payments; I also had a little birthday money put away. The classes were held once a week, in the evening, so usually Bob could baby-sit, but if he was being difficult about it, as he sometimes was, I could always leave Wayne with the Ballmaiers.

I thoroughly enjoyed the classes. They were what I imagined finishing school to be like. We learned about makeup, hairstyles, clothes and appropriate accessorizing, walking, sitting and standing correctly, how to enter and leave a room graciously, and so on. It was great fun and the class often dissolved into gales of laughter at some of our less successful attempts at graciousness. At the end of the course, the graduates' husbands, boyfriends and others came to watch the fashion show we put on and to see us get our diplomas. I was the only one there with no family in attendance, but that was nothing new: when I was a child, no one had ever come to see me in school plays.

Surprisingly, after I left Sabie's I had some calls to do modelling assignments, not runway stuff, of course, but enough to boost my confidence and morale. I mostly did catalogue work for Montgomery Ward or Sears Roebuck, or modelled at shows for the wholesale buyers' markets. I still laugh when I think of how skinny I was at the time; I sometimes had to wrap a small towel around my middle to fill out the dress or coat I was modelling. It was hard work and the pay was good but I knew I wanted, and needed, to get a full-time job.

While all this was going on, my brother Peter and his wife Brenda decided to come to America. They would stay for just a couple of years and hoped to make enough money to go back to England and buy a decent house. I was thrilled at the prospect of having some of my own flesh and blood nearby. Bob was kind enough to sponsor them into the United States and, as luck would have it, the apartment next door to ours became available so we snatched it up for them. I could never have believed I'd be lucky enough to have family close by. It was a miracle.

Peter had no problem getting a good job, as he was a fully qualified journeyman compositor and a member of the International Printers' Union. He started work just a day or two after they'd arrived in the US. Initially, he had to work night shifts, so Brenda and I spent many evenings together. We loved it when Peter stopped off at the bakery on his way home from work in the morning to pick up a loaf of freshly baked Gonnella bread, still warm from the oven and crunchy. I would go over to their apartment and we would sit at their kitchen table, eating slice after slice of bread and jam. I had missed good bakery bread since I'd been in America, so the crusty French and Italian bread we bought was like manna from heaven.

Shortly after Peter and Brenda came to the States we and our parents each bought a tape recorder. They were the reel-to-reel type and it took ages to fill one of the tapes, but at last we could actually talk to each other, hear each other's voices. I used to live for the days when a tape arrived in the mail. Mum and Dad still didn't have a telephone and had no idea when they'd be able to get one. Anyway, on a tape we could chat for hours while on the telephone we could talk for a few minutes at most. I wish I still had those tapes but they were soon forgotten after telephones and travel between the two countries became more available and affordable.

When the novelty of having my family next door began to wear off, I believe Bob became jealous of my friendship with Brenda because we spent a lot of time together. We were always nattering over cups of tea, she telling me about her family, the life she'd left behind in England, and how hard it was being in America, with Peter working nights and sleeping all day. It was wonderful to share everything we had in common, the memories of home and families, and the difficulties we faced in the States, the frequent homesickness and our guilt at leaving our mothers. We shared lots of laughter and tears, and always tried to see the funny side of things.

On one occasion the funny side was hard to find. For some reason, perhaps our janitor was away, the garbage bin, which we shared on the porch between our facing back doors, hadn't been emptied for at least a week. It was now overflowing and we couldn't get the lid to close, so Brenda and I decided to take it down to the basement ourselves. We each took a handle, and as we lifted it, it tipped, emptying the contents all over the back porch and down the stairs.

'Shit,' I said.

'Oh, my God,' screamed Brenda, and when I realized what she was screaming about, I screamed too. Millions of maggots were crawling everywhere.

'I knew that garbage had been left too long,' I said.

'Now what do we do?' moaned Brenda.

'Let's see if we can just sweep them down the stairs and over the edge,' was my first suggestion. I fetched a broom and began to sweep, but got nowhere.

'They're just crawling back,' said Brenda. 'We'll have to kill them.'

'What with?' I asked, but then I had an idea. 'I'm going to run some really hot water and put bleach in it. That should kill the little buggers.' Off I went to prepare the lethal potion.

When I came back out, I took off my shoes so they wouldn't get wet, and began swooshing the water over the maggots and sweeping them away in a tide of noxious hot water. Brenda stood and watched as I sloshed about in the now muddy, maggoty water. It took ages to sweep it all the way down two flights of stairs and off two back porches. I left the broom by the basement door, staggered back up the stairs, and told Brenda, 'If I don't get a cup of tea soon, I'm going to die.'

'Well,' she said, 'you can't come in here with those dirty feet. You'll have to wash them first.' Then she added, 'You can't wash them in the sink, Iris. That would be disgusting. You'll have to flush them clean in the toilet.' And that was exactly what I had to do before she'd make me a cup of tea. We've often laughed about that nightmare situation, but it still makes me shudder.

Brenda and I often went shopping in the evening, as girls do, and we occasionally went to see a movie. This meant Bob had to baby-sit, but he usually just wanted to watch TV anyway, while I was not prepared to sit out the rest of my life glued to a TV screen and neither was Brenda. One night Brenda and I were watching a movie when, about halfway through, the film suddenly stopped and there was an announcement over the loudspeaker, which at first I didn't understand.

'They're calling your name, Iris. They want you to come to the manager's office right away,' said Brenda.

'Oh, God, no, something must have happened to the baby!'

We scooted out of our seats and rushed up the aisle towards the exit. Scared half to death, we went to the foyer, and there was Bob, with Wayne in his arms. 'Come on,' he shouted. 'Your son's been crying ever since you left and I want to go to bed.'

Everyone was staring at us and I could have died of shame at the idea that people might think I was neglecting my baby, and at the spectacle my husband was making of himself and me. I wasn't sure if I hated Bob or myself more. On the drive home, I clung to my small son and cried. Eventually I glanced at Brenda. She looked back at me and shrugged, as if to say, 'Don't look at me. I don't know what to say or think either.' I dreaded the scene that might erupt when we got home, but there was no scene. Bob didn't say a word, just took off his clothes and went to bed, while I sat there, crying and rocking Wayne, all the time thinking what a terrible person I must be.

Shortly afterwards, Bob said he had a surprise for us. I thought he must be trying to make up for our recent trouble. 'We're going on vacation,' he said. 'Someone at work told me about a place in Michigan that's cheap and right on a small lake. They have cabins for families and you can either cook your own food or arrange to have meals included.'

'Where is it?' I asked.

'It's called Paw Paw Lake and it's in Coloma, not too far to drive, and it'll be cooler there. What do you think?'

'Sounds great.' The change of scenery would do us both good. Perhaps we'd be able to get closer again, re-kindle the flame that used to burn so brightly.

Excited, we made plans for our holiday. Summer was just about over and Bob told me it would be beautiful in Michigan, with the leaves on the trees beginning to change colour.

'Autumn comes to Michigan earlier than it does in Chicago,' he told me, 'and it won't be as crowded as it is in summer time. That part of Michigan is famous for its apples, so we'll have to bring a couple of bushels home for Mom to make into apple sauce.'

'I can hardly wait!'

So, off we went on a week's holiday. I'd be able to tell my family back home that I'd visited another of America's many states.

The resort we'd booked into was a series of small, very old cabins, furnished to a minimal standard, but it was perfectly adequate for our needs. On the first day, we drove around the area, checking out where everything was, especially the grocery since we planned to cook most of our meals. The second day was glorious: the sun was shining and it was still warm during the daytime. We borrowed a couple of inflated rubber inner tubes and floated around on the lake for hours, that being my only option since I couldn't swim.

Wayne had a grand time, taking turns with each of us to paddle around in the rubber dinghies. At one point, Bob had apparently hung around the old wooden dock with him for too long because when I hauled Wayne out of the water his little legs were covered with black things. I screamed, and soon Bob was beside me.

'Oh, my God,' he said, 'they're leeches! Quick! Get the salt!' I ran into the cabin and got the shaker. By the time I returned, Bob was pulling leeches off Wayne's legs, and when we sprinkled salt on them, they curled up and fell off.

'We can't go in the water any more,' I told Bob. I was still shaking with fright, and I knew I had nightmares to look forward to, but Wayne grinned. He didn't seem fazed by the experience at all.

'He wasn't scared until you screamed,' laughed Bob, but I still didn't think it was funny. We told the old couple who ran the resort what had happened.

'Just steer clear of the dock, honey, and you won't have to worry about leeches cos that's the only place you'll find 'em.'

The following day, the next disaster hit. I hadn't slept well on the night of the leeches. I was still upset about what had happened but I was also having difficulty breathing. Oh, no, I thought. Don't tell me I'm coming down with a cold. By morning my eyes had swollen shut and I could hardly swallow. My palate was swollen too, almost completely blocking my air passages.

Bob rushed up to the resort owner's house to find out what we should do. They told us to leave Wayne with them and get to the hospital right away, and that was what we did.

We learned that many people coming from out of the area had severe allergic reactions at that time of the year, something to do with ragweed pollen in the vicinity. They also told us that it was a particularly bad year for it.

The hospital staff shot me full of antihistamine, which knocked me out for the next two days. We felt it safer to cut short our holiday and headed home, disappointed that our attempt at togetherness had not accomplished what we'd hoped it would.

I can't deny that Bob and I enjoyed some good times together, but we were drifting apart, and rapidly, to say nothing of the disdain that I felt coming from his family. I also can't deny that it must have been difficult for him, dealing with all my emotional problems. I'm sure that at times I was hard to live with. He had slapped me now and again, and I don't believe that was his nature but I could

93

feel his frustration building into anger. We were making each other miserable and something had to change. I decided to tell his mother what was going on.

'Can you please talk to him?' I begged, through sobs. 'He's been hitting me and I'm scared.'

'Well,' she spat back at me, 'I'm sure you deserved it.'

I remembered then that Bob had told me his father would hit his mother; I also remembered seeing her once with a black eye. She'd told us she had walked into a door. How could I have been stupid enough to think she might sympathize? I'd forgotten the old saying about blood being thicker than water. I determined then to try harder to avoid arguments, to steer clear when Bob was in a bad mood or had been drinking, to try anything and everything to protect myself from further abuse. I also promised myself that I would try to be more of the kind of wife he seemed to want, and that, I supposed, was obedient.

It had occurred to me that, in marrying so young, I had given away my youth and all the activities that you normally experience in your late teens and early twenties. For months now I had listened to Cindy, Brenda and all my other English friends exchanging stories of the fun they'd had going to dances on Saturday nights, travelling to London to see shows, holidays with friends at Butlin's holiday camps. I had done none of those things, except for a couple of days out with Bob while we were courting. There seemed to be a huge chunk missing from my life, a chunk that I hadn't thought important in my haste to get married before Bob went back to America. Perhaps that was what my parents had warned me about. Perhaps this was what they were afraid would happen, that I would suddenly realize what I had missed. Of course, they had been right: all of the things they had predicted might happen were happening, but what could I do except try to make things work? Two things ran through my mind: I must not let my parents down, and they must not think of me as a failure. I hoped my connections with other GI brides, Cindy Ballmaier and my sister-in-law Brenda would help me to make up for lost time and my lost youth. I thought that enjoying a new and different kind of entertainment would enable me to forget what I had missed, but to do that, I needed the support of my husband and his patience seemed to be running out.

We did two things with other couples that made me hope our social life was improving. First, Bob invited Peter and Brenda to attend his union's annual dinner and dance, which would be held at the famous Hilton Hotel in downtown Chicago. Brenda and I went shopping for something special to wear, both choosing summery white dresses. Everything went well and we were enjoying the evening until I had to visit the ladies' room. Brenda came with me. My dress had a long red scarf-type adornment that draped round the neck and fell in a flowing tail down the back of the dress. I forgot to hitch it up when I sat on the toilet. When I stood up, the now soaked tail slapped around my legs. It soon became abundantly clear that the red dye was not colour-fast. My legs, the skirt of my beautiful white dress and my shoes were sucking up the red colour, which was about the same shade as my face. At that moment, Brenda came out of her cubicle. She just stood there, staring at me. 'Oh, my God,' she said. 'What have you done?'

'What have I done? Well, it looks like I've ruined our night out. You'll have to go and tell Bob that I can't come back in.'

'I thought you were bleeding,' she muttered, as she scurried off.

While she was delivering the bad news, I tried to wash and dry myself so that at least our miserable ride home wouldn't smell like the inside of a toilet. No one said much on the way, but I could see that my husband wasn't happy. I tried to lighten the mood: 'Well, at least we got to eat our dinner,' I said, but his response was a couple of disapproving grunts.

The next attempt at a night out consisted of eight couples going for dinner and the show at a well-known nightspot. Brenda and I were particularly excited, as neither of us had ever been to such a place. We all sat at a long table and soon the drinks began to flow. Bob and I each had one, then chose the cheapest thing on the menu because that was all we could afford. Everyone else was ordering lobster and steak. None of that mattered until the bill came and someone decided that we should just split it evenly between the eight couples. I thought Bob was going to explode. Next thing I knew, everyone was staring at us while he made his feelings known.

'There's no way in hell I'm going to contribute to your goddamn lobster dinners and your endless rounds of drinks,' he shouted. 'I'll pay for what we had and that's it.' By then, everyone in the place was staring at us. I wanted to crawl under the table, but I understood his anger: we really couldn't afford to pay for such luxuries. I just wished he could have expressed it quietly. That group of friends never did invite us to go out with them again, and I can't remember what the show was like. Bob and I certainly seemed to have a problem when it came to having fun with other people.

9: The Questionable Gift of American Citizenship

In an effort to make Bob happy, I applied for American citizenship. I had been in America for three years, and that was the only requirement I had to fulfil since I was married to an American. Secretly, I gathered the information I needed to go through the naturalization process. One of my neighbours, Pat Yuskus, agreed to help me study for the test. I began in earnest, learning about American history, the Constitution, and so on. When Pat thought I was ready, I sent in my application and waited to hear back from the Office of Immigration and Naturalization.

When I received an appointment for the test I was a nervous wreck, but off I went, with Pat taking care of Wayne. Although I didn't do all that well, I passed. I could hardly believe it when the interviewer asked me questions about the Magna Carta.

'I only studied American history and politics,' I told the bored-looking official. 'I didn't expect you to ask me about British history.'

'My dear young lady,' he said, 'the Magna Carta is very much a part of American law and history.' Then, after a brief silence, he really surprised me: 'Why don't you just go ahead and tell me what you *do* know?' he said. For a moment, I was struck dumb – this wasn't how it was supposed to go – but I took a deep breath and rattled off all the facts I could remember until he said, 'That's enough. That will do nicely.'

He began to fill in some paperwork while I gave a great sigh of relief and breathed normally again.

The final step towards citizenship was the swearing-in ceremony. Finally, the big day came: in a large courtroom in the US Federal Building in Chicago, with about a hundred other people, a judge swore me in as an American citizen.

Now, I must confess that when I had to swear to take up arms against the country of my birth in the event of war with it, I crossed my fingers behind my back. I supposed that admission could get me deported, but so be it: I never could have sworn to that.

I could hardly wait to tell Bob what I had done. I had been visualizing his surprise, pride and happiness when I showed him my citizenship papers, but when I made the big announcement and proudly produced them, he reacted as if I had told him that dinner was ready. That might have been what pushed me over the edge. I don't know if I was more hurt or angry, but the wedge between us had been driven deeper. That his family had thrown a party to celebrate their daughter's husband, Mike, receiving his citizenship made it worse, but Mike seemingly allowed his in-laws to run and rule his life. He hardly ever spoke.

In the event that Bob and I separated, I knew I would need a job so I started checking the newspapers, looking for something I might be able to do. I was interviewed at an employment agency for a receptionist position that offered switchboard training, but required a little typing. I lied, telling them I could type. I think they liked the idea of having an English voice answering their telephone so they hired me to start on the following Monday morning.

It was Thursday afternoon and I spent the next three days teaching myself to type on Bob's old portable machine. On Monday morning, off I went, nervously, to start my new job. At that point, having done nothing but practise typing, I was even typing my thoughts inside my head.

I enjoyed that job and liked the people I worked with. We were always busy and the time passed quickly. My responsibilities were gradually increased and I began to feel better about myself, developing more confidence. I was also optimistic about the future now that I had more skills.

I still laugh about the way some of the job seekers filled out their applications. When it came to the box that required them to fill in their sex, instead of writing male or female (M or F), several noted the frequency of their sexual encounters. Blimey, I thought. No wonder they're out of work.

So that I could take a full-time job, I had enrolled Wayne, who was now about two and a half, at the Gay Time Nursery School. Its bus picked him up early each morning and brought him home in the evenings. On the first day, he almost broke my heart: he cried and didn't want to go; then, when he came home that evening, he wouldn't talk to me. He cried again the next morning, but that night he was babbling about his new friends and all the fun he'd had. He was also proud of the picture he'd brought home with him. The next morning, and every morning after that, my little man went off happily on the bus.

An Italian family, who treated all the children as their own, ran the nursery school, which was very well organized. It had a large playground with lots of equipment, and the children took their afternoon naps on folding cots. The grandmother, or 'Nonie' as they called her (from the Italian word *nonna*), prepared all of their food. Wayne informed me that he had carrots every day 'to make my eyes work real good', and celery, 'for my brains'. It was often hard not to laugh at some of the things he told me, with such a serious look on his face. Gay Time Nursery School still holds a special place in my children's hearts and mine; it truly was a godsend. It was more like sending your child to stay with relatives than to an institution.

With me working full time, things at home were worsening. My new-found confidence caused conflict between Bob and me. In tears at work one day, I confided in my boss, Mr Dillon, about the situation at home following a particularly unpleasant evening and night. He had seen me crying in the staff-room and he told me that he would be there for me if I ever needed to talk. The previous night, Bob had had a few beers and had become extremely belligerent. It had taken me longer than usual to get dinner on the table for him: he had complained about having to wait for his meal and that I hadn't cooked the pork chops the way he liked them. Then he derided me for getting behind with the laundry and ironing and for my reluctance to go to his parents' house every weekend.

'How am I supposed to keep up with the chores when the only time I have is on the weekends?' I countered. 'I can't be in two places at once. Don't you think you could explain that to your folks?'

'My mother worked and kept up with everything. She even managed to tile the kitchen and hang wallpaper,' he protested.

'Yes, and you told me it had almost killed her. I don't plan on letting household chores kill me. I just need time to get organized and that means having some free time on weekends.'

'Well, if you can't keep up with things at home, you're going to have to quit that job and start doing what you're supposed to be doing,' he said, as though that was final.

'Bob, I'm not going to give up my job,' I told him. 'It will just take me a little longer to get a proper routine going. I'll soon have caught up on everything.'

Then he said something that really hurt me.

'You're just lazy,' he said. 'You can't be bothered to take care of your son or me. You're selfish.'

'I'm not selfish. I thought we were going to save up for a house, which was the main reason I started working in the first place. Have you forgotten that we even went and looked at houses?' At one time, we had looked at model homes in a new sub-division, but at thirteen thousand dollars, Bob had said we couldn't afford one on his salary of ninety dollars a week: we'd have to wait until we'd saved a larger down-payment. I reminded him of all that but he carried on berating me.

By now I was crying, deeply hurt, but I was also angry. Then he took me by the shoulders and shook me. Before I could think, I hit him. Shocked by the intensity of our confrontation, we both stepped back and stared at each other. Outwardly I was shaking, but inside I was scream-ing. I'm sure we were both thinking the same thing: what's happened to us? How had we arrived at this heartbreaking impasse in our marriage? Where was the tenderness we had once known, and why had it gone? I wanted to make him happy, but if I did it his way, I would suffocate. I simply had to have something to fill the well of despair that was threatening to drown me.

I knew Bob was having a hard time dealing with my new independence. I was also aware that I was equally to blame, especially since I was no longer the passive little girl he had married. I'd had terrible mood swings after giving birth to our son but now I was dogged by depression, excruciating loneliness and frustration. I couldn't seem to do anything right. Every time I thought I had moved a step forward, his criticism and negativity brought me crashing down to an ever deeper place. Emotionally, I wasn't walking through each day, I was crawling.

The fact was that I was outgrowing him and his work-eat-sleep routine, and neither of us knew how to deal with it. I suppose that's one of the dangers of marrying too young. Just before our wedding Nat King Cole's 'They Try To Tell Us We're Too Young' was popular and I'd often heard Dad singing it. Now those words haunted me daily.

My boss, Mr Dillon, had listened patiently as I explained some of what had been happening. Eventually he told me his wife's brother was an attorney and, if I wanted, he would arrange for me to see him.

For the next few days I continued to work and tried to catch up on the household chores that Bob complained I'd been neglecting. I was exhausted from lack of sleep. My mind was in turmoil. Bob and I fought about every little thing and I was sure he was just as miserable as I was. Soon I realized that I couldn't live like that any longer: it was destroying both of us.

The following week, I told Mr Dillon it was time for me to talk to his brother-in-law.

My meeting with the attorney was difficult. He told me the grounds for divorce, if not adultery, would have to be physical cruelty. I didn't want to accuse Bob of physical abuse because I knew he wasn't an abusive person. The only times he had struck me were in moments of frustration, nothing like the violence you read about in the newspapers. Besides, I had hit him back, and that made me as bad as he was, didn't it?

When I broke the news to Bob that I had talked to an attorney, he was devastated.

'You can't do that, Iris. Please give us another chance,' he said. 'How can you possibly think you can make it on your own? How can I, for that matter?'

'It's too late, Bob. You've told me over and over again that you don't want to change just to make me happy, but I *have* changed,' I told him.

'What about Wayne? You can't take my son away from me. How do I know you won't take him to England?'

'I have no intention of taking Wayne from you. You'll still see him and maybe he'd like to have parents who aren't fighting all the time.' The arguments went back and forth for hours, but we were both aware that the conversation was going nowhere. In the end we just sat there, holding hands across the table, and cried until there were no tears left.

We had those conversations more than once, and I'm sure he knew we couldn't go on as we were, but when I finally told him I was taking action, he took it badly. Again, we cried together but I told him we had shed enough tears and that it was time for both of us to have another chance at happiness.

The divorce went through with no complications since Bob did not contest it; he hadn't liked the reference to physical abuse but, of course, he knew it was true. There was nothing in the decree to prevent me taking my son out of the country and I received full custody of Wayne. Bob was granted 'reasonable visitation rights', but he and his family told me to remember that it would be illegal for me to return to live in England; if I tried to do so, they would fight for custody of Wayne. I believed them. With our marriage over, Bob went to live with his parents while he sorted out his life, and I had to decide what I was going to do.

Bob and I amicably divided furniture and household items, each claiming odds and ends that were uniquely our own. His parents demanded the return of anything valuable they had given us, particularly the silverware they were buying for us, piece by piece. By then, I believe we had two place settings, in a pattern they had selected, which was the same as theirs. I returned them happily. I would have hated going through the rigmarole of washing and wrapping each piece separately every time I used it, as they always did. I'd much rather have some good old stainless steel that I could just throw into a drawer; I certainly didn't feel the need to impress anyone with such pretentious nonsense.

Then I planned my next move. I wanted to go to England for a while. When I told the Ballmaiers, who had recently moved into a big old rambling house nearby, they offered to store my furniture and put me up until I left. Wayne and I shared a bed in one of their spare rooms.

At around that time, my lawyer, Charles B., called and asked me to have lunch with him. He said he had to talk to me about something and, wondering what the mystery was, I agreed.

'You'd better start looking for a new job,' he said.

'Why?' I asked.

'Well, no one knows it yet, but my brother-in-law [who owned the employment agency where I worked] is bankrupt. You won't be getting any more pay cheques, and even if you do, they'll bounce.'

'Thank you for warning me, but maybe it's not as bad as you think. I want to go to England anyway so I'll take off sooner rather than later.' I was extremely grateful that I had been warned – I'm not sure I could have handled working for nothing: I'd already had enough bad news.

10: Divorce, and Home for Christmas

It was almost Christmas and, I thought, a good time for me to be with my family. My divorce would not be final until January but I didn't need to be in Chicago for that since we'd already had our court appearance and had signed the papers. Each Christmas since I had left England I had longed to spend it with my parents; I had cried whenever I heard such songs as 'I'll Be Home For Christmas' played on the radio or television. Christmas had never been a grand affair at home. My family couldn't afford to spend much but we always had a bottle of sherry on the sideboard, a bowl of fresh fruit and nuts, and a roast chicken for dinner followed by Christmas pudding. Before digging into the feast, we pulled the traditional crackers and enjoyed the meal wearing paper hats. No, it had nothing to do with all those trimmings: it was the thought of being at home with my own family whom by now I hadn't seen for two and a half years. This would be my dream come true, and I arranged for Wayne and I to leave Chicago on 22 December 1959 and arrive in London the next day.

My plan was soon shattered.

In the late afternoon of 21 December, even though it was still light outside, I tucked Wayne into bed.

'It's not dark,' he said. 'Why do I have to go to bed?'

'We have to go to bed early because we have a big day

tomorrow. We're going on a plane to see your nanny and granddad and they live far, far away,' I told him. He looked satisfied and snuggled down to sleep . . . or so I thought.

I went downstairs to watch TV and have a snack before I joined him. Eventually, knowing I probably wouldn't sleep, with my stomach in knots of excitement, I said goodnight to Cindy and Phil and went upstairs. When I opened our bedroom door, I screamed. 'Oh, my God, what have you done?' My head felt as though it was about to explode.

Cindy and Phil came running up the stairs to see what had happened, and when they did, they pulled me away from the room. They were afraid of what I might do.

My darling child had not gone to sleep. Instead, he had decided to play. He had torn up our passport (a parent and child shared one in those days) and painted everything on the dressing-table with red nail polish. I thought I'd go mad. Wayne, who had been grinning when I opened that door, was now howling. Phil gathered him up in his arms and removed him from my sight. By now, I was crying – wailing might be more accurate. Cindy dragged me downstairs and made me drink a shot of whiskey, telling me that we would sort it out, but at that moment, I couldn't see how. I just wanted to die.

When I had calmed down to some degree, I realized we would need a new passport, and a plan began to form in my head. First things first, I thought. I phoned Ebert Photography Studio, which had taken our passport photo, but it had closed for the day. Fortunately, I had become friends with the studio owner, Will Ebert: he had taken the photos for my modelling portfolio and had used one of my portraits in his advertisements. I looked his name up in the telephone directory and, luckily, it was listed. Taking the bull by the horns, I phoned him. Stifling sobs, I explained what had happened and that I had to be at the passport office first thing the following morning. Could he possibly go to the studio and print some copies of the passport photo for me? With no hesitation, he agreed to do so and I arranged to meet him there. I already knew that, no matter what, we would not catch the booked flight; I called the airline and asked that they put our reservations on hold until I had the new passport.

After what seemed an eternity, I had the new photographs. There were no words to express my gratitude to Will Ebert for his kindness, but I've never forgotten it.

The next morning I was at the passport office in downtown Chicago when it opened its doors. With tears streaming down my face, I showed them the damaged passport and explained what had happened. At first, they said there was no way they could help me, but a senior clerk overheard our conversation and stepped in. 'Don't panic,' she said. 'Let me call Washington to see if we can get around it. I seem to remember doing this for someone before.' She vanished into an inner office. When she reappeared, there was a grin on her face.

'Good news! I've been given permission to issue you an emergency status passport and we can have it ready for you by late this afternoon.' I thought I would implode with relief as I thanked her and cried some more. I wanted to leap over the counter to hug that wonderful woman.

Back home, Cindy made cups of tea and encouraged me to be positive. 'Everything's going to be all right,' she told me. 'You'll see. The worst part's over. You'll soon be on a plane heading for England.' I wanted and needed to believe her so I just gave her a hug and told her how much I appreciated her. Then I went and put my arms around Wayne.

He had been sitting quietly, just staring at the floor while Cindy and I talked. Now, he looked up at me with tears in his eyes. 'I'm sorry, Mommy,' he whispered, and I just held him in my arms and rocked him, knowing how awful the little fellow must feel and how frightened he must have been at my reaction to what he had done.

'It's okay,' I told him. 'Everything's going to be just fine.'

The next step was to contact the airline again, to see when they could get us on a flight. They gave me little hope since it was Christmas and everything was booked solid, but they promised to call me if anything opened up. I sat beside the telephone, willing it to ring. When it did, I jumped a foot in the air, and my heart was in my throat. It was good news. They had us booked on a flight that left Chicago on Christmas Eve and would get us to London on Christmas Day. It wasn't perfect but it would do. We were finally on our way home.

The flight was long and I was exhausted, but as we approached my beautiful England, my heart was bursting with joy: I would soon be with my family. Then, after we'd begun our descent into Heathrow Airport, the captain made an announcement that changed my joy to despair: 'Good morning, ladies and gentlemen. We've been informed that we cannot land at London's Heathrow due to heavy fog. We're going on to Frankfurt,

Germany, where we'll stay until weather conditions in London change.' Groans came from all around but none was more desolate than my own. How could this be happening after all we had already gone through? I was numb with disappointment.

We landed in freezing Frankfurt, where buses transported us through heavy rain to a small, luxurious hotel. Here we were to remain until further notice. Our stranded group appeared to be the only people staying there. Of course we are, I thought. Everyone else is enjoying Christmas at home with their families. A thoughtful older man offered to help me with Wayne but I declined. I had sat next to him on the plane and, looking over his shoulder, I'd seen in his passport his profession listed as 'Executor'. Just the thought that he might be a hangman gave me the willies. I felt a bit silly when I later learned that he was an executor of estates and wills.

The hotel's limited staff were kind to us, understanding our plight, and we passengers tried to enjoy our delightful surroundings, but we were frustrated and frazzled. The most memorable part of my stay was being served pheasant-under-glass for our Christmas dinner. I had never had it before, and have never had it since.

The following day, we had been cleared to fly, but this time to Glasgow; more groans. From there we would travel by train to London. Could it get any worse? We trundled back to the airport and were soon in the air again, this time filled with dread at the thought of the circuitous journey that still lay ahead.

It was inky black as we flew over England. My eyelids were heavy from lack of sleep but Wayne had slept all the way. Suddenly I was wide awake. The captain was making another announcement: 'Good evening, ladies and gentlemen. We have good news for you. The fog has lifted at Heathrow and we will be landing there shortly.' A great cheer went up throughout the aircraft. We were no longer on our way to Scotland. We were finally going home.

I looked down at my little boy, who grinned up at me. 'Are we nearly there, Mommy?'

'Yes, we are.'

Theoretically, that was true, but the adventure, or misadventure, was not yet over. After gathering our luggage and clearing Customs, we emerged into the airport. I scanned the few people waiting there but saw no familiar faces. By now, it was after midnight. Where was my family? The airline and hotel had promised to send telegrams, notifying them of our new arrival time. My family still had no telephone so I couldn't call them. What could have happened? We sat on our suitcases and waited until we were the only two people left in the terminal. It was an eerie feeling, sitting alone in that alien place. I found a member of the airport staff; few were working at that time of the night – it was the wee hours of 27 December.

'Sorry, love, there ain't no transport at this time of night. You'll have to wait till mornin' unless you can get a taxi willin' to take ya,' he informed me.

Where are they? Have they forgotten we're coming? My emotions ran the gamut, from anger to disappointment and back again. What about my poor child? Didn't anyone care about him? I'd been sure they were as excited as I was. Could I have been wrong? I sat Wayne on a bench just inside the terminal door, went outside and vomited.

The stress had finally got to me and at that moment I wanted to scream. As I stood at the kerb, wiping tears, snot and vomit from my chin, a small miracle happened. A taxi pulled up in front of me and the driver rolled down his window. 'You look like you need 'elp, mate,' he said, and I proceeded to explain my predicament. 'Where do you need to go?' he asked, and I gave him the address.

'I know just about where that is, and it ain't all that far. Do you want me to take you?'

Oh, my God, did I! 'Yes, please,' I replied. He got out of the cab and helped me gather up my son and the luggage, and off we went. I hadn't a clue how much it would cost, and at that point I didn't care.

With little traffic on the road, it was about half an hour later when we arrived at Little Oxhey Lane, where Mum and Dad had recently moved into a new council house.

'What number is it?' the driver asked.

'A hundred and three,' I replied.

There were very few houses on this new residential stretch of road but it was pitch dark and we couldn't read the numbers. The taxi stopped. 'I'll wait while you find the right 'ouse, mate,' he offered. 'I can't just drop you off and leave, can I?'

I left Wayne in the taxi and went to find number 103. It wasn't there. None of the houses had numbers. The doors were freshly painted and all the numbers had been removed. I went back to the taxi and told the driver, who agreed to wait a little longer. My only hope now was to peer through any open-curtained windows to see if I could recognize anything inside. Why was this happening to me? I wondered. Did they still not care enough to be there for me? Had nothing changed? Then, at last, I noticed something on the windowsill inside one of the houses that I was sure I remembered.

'This is it,' I called to the driver.

'Hooray.'

The kindly taxi driver unloaded our luggage, brought Wayne to me and perched him on a suitcase, while I knocked on the door. There was no answer. I told the driver it was okay for him to leave, that it might take a while to wake someone, and I felt sure everything would be fine. I paid him, thanked him for his help and patience, and he drove off into the night, leaving a forlorn twosome standing in the lonely darkness. The cold began to penetrate my coat and I started to shiver. I crouched down, unlocked our large suitcase and, after rummaging for a while, found what I was looking for, a thick woollen cardigan, which I wrapped around Wayne – he was shaking with cold, too.

I continued hammering on the front door, then went around to the back and pounded on that. I tried calling through the letterbox and throwing gravel up at the bedroom windows but to no avail. By now, Wayne was crying so I sat next to him, put my arms around him and tried to comfort him by telling him what a grand adventure we were having. It occurred to me that with my big woolly cardigan wrapped around him, he looked like a little old man as he sat there, trying to be brave. I had dressed him in the American style of the day: he was wearing long grey flannel trousers, a red blazer with a crest on the breast pocket, a white shirt complete with clip-on tie, all topped off with a little fedora hat. The poor lad still looked amazingly fresh and smart while I'm sure I looked, as my mother would have said, like something the cat had dragged in.

'I'm sorry, Wayne, are you warm enough? I can get something else out of the case if you like,' I told him.

'It's okay, Mommy. I'm just tired and I want to go to sleep.' He choked back a sob. He'll get pneumonia if I don't do something soon, I thought, but what could I do? My teeth were chattering so I knew Wayne must be freezing.

Fear gripped me. What if no one's at home? I thought. What if we'd passed each other on the road and they'd gone to the airport and wouldn't be back for hours? What if they'd had an accident? Perhaps I should start knocking on other doors. Maybe someone would have a telephone and I could call the police. Just as that thought entered my mind, a car pulled into the driveway, which was shared with the house next door. I jumped up, my heart almost leaping out of my chest.

'They're home, Wayne! Nanny and Granddad are home!' I shouted to him, but I was wrong: it was the neighbours coming home from a late-night party and they were very drunk.

When they learned who we were, they invited us into their house, made me a cup of tea, then laid Wayne on their sofa and covered him with a blanket. In seconds, he was asleep. They told me that they knew we were expected and that Mum and Dad had made two trips to the airport to meet us but each time they'd been told that there was no information as to when our plane would arrive. In fact, they'd been led to believe that we were still in Germany. The airline had promised to phone them when more information became available but, of course, Mum and Dad had no telephone: they'd had to rely on calling the airport or airline from the corner phone box. By that time, and completely exhausted, they had gone to bed, planning to start ringing for information early the next morning. No wonder I hadn't been able to rouse them.

It was several hours before we managed to wake Mum and Dad. There were lots of apologies and tears, but they were tears of joy: I was home. The last thing I remember from that traumatic night was Mum telling me how sorry she was that they'd already eaten our Christmas dinner.

Wayne and I slept well into the next afternoon and only woke when Mum came upstairs with a cup of tea and said that everyone was anxious to see and talk to us.

After more tea, 'breakfast' and everyone trying to talk at once about our nightmare journey, I wandered around the house, touching and looking at everything, as I had done on my last visit home. I grinned and cried alternately at the sheer joy of being at home, the simple pleasure of familiarity, hearing my family's Cockney accents, gazing into their eyes and smelling the usual smells. The thought of having to leave it all behind again crept into my consciousness and I had to blot it out. I'd worry about that later.

My time in England was all I'd hoped it would be. It was wonderful visiting my relatives, all of whom seemed eager to hear about my life in America. Wayne had his fourth birthday while we were there and the family made a big fuss of him. I also visited as many of my old friends as possible but mostly I spent time with my school pal Sheila McDonald, who was now married to Ray Jukes, a friend of my older brother Peter. They were still living, with their baby, Jane, on the Oxhey Estate with Ray's parents.

Besides having Sheila, Ray and baby Jane living with them, the Jukeses also had a lodger. He was a nice-looking man named Chuck and I developed a bit of a crush on him; my visits became even more frequent, always in the hope of seeing him. Finally, Sheila suggested he should ask me out, which he did. We had several dates, and he was kind to my son. Dad didn't like him at all and I had a big falling-out with him when he called Chuck 'a toe-rag'. The pot was calling the kettle black – I hadn't forgotten about Dad's past.

I continued to see Chuck, even though a cloud now hung over my stay at home. I probably spent too much time with him. He took me to nightclubs and occasionally we didn't get home until the wee hours of the morning. We sometimes made love on the couch in the living room, only parting when we heard sounds upstairs. I knew that, in my parents' eyes, what I was doing was wrong, that it was unfair to them, but I had missed so much by marrying so young. I suppose I was just trying to make up for it. I couldn't expect them to approve: they saw only a fun-loving man who was still single at the age of thirty – there had to be something wrong with him. They couldn't understand that, in a way, Chuck had become my lifeline. He was giving me some of the fun I had missed as a teenager, some excitement and a break from the depression of the years spent trying to fit in with life in America and a family who couldn't accept me for who I was. I knew he was no angel, but he had a well-paid job and no other obligations, he was known to be a one-woman man, and best of all, he seemed to care about my son. At the time, most importantly, he gave me back my confidence. He also gave me hope.

Wayne and I had been in England for about two months when Bob, who had written to us several times, insisted that we return to America. He reminded me that it was illegal for me to keep his son away from him and that he might have to take legal action. My parents concurred: they thought I should return to the States and to my obligations. I later learned that it was not illegal for me to stay in England with our son as long as I made every effort to ensure that he saw his father.

I will never forget going down on my knees, sobbing my heart out and begging, 'Please don't make me go back, please let me stay with you.' Dad cried too, but Mum, stoic as ever, reminded me that I had made my bed and had to lie in it. All I could think was that she didn't want me, that nothing had changed, that she still didn't care about me. Were my parents worried that they might have to help support my child and me financially? I knew that my mother didn't approve of my divorce or of me; she was ashamed, and I was sure she thought that everything had been my fault. At that time, in Britain, the only grounds for divorce were adultery, and abandonment or separation that had lasted at least seven years; the 'other woman, or man', referred to as 'the co-respondent', had to be named in the decree and the story usually appeared in the newspapers. Divorce was scandalous.

Chuck had made it abundantly clear that he had no intention of marrying or settling down and said nothing to dissuade me from leaving. Sheila had warned me not to become too fond of him; he was an old friend of hers and she knew he was not interested in having a permanent relationship with anyone, even though he only ever dated one woman at a time. He had actually told me that he couldn't understand how anyone could juggle more than one relationship. And so the time came for us to part. We said goodbye with tears in our eyes, promising to keep in touch. He had never said he loved me, but while we were together I knew he cared about me; I also knew I would miss him and hoped he might miss me too.

Having postponed the inevitable for as long as possible, I booked our flight back to America and wondered what lay ahead for my little son and me. I knew Wayne's father would always be good to him – he was a good man – but the rest was up to me. I just hoped I could do it on my own. Over the years, I often wondered how my parents could have allowed me, a sixteen-year-old girl, to get married and move to another country, but it was far more agonizing to recall that they made me go back to America and virtually nothing. I had nowhere to live, no job and no money, except the small amount I was supposed to receive in child support from Wayne's father – and how could we even be sure of that? The pain of the perceived rejection still lives in me, an ugly scar.

It is impossible to describe the heartbreak I experienced at leaving my old home again. I remember only the all-consuming fear of facing life alone, and the ache in my heart as I said goodbye to my family, my true home and my beloved country. I didn't know who I was any more. I was no longer a GI bride; I was divorced, a *former* GI bride. Did that make me a GI divorcee? I wondered how many other GI divorcees were out there. Had they faced the same fears that I now faced? Had any of them returned to their families in England, or had they been forced to live with the consequences of their mistakes and decisions? I didn't seem to belong anywhere now, and I felt as I had when I was an evacuee during the war: desolate and in despair.

As the plane rose into the air I watched the British coastline disappear beneath the clouds, and a new, greater fear gripped me: what if I could never afford to make another trip home? What if I had just said goodbye to my family for the last time?

11: Single and Alone

Back in Chicago, the Ballmaiers agreed to let me stay with them until I found a job and an affordable apartment. My furniture and other belongings were still stored at their house so Wayne and I moved back into our old bedroom – the scene of a destroyed passport and almost-aborted holiday plans.

I don't know how I would have coped without the Ballmaiers. My brother Peter and his wife Brenda now lived in a distant suburb with their two children and they were expecting another, so I saw little of them. I wished they still lived next door: I missed having them nearby. I couldn't sit around feeling sorry for myself, though. It was time to get some money coming in and I had to find employment.

I'd always fancied working for a doctor so when I found the help-wanted advertisement for a receptionist in a surgery, I applied. The doctor hired me on the spot and I was soon working in downtown Chicago. Over the years, it always proved easy for me to secure such positions: Americans seemed to love having an English accent answering their telephones.

I still had a little money saved from the divorce settlement and, after I'd received my first few pay cheques, I could afford the security deposit on a small apartment close to the Ballmaiers. Bob, my now ex-husband, was always faithful in sending us Wayne's allowance; the amount was not huge but it made all the difference in that we could live in a decent neighbourhood and apartment. He always made sure Wayne didn't have to go without, and his parents were good to their grandson too. Bob was also conscientious about his visiting rights; he always picked his son up punctually and brought him home at the agreed time; he did fun things with him, and often took him for the whole weekend so that I could have a little break. I couldn't have asked or hoped for a more congenial arrangement and considered myself lucky that it was so.

The apartment I rented was near the elevated train to downtown, and Wayne could once again attend the Gay Time Nursery School. Everything seemed to be falling into place, but it was still a struggle and I worried about our future. I had felt secure while staying with my family in England and, to a degree, while I lived with the Ballmaiers, but it was frightening to be alone, and I wondered if I'd be able to cope with the responsibility.

The second-floor apartment I rented was the smallest of three in an old house. It consisted of a bathroom, then a large room divided into kitchen, dining area and living room. A small bedroom led off the living room so Wayne and I had to share the bed. My double bed took up the entire bedroom and there was little storage space; the only place for the rest of my bedroom furniture was in the dining area. Wayne's bed, plus a few boxes of miscellaneous belongings, had to stay in storage until I had a bigger place. I had no idea when that might be.

Luckily, a single girl in her thirties, Joan Witek, lived in the next-door apartment and we soon became friends. Joan worked as a secretary in downtown Chicago. She was also director of music for a large Catholic church and school in the city; she worked long hours but when she was at home she was good company. Sometimes I dog-sat for her, and occasionally she baby-sat for me.

Joan was not particularly attractive. She fought a constant battle with her jet-black facial hair, and she was what you might call a big girl. She was madly in love with one of her bosses and thought he felt the same about her. I was sure that he was using her. There were many times when she prepared dinner for him and he didn't show up, which was lucky for Wayne and me because she would invite us to eat the food. Joan was an excellent cook; the aromas of whatever she was cooking would drift into my apartment and make my mouth water.

She tried to fix me up with one of her boss's friends. 'Maybe if Clare [Clarence!] comes over to see you, Jim will be less likely to stand me up,' she said. I sensed there was method in her madness and agreed to meet the man. We double-dated a couple of times, and we even went to Lake Geneva for the weekend once while Wayne was away with his dad, but for me, there was too much drinking, which I found a giant bore. One dreadful thing happened while this liaison was going on. The four of us had been out for dinner and had come back to Joan's apartment for a nightcap. Jim took the key from her and unlocked the door. We all piled in, expecting to hear her little dog yapping, but we were met with silence and a foul stench. When she turned on the lights, there was the dog, quivering and cowering under the kitchen table. All over the floor lay the torn-up remnants of several sanitary towels. He had been in the garbage can and, to top it all, had messed on the floor. No wonder he was shaking.

I was mortified so I can only imagine how Joan felt. I immediately excused myself and went next door into my own apartment, leaving Joan with two shocked men and the most embarrassing situation imaginable. Soon I heard doors banging, and knew the men had left; the last thing I heard was one of them saying, 'Jesus Christ, that was disgusting,' as they went down the stairs. I went back into Joan's apartment to see if I could help her, but she was inconsolable as she began cleaning up. I could only wonder how she'd ever be able to face her boss again, but she'd have to if she wanted to keep her job. For days after that, the only smell coming from Joan's apartment was that of burning incense.

Dr H., my boss, had his office on the mezzanine floor of a hotel on the near-north side of Chicago. It was close to Lake Shore Drive, which was where many of the city's elite resided. Dr H. had numerous wealthy patients, including some members of Chicago's illustrious high society. He was also physician to the Chez Paree Adorables, who performed at the city's most famous nightclub, the Chez Paree. Many of the girls lived in the hotel and I often found them sunbathing nude on its rooftop terrace when I went up there to eat my lunch. On one occasion, I would have crawled over them to the rail, if I'd had to: the Queen and Prince Philip had arrived in Chicago on their tour of Canada and North America. They had sailed on the royal yacht, *Britannia*, down the St Lawrence Seaway to Lake Michigan, and had disembarked at Buckingham Fountain.

I had read in the news that their motorcade would be passing the hotel and there was no way I was going to miss that, nude sunbathers or not. It was one of just two occasions in my life that I was privileged to see the top of Her Majesty's head. (The second time was many years later at the Gare du Nord in Paris. She had travelled on the Eurostar, which takes you from London to Paris direct, passing under the English Channel.)

After a while, Dr H. decided I could start helping his two nurses. His practice was close to the historic Navy Pier, and he had a contract to treat minor injuries incurred by the construction workers involved with renovation and restoration work there. Between the regular patients and treating injuries, the nurses were often swamped. They taught me to change wound dressings, remove sutures and deburr needles. Yes, in those days, they reused needles, which had to have any microscopic burrs filed off before they went into the sterilizer. I say microscopic but all we did was test the end of the needle with the tip of a finger. No wonder injections were so painful back then.

One of the doctor's friends, who came in regularly, began flirting with me. Byron H. was probably in his sixties, but I knew he was a wealthy widower. At that time, I had begun to think I should look for a rich man rather than elusive and often disappointing love so I flirted back. On one of his visits, he told me he was going to the hospital to have some tests.

'How come?' I asked.

'How come you come, I come, baby come,' he said, laughing like a banshee. What a jerk, I thought. How crude. I made up my mind right then that I wouldn't go out with him if he was the last man on earth . . . but I did, just once. We went to a smart restaurant and shared pleasant conversation; he even told me about his wife and how she had died. He was so much nicer than I'd thought, and when he invited me back to his house to see his collection of old jukeboxes, I went. His home was sumptuous and the antique jukeboxes were impressive. I thought I had misjudged him. I was relaxed and comfortable – until the mood changed drastically.

'Well,' he said, 'I've been nice to you and now it's your turn to be nice to me.'

How could I have been so naive? That's what I get for being so trusting, I thought. Now what do I do?

'What do you mean?' I said, acting as dumb as I now felt.

'I'm taking you to bed. That's how you're going to be nice to me,' he replied, and pushed me towards the stairs.

I was petrified. 'No, I can't – please. I have to get home. I promised the baby-sitter I'd be home by now.'

'You should have thought about that before,' he all but snarled at me.

Roughly, he grabbed me. His fingers dug into my arms and his manicured nails were hurting me. Oh, my God, I thought, he's going to rape me, but then I had an idea. 'If you don't take me home right now, I am going to tell your friend Dr H. and the girls in the office that you tried to rape me.'

'You bitch,' he spat out. 'I believe you would, wouldn't you?'

He was right. I didn't care who he was or what his connections were, I was not about to be bullied by a jerk like him. Yes, I was stupid to have put myself in such a situation and I had a lot to learn, but I was learning fast. I would never allow myself to get into such a fix again.

One day at work I felt terrible – I had been up all night with a sick Wayne and could hardly keep my eyes open. One of the nurses, a second-generation Lebanese girl with great almond eyes and jet-black hair that came down to her waist, told me she had something that would help me get through the day and handed me a capsule. She didn't tell me what it was but assured me it was safe and that she often had to take one. I swallowed it and was soon wide awake and blabbering away like a chimpanzee to anyone and everyone. I was in love with the world and everyone in it. I thanked Faith, the nurse, for saving my life and for helping me to survive the day. It was nothing short of a miracle.

When I got home that night, I crashed. I was so tired that Wayne and I went to bed at seven o'clock and slept straight through – I hadn't even undressed.

'What the heck did you give me?' I asked Faith the next day.

'Just Dexedrine,' she said. 'It's a stimulant. We keep loads of it here. Doc gives it to the Chez Paree Adorables. It gives them energy and keeps the weight off. Lots of his patients come just for that, but keep it under your hat,' she added.

Well, I certainly didn't need to lose weight: I was still skinny as a rail.

Faith was to surprise me again. One day, she asked me if I was interested in becoming an escort.

'What's an escort?' I asked.

'Well,' she explained, 'it's someone who goes out for dinner or to a show with men who are in town and don't want to go out alone.'

'Are you kidding? Isn't that prostitution?'

'No, no, no,' she said. 'It's nothing like that but you can have sex with them if you want to. They're just lonely men, mostly travelling executives, who want to be seen with a pretty girl on their arm, and you get to have a good time and go to places you couldn't afford to go otherwise.' Hmm, I thought. Sounds fishy to me.

'Here, look at this,' she said, and pulled a fabulous piece of jewellery out of her pocket. 'I got this from the guys I spent a little time with last night.'

'What guys?' I asked.

'There's a huge luxury yacht moored down by Navy Pier. It's owned by some very wealthy Arabs. I went to a party there, had some drinks, danced, had a fabulous meal prepared by their own chef. It was amazing. When it was time for me to leave, they gave me this gift, in appreciation of my company.'

I was flabbergasted. 'You didn't have to have sex with anyone?'

'Oh, no,' she said. 'They're having another party tomorrow night and they've asked me to bring some friends. Do you want to go?'

Well, it sounded interesting, but suspicious. I declined. I'd been single for just a short time, but I'd already had enough of going out with strangers.

At about that time, Dr H. started asking me to deliver packages to rooms in various hotels. At first I didn't think anything of it, but one day I peeked inside a bag. I had learned a lot about prescription drugs while I'd been working for him, and I recognized the names of many. The bag was full of amphetamines. Oh, my God, I thought. He's using me to deliver illegal drugs. What would happen if I was caught? I should look for a different job, I decided, but in the meantime I just had to be careful.

During the time I worked for the doctor, certain men came in regularly, supposedly to be sobered up. I had learned this from the nurses. They were, most often, politicians and bigwig executives and, for the most part, disgusted me. Usually they'd had too much to drink at lunchtime and now had meetings to attend, or speeches to make, and I'm sure they paid dearly for the doctor's services.

One of the regulars was the executive director of the Chicago Convention Bureau, whose assistant always accompanied, supported or dragged him in. Occasionally, they both needed treatment.

The assistant was good-looking. He was about thirty and, according to his file, single. A closer look revealed that he lived just a few streets away from me. While he waited for his boss, he'd chat to me and he seemed like a nice person. He was always polite and always wore a big grin. I was intrigued. One day while we chatted, I mentioned that I'd noticed we lived a few blocks apart.

He laughed. 'Maybe I'll have to come over to borrow a cup of sugar some time,' he said.

'Why not?' I answered, and that, I thought, was that.

It was shortly after that that I quit my job with Dr H., and went to work as receptionist for a company called

Owens Corning Fiberglass in Chicago's 'Loop' – the downtown area defined by the overhead train tracks that circle it. It was closer to my apartment, so I cut down on my travel time, and my working hours were shorter, which helped with the childcare situation. The office staff and salesmen were pleasant, with one exception. Today he would have been fired for his lewd comments and constant pawing of the girls in the office. I became frightened to go into the file-room because he would soon be breathing down my neck. I talked to the office manager about it but he laughed and asked where my sense of humour was.

While I was working at Owens Corning, my good friend Bobby McCarthy was working nearby for Mitsubishi's Chicago headquarters as the receptionist. Since she and I both operated switchboards, we often chatted when the bosses weren't around, but I'll never forget one particular call I made to her some time after I'd left my job. It was 11 November, Election Day in America. The phone rang for an unusually long time before someone answered, and it wasn't Bobby. A Japanese-sounding male voice said, 'Mitsubishi International.'

'Hello, is Mrs McCarthy there, please?' I replied.

'So solly,' said the voice. 'All of Mitsubishi crose today in honah off National Erection.' I thanked him, hung up and almost fell out of my chair laughing. I couldn't wait to tell Bobby. After that we always called each other on Erection Day.

Bobby also told me of the time that the president of Mitsubishi Chicago showed up unannounced at her apartment one Sunday afternoon and scared her half to death.

'I come because I hear your morals are low,' he told her,

but how wrong he was: her immediate boss had reported that Bobby's 'morale' was low due to her recent divorce.

'I sent him away,' she said, 'telling him I was expecting company, but I was never sure if he'd come to take advantage of my low morals or to offer support after hearing of my low morale.'

In those days, we were naive about many things and often embarrassed due to our ignorance of worldly matters.

'I've been dating a Sikh Indian,' Bobby told me one day, soon after the Mitsubishi incident.

'What's wrong with him?' I asked.

'You idiot,' she said, exploding into laughter. 'He's not ill. Sikhism is an Indian religion.' Well, how was I supposed to know that?

It was around that time that I learned Bob Irvine had remarried. Wow, I thought, that was fast, but when I talked to him, I wished him all the luck in the world and told him that I hoped he would find true happiness in his new partnership. About a month later, I received a phone call from his wife, Rosemary, asking if she could see me. Confused but curious, I agreed and arranged a time. She arrived at the apartment looking as nervous as I felt. What could this be about? I wondered.

We had coffee, to give us time to settle down, and then she burst into tears. As she dabbed her eyes with a handkerchief, I noticed that she was wearing my old wedding and engagement rings. I wonder if she knows he didn't buy them new, I thought. I couldn't believe anyone would be callous enough to give his ex-wife's rings to someone else. Then I realized: it was something else Bob's parents must have been behind. I'd had to return other valuables to them and the rings had been included on the list.

Finally, when she stopped crying, we got round to the reason for her visit. 'I don't know how to make him happy, Iris. He keeps talking about you. He's still in love with you, you know, and I wondered if you could give me some advice on how to deal with him, what I need to do to make him love me.'

What could I say to her? Bob and I were divorced. I hadn't known how to make him happy and he hadn't been able to make me happy. How did she think I could help? 'Look, Rosemary,' I said, 'I doubt very much that he's still in love with me.'

'Oh yes he is,' she interrupted. 'I hear it from him all the time, especially if he's been drinking. He keeps telling me I can't hold a candle to you.' Now she was sobbing again and I had a hard time keeping my own emotions in check. I felt so sorry for her. 'Do you think he remarried too soon? Do you think it was just on the rebound?'

'I can't answer those questions,' I told her, 'and all I can tell you is that he's a simple man with simple wants and needs. He wants a clean house, dinner on the table when he gets home from work, and he doesn't particularly like going out. Oh, and he wants sex often.' Then it was my turn to ask questions. 'Does his family still expect you to come for dinner every weekend?'

'We go there pretty often but not every weekend.'

'Lucky you,' I said, and that brought a laugh from her.

We continued talking for some time. I don't think I gave her any real answers but I think she was relieved to have shared her problems with someone who understood.

Shortly after our little meeting, I learned that Bob and she had split up. Apparently, after one of their fights, she had followed him to the bar where he hung out and hit him over the head with her stiletto-heeled shoe, leaving a rather nasty hole.

My letters home were probably giving clues as to how unhappy I was and how hard I was finding it to manage, both physically and financially. My parents' letters back to me were encouraging and they tried to cheer me up, but I was still hurt that they hadn't supported me when I'd begged to stay with them in England. If it hadn't been for the other GI brides I had met, I'm sure the situation would have been far worse. Our shared stories, both funny and heartbreaking, helped me. I'm not sure how I would have coped without those girls: they were a lifesaver. Occasionally, I saw my brother and his wife, but with them now living in the suburbs, our visits were rare. I had no car and there was no public transport to where they lived.

It was about that time that I first applied for credit: if I had to stay in the US, I should try to make a real home there. I was now twenty-one and living in my own apartment; it was time to put my own mark on the place. Goldblatt's Department Store granted me fifty dollars' worth of credit and I bought a large picture to put on the wall over the apartment's non-functioning fireplace. Now it felt a little more like home, so I dug my heels in and decided to get on with it.

12: Enter Robert Lee Palmer

As I tucked four-year-old Wayne into bed for the night, the telephone rang. I dashed into the kitchen and picked it up. The man's voice at the other end was unfamiliar.

'Do you think you could spare a cup of sugar?' he said.

At first, I thought it was a crank call and was about to hang up when it suddenly dawned on me who he was: Bob Palmer, the nice-looking man I'd met in Dr H.'s office. I laughed, and we talked for half an hour. 'Oh, for goodness' sake, why don't you just come over and get the cup of sugar?' I said eventually.

Bob lived within walking distance of my apartment and was soon ringing the doorbell. We drank coffee and talked for hours until I finally had to put a stop to it – it was after midnight. 'Look, I don't know about you but I have to get up early for work. You'll have to leave now or I'll be a dead duck tomorrow.'

He apologized for keeping me up so late and, with no fuss, off he went. 'I'll call you again soon, if that's okay with you?' he called back to me. I said that would be fine; he had been so polite, and I'd been interested in all he'd told me about himself and his life. I'd learned that he was an only child, that his parents, Dan and Esther Palmer, lived in Peoria, Illinois, and that his father worked at Hiram Walker Whiskey Distillers. His millionaire Uncle Art, his father's brother, had put him through college at

Bradley University in Peoria. He had lived with this uncle and aunt for much of his life and claimed that if I ever met them I'd be far more likely to think he was their son and not the son of his actual parents. I got the distinct impression he was ashamed of his parents and considered himself better than them. I also discovered he had served his two years of national service in an office in California doing accounting and negotiating military contracts. Apparently, Uncle Art had connections in all the right places and he had used them to keep his favourite nephew out of active service.

Bob, I learned, was a bit of a namedropper. It was obvious that he was trying to impress me. He told me that his uncle had initially made his fortune in whiskey distilling and filmmaking, but was now a major shareholder in Phillips Petroleum Company; he was also part owner of the Houston Oilers football team. I could certainly understand why Bob preferred to consider himself his uncle's son, rather than the son of a lowly labourer who lived in an attic apartment. He made a point of telling me that his uncle and aunt had no children of their own and, since they had practically raised him, he would inherit most of their fortune.

Bob, or Palmer as I came to call him (it was less confusing since I had just been divorced from a Bob), was at the time second in command at the Chicago Convention Bureau. His position afforded him the privilege of wining and dining many of America's rich and famous people on his seemingly limitless expense account. The responsibility of the Bureau was to woo corporations and organizations to hold their meetings, conventions and exhibitions in Chicago. There were many millions of dollars at stake each year so it had carte blanche to do whatever was necessary to persuade groups to make Chicago their choice of venue. At that time I knew little about the use of credit cards and was shocked to see how many Palmer had in his wallet. The only previous knowledge I had of credit was my recently acquired fifty-dollar account with Goldblatt's and buying things on the never-never back in England – never-never meant you never finished paying for whatever you had purchased and the 'tallyman' came to the door every week to collect the instalments. Things were different in America.

Palmer wined and dined me in grand fashion, and from the first week of our friendship, I received a dozen red roses every Friday. He bought little gifts for Wayne too. He had once been engaged to a Jewish girl, but for a very short time. They had met at college but her Orthodox family had threatened to disown her if she married outside the religion so the romance had ended. He explained that in Orthodox families, if someone married out, the family sometimes held a funeral and considered the person dead. I had never heard of such a thing and was shocked.

Another thing that impressed me about Palmer was that sex wasn't high on his list of priorities. When we eventually made love, it was not particularly successful. I put that down to us both being nervous.

Palmer was an avid golfer, card player and drinker. I didn't recognize that his drinking might become a problem: I thought it went with dating, socializing and his job. There were a number of times when he failed to show up for a date, or was extremely late and had obviously been drinking, but the excuse was always that he had been with clients. I came to accept it, but hoped it wouldn't happen too often.

Palmer had a small circle of male friends whom he golfed with, and all but one were unmarried. His poker-playing friends, most of whom lived in a funky old residential hotel called the Central Plaza, were what you might call classic Damon Runyon-type characters. The hotel was where many of the racetrack crowd stayed during racing season – it was always full of colourful characters.

One of Palmer's friends, an elderly Jewish woman named Merle Schneider, had lived in the hotel for many years, and worked for the City of Chicago in the Mayor's office. Merle had a deep, gravelly voice, always had a cigarette hanging from the corner of her mouth, and called everyone 'kid'. She often called Palmer in the evening, sometimes even if it happened to be one of our date nights, when Wayne and I were at his apartment sharing a pizza or such.

'Hey, kid, ya wanna play a little poker?' she'd ask, and if a game started, it would invariably end up an all-nighter. Wayne and I would leave them to it and walk home. Merle wasn't happy when I came on the scene: it interfered with her social life. She'd shuffle into the apartment, cigarette dangling. 'Hiya, kid,' she'd say to me. Then, 'Hey, kid,' to Wayne.

Joe Kalny, a travelling salesman, was another character. I'll never forget him telling us that, when he travelled, he travelled light. 'Yeah,' he said. 'I just take one white nylon shirt with me. I wash it on my body when I take a shower at night, and then I hang it up to dry and it's ready to wear the next morning.' I thought, Wow, that's clever, but I also thought it a bit weird.

Then there was Pete Huber, one of the nicest people I've ever known. Pete, to the envy of the rest of the group, made tons of money selling Titleist golf balls. His job was to travel the golf-tournament circuit and socialize with the big-name golfers. Everyone teased him about his easy life and the fact that Titleist golf balls didn't need anyone to sell them: they sold themselves.

Yes, most of the people in Palmer's circle of friends were not only single but also heavy drinkers who played hard. I was never aware of any of them dating – they probably didn't have time – and I'm sure it came as a shock to the group when Palmer suddenly produced a girlfriend. I sometimes got the feeling I was messing up their routine but they always treated me with the utmost respect, especially since I didn't interfere with their golf or card games. Wayne was the only child around and everyone made a fuss of him, which he thoroughly enjoyed; Palmer would even take him to the golf course on occasion, which I thought was sweet. I began to think that this relationship might be worth keeping.

After Palmer and I had been dating for a couple of months, two things happened that just about knocked me off my feet.

It was Saturday morning. I opened my mail to find a sizeable international money order from Chuck, the man I'd dated in England who was not interested in marriage or a serious relationship. There was a letter with it saying he'd visited my parents, who had told him I was struggling financially and that they were worried about me. The letter went on to say that he just wanted to help since he made more money than he knew what to do with and that this was a gift. As I sat there staring in disbelief at the money order and the letter, the doorbell rang. It was Western Union, delivering a telegram.

WANT TO MARRY YOU STOP IF YOU SAY YES WILL ARRANGE TO COME FOR YOU OR USE MONEY TO BUY TICKETS HOME STOP REPLY BY RETURN PLEASE STOP MISS YOU STOP LOVE CHUCK

I sat there in stunned silence. My head felt as though a herd of wild horses was stampeding inside it. The shock had paralysed me. I don't know how long I sat there, shaking from head to toe. The telephone rang, bringing me back into the moment, and like a zombie, I stood, walked to it and picked it up. At first I couldn't speak.

'Hello, is that Iris? Can you hear me? This is Chuck. Did you get my letter? Did you get the telegram?' He sounded nervous and excited.

'Yes,' I managed to croak out.

'I couldn't wait for your answer,' he said. 'What do you think?'

'I can't think,' I told him. 'I've only just got your letter and telegram and it hasn't sunk in yet. It's too much of a shock. I don't know what to think, I just don't know, I'm sorry,' I blabbered, then broke down and cried. Oh, my God, I thought, I've just got over him, pushed him out of my mind, and now this. At last I was able to gather my thoughts. 'It's too much to take in right now, Chuck. Please don't do anything drastic. You have to give me time to think. It's all too complicated – there's so much involved.'

'Shall I call you back? How long do you need?' he asked, and of course, I couldn't tell him because I didn't know the answers. I said I'd be in touch as soon as I could, and promised not to keep him waiting.

After we'd hung up, I sat there, hardly able to breathe. My heart felt as though it was going to burst out of my chest. I tried to concentrate on taking deep breaths but it was impossible: there were iron bands around my ribs and they were crushing me. I was glad Wayne wasn't at home to see me like that: it would have scared him. At last, I managed to get myself into the bedroom, where I curled up on the bed and pulled the covers over my head, hiding from a world that had suddenly spiralled out of control.

Later that evening, I went next door to see Joan and spilled out all that had happened. We talked for a long time, discussing the situation over a few strong drinks, and then she took both my hands in hers and looked me straight in the eyes.

'Are you in love with this man? Even if you do love him, are you willing to face the legal battles involved with taking Wayne out of the country? Do you love Chuck enough to take Wayne away from his father?' Her questions stunned me into reality. They were the questions I'd needed to ask myself, the questions I would have to answer honestly before making such a monumental decision.

The following day, I called Chuck and told him I had already begun seeing someone else, that it was obvious I didn't know my own mind. I told him of my concerns about taking Wayne to the UK, but he counteracted by offering to move to America. I wondered if he really loved me or just felt sorry for me. With that in mind, I said it had all happened too suddenly, that both of us needed time to think before we jumped into something we might later regret.

I sent Chuck's money order back to him and told him I thought we should forget the idea of getting together, that I wasn't convinced we could make each other happy. I never heard from him again. Some time later, I learned from my friend Sheila that Chuck had moved to another town and had left no forwarding address. I felt terrible, but still believed I had done the right thing.

While I was still reeling from what had happened between Chuck and me, the next bolt of lightning struck. Palmer asked me to marry him *and* he had already bought the ring. I told him it was much too soon and that I would have to think about it. In addition, I still hadn't met his parents. When I mentioned that, he told me they'd probably think no girl was good enough for him, and they would never approve of him marrying a divorced woman, especially one with a child.

I wasn't sure how I felt about the prospect of yet another rejection but Palmer was pressuring me to accept. He assured me that his parents would rarely visit Chicago, so why worry? I wasn't sure how I felt about him, but after the Chuck incident, I was vulnerable and insecure. Palmer was good to Wayne and me, we had great times together, he seemed genuinely to care about Wayne and, of course, he was here. After much deliberation, and taking everything into account, including the security of his impressive job, his treatment of my son and that he was so much more sociable than my first husband had been, I accepted his proposal. His friends were flabbergasted. They'd been convinced that confirmed bachelor Palmer would never marry. And I felt quite special to have landed such a prize catch.

Not long after that, Palmer showed up at my apartment, stinking drunk from one of his 'business meetings'. He stumbled up the stairs and fell on the floor, slobbering and blabbering about how sorry he was and how much he loved me; he had also wet his trousers. I wasn't sure if it was beer or urine, but whatever it was, he stank, and I was disgusted. I threw his ring at him, told him to leave and that I never wanted to see him again. I don't remember ever being so disappointed, angry or hurt before. I didn't need that crap in my life and especially not in my son's life.

He went away for a while, I supposed to have more to drink, and then he was back, banging on the door, throwing pebbles at my window, crying and begging for forgiveness. The neighbours threatened to call the police so I relented and let him in. He went to sleep on the couch after blubbering for a while, and when he woke up, in a more sober condition, he was contrite and embarrassed, promising never to do such a thing again. I didn't take the ring back right away, but after a few days of bouquets and other peace offerings, I gave in. I didn't understand the signs, couldn't read the writing on the wall – otherwise I'd say I must have been mad. We tentatively set a wedding date.

I met his parents when they came to town for a weekend, I supposed to inspect me. We had dinner together and were all visibly uncomfortable. They didn't have a lot to say and I was grateful that Palmer did most of the talking. His mother, Esther, was on the dowdy side and kept her lips pursed, which told me she was trying to hold her tongue so that she didn't say something she might later regret. It was fairly obvious that she had decided not to like me. His father, Dan, was quiet until he had a few drinks in him, then proceeded to talk about life in Peoria, or perhaps I should say death in Peoria, since he went on about all the people he'd known who had died there. Later, he began to ask me a lot of personal questions and I was grateful that Palmer put a stop to the interrogation. Dan also had a nervous tic, which was a little unsettling. I later learned he had undergone several operations on his nose, supposedly for a deviated septum. The result was that he snorted like a pig all the time.

Apparently, his parents had not lived together much when Palmer was a child, as his father had been sickly and had always gone to stay with his own mother when he was feeling poorly because he thought she took better care of him than his wife did. I found that most peculiar but at last I understood why Palmer had spent so much time living with his Uncle Art and Aunt Gladys.

I had been divorced for less than a year when we were married in the private chambers of Judge Abraham Marowitz, a well-known political figure in Chicago; I also heard that he was a major figure in the city's Machine. Palmer's friend Merle Schneider had arranged for the marriage to take place 'in chambers'. She knew all the political bigwigs in Chicago from working in the Mayor's office and having also been active in the Democratic Party. The only people to attend our wedding were my brother Peter, one or two of Palmer's colleagues from the Convention Bureau, Merle Schneider and Pete Huber's brother, Joe, another of his golfing friends. His parents didn't come. His colleagues gave us a lovely wedding luncheon at a downtown hotel, plus two nights at the grand old Edgewater Beach Hotel.

Staying at the Edgewater Beach was like living inside a scene from a movie. It was very elegant and we stayed in a magnificent penthouse suite. I had my first room-service meal there, complete with champagne. Palmer looked handsome and debonair with his dark brown eyes and slicked-back black hair; he wore silk pyjamas and a matching bathrobe, and I felt like a movie star in my diaphanous white peignoir. It was like a fairy-tale. As I stood at the vast walls of glass that looked out over the lights of Chicago, I kept thinking, If they could see me now. However, the wedding night was not the success I'd hoped it would be. The romance fizzled out because Palmer seemed more interested in guzzling champagne than he was in making love to me. I almost had to force myself on him. He tried to make a joke of it, telling me we had all the time in the world for lovemaking; I should relax, drink some wine and enjoy the luxury while I could. I don't remember much more about that night. What I do remember is that the day had been seriously marred earlier. Palmer and I were on the Lake Street elevated train, on our way into Chicago to be married, when he turned to me with a very serious look on his face. 'I have an important question to ask you before we get married,' he blurted out.

'Now?' I said. 'Sure, ask away. What is it?'

And then he dropped the bomb.

'Can you swear to me you're not marrying me because you're pregnant with someone else's child?'

The air went right out of me and I could hardly breathe. I felt as though he'd punched me hard, right in the solar plexus. When I was able to speak, I choked out, 'You're joking, right?'

'No, I'm very serious,' he replied.

Who is this man I'm about to marry? I thought. Who is this stranger? I should have jumped off the train at the next stop. However, all I could think was that it was too late for me to turn back, and so, after I'd caught my breath, I assured him that I was not pregnant, and on we went.

To this day, I cannot believe that I still went through with the wedding. If there was one piece of advice I could give to anyone getting married today, it would be this: for God's sake, if you have any doubts or fears about the person you're about to marry, or about the marriage itself, it's never too late to back out, even if you're standing at the altar.

I was eventually able to push the incident to the back of my mind, and I comforted myself that his parents had undoubtedly put that thought into his head and he had asked me for their sake.

13: The Palmer Saga Begins, and Meeting a Royal Butler

After Palmer and I were married, I opened the mail each day and was horrified to discover that he was in a far worse financial situation than I was. I simply had a difficult time making ends meet, but he was up to his neck in debt. One of the first bills I opened was from a downtown Chicago florist – for all the flowers he had sent to me during our courtship. It came with a threatening 'past due notice'. That bill was a shock, but not nearly as shocking as some that came later.

That evening, after we'd had our meal, I presented the bills to him, pointing out the demand from the florist. 'What's all this about?' I asked him.

'Don't worry,' he said. 'It's just temporary, a misunderstanding I'm trying to get sorted out with my bank.'

Another thing I found strange after we were married was Palmer's compulsive behaviour. For instance, there was his bedtime routine of checking the locks on the doors and windows. First, he would lock them, then tug each handle exactly twelve times to make sure they were secure. Sometimes, if he wasn't sure he had counted correctly, or if he lost count, he would start again. Not of major importance, I suppose, but if I had known then what I know now, that behaviour would certainly have rung warning bells for me. Occasionally, I would tease him. 'I don't think you counted right,' I'd say. Not that I actually knew, I just wanted to see what he'd do. I knew it was mean to do that, but what the heck? I had little else to laugh about.

'Goddamnit,' he'd say, and check them all again. Once, I couldn't stop laughing, and he became so angry that I thought he was going to punch me, so I decided it safest to ignore his weird behaviour. After all, what harm was it doing?

We had managed to find a much nicer apartment to move into after we were married. It had two bedrooms, a huge living room with a dining area, a modern bathroom, a smallish kitchen with lots of cabinets, and there were huge wardrobe-type closets throughout.

There was plenty of room in the second bedroom for Wayne, his toys and clothes; the walk-in closet was as big as a small bedroom, and he often used it as his den. We'd had little money to spare so he'd never had his own space before, a place where he could invite friends to play. The little guy had adapted to our compromised situation since his father and I were divorced, and now I was happy to be able to provide such a lovely spacious room for him. I let him help to pick out the bedspread and curtains.

The apartment, considered a basement apartment since it was partially below ground level, had large picture windows and was light and cheery. The building was almost new and was in a great neighbourhood. We were about half a block from the elevated train, the library, the YMCA and the Chicago Park District Recreation Center. There was also a children's playground across the street and two parks nearby. Then, just one block away, was the school and all the shops we could need. It was perfect, especially since we had no car at the time; we certainly didn't need one as long as we lived there.

We soon met our next-door neighbours, Mary and John Nicholson. They were also newlyweds and both worked for airlines. Mary soon became my best friend. Other people in the building included a novelist and an advertising man, an artist and a furniture designer, Greek restaurant owners, Jewish dress-shop owners, and a beautiful model who was the mistress of an infamous union leader and mobster. Later, another newlywed couple moved in – a May and December match: she, another Mary, was just twenty-one and he was over fifty. Within nine months of their marriage, they had a baby, and then, little more than ten months later, they produced twins. Jack was already a grandfather so this new family must have been quite a shock to him, and to his adult children. We never understood what Mary saw in him. Every time we met, he was drunk, not pleasantly so. He always became obnoxious and often demeaned and insulted Mary in front of us.

'Look at my wife's fat ass,' he'd say. 'She's got nice big tits, though.' He'd be laughing as poor Mary cringed.

Overall, it was a most interesting group of people; we all got along well and had great fun together. Our neighbours were like an extended family; even the wife of our Italian janitor, who baby-sat for us regularly – another Nonie to Wayne – seemed part of the family.

There was another apartment building next door where a number of children lived, so Wayne had plenty of playmates. One of the families in that building was Greek and their *yia-yia*, Greek for 'grandmother', lived with them to take care of the children while the parents worked. Yia-yia also took care of any other neighbourhood children who happened to be around. Every morning she would cut a fresh long switch from the lilac bushes that ran along the edge of our properties, and she would use it much as a goatherd would in rounding up the goats. She couldn't speak a word of English but jabbered away in Greek all day long, waving her switch menacingly at the children. The children adored and respected her. We never had to worry about them – they could be outside from dawn to dusk, only coming in for meals, and we knew they were safe with Yia-yia. I remember telling Wayne, 'You are such a lucky kid.'

'Why?' he asked.

'Well, you have an American grandma, an English nan, an Italian *nonna* and a Greek *yia-yia*.'

He looked puzzled. 'How come I've only got one horrible grandpa, then?'

Hmm, I thought. I'd better change the subject, but first I reminded him that he had a nice granddad who lived in England.

'Oh, that's good,' he said, 'but I wish I had one here.'

Besides school, there was an abundance of free or cheap activities for children nearby. They could swim in the indoor pools at either the YMCA or the Park District, listen to stories at the library, play basketball at the court across the street and attend all kinds of fun classes at the Park District, which ran a day camp when school was out for the summer. There were just as many activities available for adults. Living in that kind of old neighbourhood, which is rare today, was much like living in an English village.

None of us ever had much money and our entertainment was simple. We had dinner parties within our building so we never had to worry about driving under the influence of alcohol. We would get together with Mary and John Nicholson almost every weekend and usually had baked beans, date bread and hot dogs for dinner. John was from Boston and baked beans were a weekend tradition. Sometimes the men would play basketball across the street or we would go for walks together around the neighbourhood. Usually on those promenades, Palmer would end up saying the same thing: 'You know what they say. You can travel widely on your own block.' We'd all nod and grunt in agreement with his words of wisdom.

A day or two after one of our neighbourhood strolls, I was having coffee with Mary Rogers, the girl with three babies, and she said something that shocked me. 'I was watching you guys walking up the street last weekend and couldn't take my eyes off Palmer. He walks funny, like a girl,' she said. 'Have you ever noticed how he bobs up and down? And my Jack was just saying that he thinks he's a bit limp-wristed.' Without hesitating, she continued, 'Do you think he might be queer?'

'Don't be ridiculous,' I protested. 'We have a very healthy sex life. There's nothing wrong with Palmer, I can assure you. He's all man. He plays golf and poker, and homosexual men don't do that.'

'Hmm, well, I was just saying,' she said.

Just saying, my foot, I thought. How dare she say such a thing about my husband? I wanted to tell her what I thought of her drunken poor excuse for a husband, but I held my tongue. Least said, quickest mended, I thought. Although, I must admit, I had often watched Palmer and thought how oddly he walked. It really did look a little effeminate. And I had lied about our sex life: it was almost non-existent.

I honestly don't think Palmer was homosexual. If anything, he was asexual. An online encyclopedia seems to confirm my conclusion: Wikipedia says, 'Asexuality (sometimes referred to as non-sexuality), in its broadest sense, is the lack of sexual attraction to others or the lack of interest in sex.' That certainly seems to fit.

On many occasions, I tried to entice him into having sex with me. I would try to emulate the seductive poses I'd seen in magazines and movies, wear sexy nightwear and such, but he simply wasn't interested. I often cried myself to sleep. I discovered after I'd lived with him for a while that he had a strong dislike of women: he seemed to have no respect for them and often said demeaning things about them. I'm sure his beliefs and behaviour had something to do with his childhood and upbringing: I knew he had no respect for his mother – but, then, he had even less for his father.

On a couple of occasions, we went to Peoria, Illinois, to visit Palmer's parents. The fun part, especially for Wayne, was travelling on the Peoria Rocket, which had run from Chicago to Peoria for many years. Palmer would book us into a private carriage, which made it even more of an adventure. It wasn't a long journey, but there was enough time to have a meal on board, which seemed a luxury to me. Peoria, though, was dreary, at least where the Palmers lived in their converted attic apartment. Mrs

Palmer made a special tomato soup every time we visited; apparently, it was one of her son's favourites and she made it with milk. I tried to duplicate the recipe several times but each time it curdled; I was sure there was a secret ingredient that she hadn't divulged. We ate most other meals out, usually at my father-in-law's local tavern, which stank of stale smoke and spilled beer.

One Peoria visit stays with me. I had to confide in my mother-in-law that I was terribly constipated and asked if she had any medicine I could take for it. I don't remember if she did, but later that day, as we were all sitting around the table playing a game, she brought up the subject of constipation. 'If you don't get relief,' she said to me, 'for goodness' sake, don't do anything drastic.'

'What do you mean?' I asked, already embarrassed at having my problem discussed in front of the men.

'Well,' she proceeded, 'someone we knew years ago had a terrible problem with constipation. He got so desperate that he dug around down in there with a rusty nail file. He got blood poisoning and died.' I had to excuse myself and only just made it to the bathroom before I threw up. These people are weird, I thought. Did she really think I might be stupid enough to resort to such bizarre methods to relieve myself?

We had some good times living at 431 North Central Avenue, even though Palmer was already creating problems with his drinking. I believe the support system within the apartment building kept us going for as long as we did.

While we were living there, I made a concerted effort to gain favour with my in-laws by inviting them and a few more of Palmer's relatives for Christmas dinner. Seven came, including a couple of aunts and cousins. With my own family and friends, we had about eighteen in all, including small children. With an additional borrowed dining table, we managed to squeeze in to eat together and, from what I could tell, a good time was had by all. I had spent days preparing food and presented an impressive feast, but on Christmas Day, as I cooked the turkey and brought the meal together, I began to feel very ill. How I got through it I don't know, but it was a great relief when some of the guests offered to help with the clearing up. By the time everyone left that night, I was dizzy and had a splitting headache. I took my temperature and discovered I had a dangerously high fever. Then I must have fainted. The next thing I knew, I was in the hospital with pneumonia. No wonder I'd felt so ill. Almost everyone who had been at our Christmas dinner sent thank-you cards and said what a wonderful day it had been; we heard nothing from Palmer's parents.

I couldn't believe it when they arrived unannounced at our apartment while we were having our traditional Saturday-night hot dogs and beans with the Nicholsons. We invited them to join us, cooked more hot dogs and beans and opened another tin of date bread. Seemingly, the meal went well and we had pleasant conversation, but we later learned that our uninvited guests had bad-mouthed me to anyone who would listen, telling everyone that they had travelled all that way from Peoria only to be fed 'lousy hot dogs'. You could have knocked me down with a feather when I heard that. I was livid. Did Palmer come to my defence? Never.

'Did they think I could pull a special meal out of the air for them?' I asked Palmer (I might have said something other than 'out of the air'). He had no answer, just shrugged his shoulders dismissively.

One of the many interesting things that happened during our time on Central Avenue began with an evening stroll that took me past the Central Plaza Hotel. A small knot of people was standing outside, chatting on the sidewalk. As I passed them, I thought I recognized one of the men in the group. I couldn't remember where I had seen him before until several minutes later. When I was about a block away, it came to me. He was Thomas Cronin, a hot item in the press and on television in 1960. He had been butler to Princess Margaret and Antony Armstrong-Jones and had recently left their employ to write a tell-all book about life with the couple. He was presently on a tour of America's television talk shows. I turned around and went back.

When I got to the hotel, he was standing alone so I decided to speak to him. 'Excuse me, sir, my name is Iris Palmer. Aren't you Thomas Cronin?'

'Yes, madam, I am indeed,' he replied, in a posh British accent.

'I'm from London,' I told him, 'and I've been following your story in the magazines and newspapers. It's all very interesting and exciting.'

'Oh, thank you,' he said. 'I'm just enjoying a little break.'

'I'm sorry. I hope I haven't offended. I always like to talk to anyone from home,' I blabbered. 'I didn't mean to intrude on your privacy.'

'You haven't intruded in the least. I'm glad to talk to

someone normal for a change, without cameras flashing in my face.' We both laughed.

'Well, my husband and I live just along the road, and if you should get fed up with all the fuss and want a quiet cup of tea, you'd be very welcome,' I told him, and gave him our phone number and address.

The following day, quite by chance, Palmer met the same man in the hotel bar where he often stopped on the way home from work. After some conversation, Cronin realized that he had already met this new acquaintance's wife. Surprised by the coincidence, Palmer invited him to have dinner with us.

I was a wreck about serving dinner to someone who had been a royal butler. I was even nervous about serving him tea, which never happened anyway since he preferred very expensive Scotch. Over the next two weeks, we ended up spending a lot of time with Thomas Cronin and I came to realize he was nothing but an opportunist and mooch. I remember thinking, as I waited on him hand and foot one evening, how ludicrous it was that I should be serving someone who had never been anything but a servant himself. Palmer and his cronies even took him to a strip show, which was something the man had never before experienced. In all the time he was around, he never offered to pay for anything or even bring a bottle of wine to dinner. The only redeeming feature of his visit was the stories he told about working for royalty and other prominent figures.

He said he had worked a five-year term for the American ambassador to the United Kingdom, and, of course, he had worked for Princess Margaret and

Antony Armstrong-Jones. At the time, there had been much speculation about the princess and her husband's relationship.

'Did Armstrong-Jones have much say in things? Did he wear the pants in the family?' I asked.

'Well, I wouldn't use such an expression,' he huffed, 'but I will say that, unfortunately, not only did Mr Armstrong-Jones want to be the master of the household, he also wanted to be the mistress. You must understand that I was very protective of Princess Margaret and her royal standing, especially in view of her fondness for drink. I often clashed with Mr Armstrong-Jones over household decisions to the point that I felt it best to seek alternative employment.'

Aha, I thought. Perhaps all the rumours about that particular royal marriage were true.

Of course, when the press got wind of Cronin's sudden departure from Kensington Palace, they jumped on him to get the inside scoop. Apparently they'd made him an offer he could not refuse. Now, having betrayed the royal family's trust, he could probably never work as a butler in Britain again. I believe that after he finished his tour of America Thomas Cronin went to work as a maître d' at one of the big Jai Alai hotel casinos in Florida, and that was the last anyone ever heard of him. While I was checking the accuracy and dates in this part of my story, I learned two things: first, he had been in the employ of Princess Margaret for just one month, and second, he was purported to be a spy.

On 20 February 2000, the *Mail on Sunday* published an article written by Jason Lewis, an investigative editor. The headline reads:

THE KGB'S SPY AT THE PALACE: Soviet intelligence files reveal the extraordinary story of how Princess Margaret's butler and top author Derek Tangye sold secrets to Moscow.

The article in part reads:

The Soviet Union spied on the British Royal Family during the height of the Cold War and even succeeded in getting an agent employed as Princess Margaret's butler, the *Mail on Sunday* can reveal.

Today we unmask Thomas Cronin – code name Rab – as the key agent in an audacious plan that led to the Royals' most intimate secrets being sent to spymasters in Russia.

Highly classified files in Moscow reveal how Cronin, who also served a five-year stint as butler to the American Ambassador, was just one of a number of Soviet spies given the mission of infiltrating London high society.

Wow, what a surprise. There we were, unsuspecting and naive, thinking it was a bit of a privilege meeting a royal butler when all the time we'd been entertaining a spy!

Meeting Cronin had been the hot topic of conversation at my next meeting with all my GI bride friends; I wonder what they would have thought if we'd known about this side of the infamous butler, and the threat to our royal family!

14: The TBPA and Convention Capers

By this time, as well as belonging to the Daughters of the British Empire (DBE), I had discovered another organization for British women. I'm not sure if my parents heard about it first or if I learned of it from my friend Bobby McCarthy. The Transatlantic Brides and Parents Association (TBPA) was founded to provide GI brides in America and their parents in Britain with a meeting ground for mutual fellowship and support. I knew how much it meant to me to have other girls like myself to talk to but it had never occurred to me that perhaps the parents we had left behind might need the same kind of support. I thought it was wonderful that someone had thought to include them. I later learned that the parents had started the club. The added bonus of belonging to the TBPA was that, because of the large number of members, they could organize and offer charter flights between the two countries. With commercial airfares being out of reach for most of us, the cut-rate charters were a boon.

The girls I met in this new club were, for the most part, younger than those in the DBE. Members of the DBE were almost all war brides, but those of us in the TBPA had married servicemen after the war had ended. We seemed to have more in common, especially since most of us had younger children. Our meetings were always great fun: we'd chatter and laugh over tea, cucumber sandwiches and homemade cakes and biscuits, all the things our American counterparts didn't understand.

'Cucumber sandwiches?' one American woman said. 'With no meat? It sounds dreadful.' And I'll never forget the reactions when I mentioned such delicacies as fish paste, bread and dripping, and toad-in-the-hole.

'I always thought you English were weird, but that is just plain disgusting,' our friend Cindy said, when my sister-in-law, Brenda, and I were talking about the food we missed.

'Well, do you want a list of all the things we think are weird over here?' said Brenda. We were always laughing about such things, and we could never have had such laughs without other English girls to share those things with. So many conversations began, 'Do you remember this or that?' We bonded through our mutual reminiscences. Without those shared joys and sorrows, I'm sure many of us would have found life in America far more difficult, especially if they'd had the misfortune to acquire in-laws like the two sets I'd had. Most of us missed our families, and many British girls I met had never been home for a visit; a very few didn't want to go, but others yearned for the opportunity. I used to watch a TV programme called *Queen for a Day* in which if your hard-luck story was that week's winner, you wore a crown, received a bounty of gifts and had your wish come true. My wish would always have been the same: an all-expenses-paid trip home to visit my family or to bring them to me. The longest I ever went without going home was seven years. I was frightened I might never see my family again.

One thing I believe we all agreed on was how lonely

and isolated we felt when we had given birth to our children and didn't have family, especially our mums, with us to offer support and share the joy. Until I met all those other GI brides, most of whom were in the same or similar situations to my own, I had often felt sorry for myself about the conditions I had married into. All of us had had dreams that were shattered by reality. I felt foolish when I heard some of their stories, and wondered at their ability to laugh about them.

'You think you married into a bad situation, Iris,' said my dear friend Shirley Ashburn, who had arrived in America just a few months after I had in 1955. She continued, 'After Wayne [her husband] was processed out of the army in New York, we bought a used car and drove it to Tennessee, which was where we'd be living. On the way, he said he'd forgotten to tell me that the house had no indoor plumbing. Well, that was a bit of a shock. His parents did get plumbing fairly soon after that, but while I was there, I had to go to a neighbour's well to fetch water. It was down by the river, and because I was scared of all the creepy-crawlies I'd heard about, I'd run all the way back. By the time I'd get there, most of the water'd be gone out of the bucket. They must've thought I was crazy, but Wayne had told me all about the poisonous snakes. They had rattlers, water moccasins, copperheads, the lot. I wasn't taking any chances,' she said. She deserves a medal, I thought. I bet she was glad when they moved to Illinois!

Another friend, June Hegedus, told me she'd been so unhappy in America that her husband had rejoined the air force in the hope of being stationed back in the UK. She said they'd had two other postings, one in the US and one in France, before finally getting to the UK.

Yet another GI bride friend, June Gradley Armstrong, said it had been seven or more years before she'd made the trip home. She told me that if she had gone during the first few years, she wasn't sure she would have returned to America. That she couldn't go back forced her to adjust and settle into American life. June's mother and mine had been neighbours in England, and June and I were old friends from the South Oxhey council estate.

There were so many stories like that and it certainly put mine into perspective. I felt especially sorry for the unsuspecting girls who had married African Americans. They wouldn't have had a clue what lay ahead. Thankfully, things are different now, but back then, a white girl married to a black man was ostracized by the black and white populations alike; they would have been labelled white trash. I can't imagine what they went through. I wondered what, if any, support they had received, and was relatively sure they wouldn't have had anything like the TBPA or DBE to turn to. I considered myself fortunate to have such a valuable support system. In addition, if it hadn't been for the TBPA, I'm sure my parents could not have afforded to visit me in the States, or I to visit them.

The person who began organizing charter flights for us in Chicago was a Scot, George Hudson. We also had him to thank for starting up a business importing British food products. We used to flock to his little shop when we learned he'd had a new shipment of goodies. The prices were high because of shipping charges, but we all thought we deserved a little splurge after giving up so much for so long. At last we had real British tea, Irish sausages, lean back bacon, Cadbury's chocolate and Marmite. We could even buy a new tea-cosy, and tapes of our favourite British music.

A Welsh couple opened a fish and chip shop; I believe it was the first ever in Chicago. Again, the prices were a bit steep – after all, they'd had to import the deep-fat fryers, not to mention the malt vinegar. As I'd approach their shop, the smell of fried fish and malt vinegar invaded my senses and I'd be salivating before I even got there. I loved that aroma. It had everything to do with memories of home. That smell still has power over me, and if it wasn't for all the health warnings, I'd probably be eating dinner out of newspaper on a regular basis. I can close my eyes and smell it now.

The owners did a roaring trade and worked so hard that it ended up wrecking their marriage and, alas, our fish and chip shop closed. We were devastated. Someone else eventually bought the equipment and reopened at a different location, but it was never the same without our Welsh friends.

I became very involved with the TBPA, and because of my knowledge of the convention business and the connections available to me through Palmer, I was instrumental in bringing one of the first TBPA conventions to Chicago. The organization sent me to Columbus, Ohio, to put in a bid.

Bobby McCarthy, Pat Connolly (another GI bride) and I set off for Columbus. We were all lucky enough to have friends or family to take care of our children for the long weekend. Pat had offered to drive us there. Her car was a new white convertible, and off we went, top down, just like

Thelma and Louise, plus one. It was a glorious day, and we sang as we whizzed through the countryside. Suddenly smoke started coming out from under the car's hood. We pulled off the road as soon as it was safe to do so. Pat went around to the front of the car and threw the hood up. Flames shot into the air. She screamed, we screamed, and as fast as we could, we got away from the car. I don't know how it happened but soon a fire truck came barrelling towards us, sirens wailing. The flames were soon extinguished. A tow truck took us to the nearest town where the car was repaired. Finally, in Pat's brand new now-scorched car, we resumed our journey. Pat was distraught but at last we reached our destination in the wee hours of the morning. Thank God, we still had one free day to recuperate before the convention's general meeting began.

That evening, as we congregated in the lobby and bar of the hotel, we found ourselves surrounded by gorgeous young men. We soon learned that they were members of a baseball team. I tired eventually of the banter and, since I still had to practise my speech for the next day, retired to my room early. Exhausted after the excitement of the day, I climbed into bed and, since I'd had a few drinks, was soon sound asleep. Bobby shared the room with me, and I thought I heard her come in later. When I woke up the next morning, I looked at her and had the shock of my life: one of the baseball players was in bed with her. I coughed loudly. Bobby sat bolt upright. She was naked, with makeup smeared all over her face and her hair sticking out in every direction. I'm not sure if she looked more like a raccoon or a porcupine. She stared at me, then turned. I will never forget her reaction.

'Good heavens,' she said. 'How did he get here?' Bobby's language reflected her background and her choice of words was quite different from what mine would have been. I made a dash for the bathroom. When I emerged some time later, Mr Gorgeous was gone, and there sat Bobby, a sheet wrapped around her.

'I'd prefer that we don't speak of this again, ever,' she said, somewhat sheepishly. I couldn't answer her: I was laughing too hard.

I'm sure that my bid to win the next convention was successful because of the coaching and advice I'd received from Convention Bureau staff. I made the most professional presentation of the day and they selected Chicago unanimously for their next national meeting. When I returned with the good news, my home group elected me to organize and chair the convention. Oh, Lord, I thought. Now look what I've got myself into.

After we'd chosen a committee to help with planning the convention, word about our coming event went out to all the Chicago hotels. We immediately began to receive proposals and invitations to tour the possible city venues. My committee and I were wined and dined by hotel sales teams, and you wouldn't believe the bribes we were offered. They came mostly in the form of monetary kickbacks, but although Palmer and I were always broke and up to our eyes in debt, I could never have accepted a bribe: I was too afraid of being discovered. Palmer had warned me that it might and probably would happen, and I wondered how he resisted the temptation but, of course, he never had to pay for meals or drinks at the Chicago hotels: they relied on him to bring them business. We girls had a

164

grand time and, although we never succumbed to financial bribery, we took full advantage of the benefits. The fact was that I was playing Palmer's game, and enjoying the attention.

The committee and I had plenty of laughs at some of the menus included in various hotel proposal packages. In an effort to appeal to the British tastes of our organization, selections like cock-a-leekie soup and trifle appeared on several offerings.

'Blimey,' said one of the girls. 'Next thing you know they'll be suggesting toad-in-the-hole or even spotted dick!' We roared at that idea. We really lost it, though, when one catering manager told us he had done his homework thoroughly.

'Ah,' he said, with a knowing wink, 'not many people would know you Brits like to have a prune in your cock-a-leekie.' I almost choked on that one. None of us had ever heard of putting prunes in cock-a-leekie soup, but when I checked it later, I discovered that the original recipe did have prunes, or pieces of prune, in it. We certainly had learned something new, and from a Chicago hotel sales rep!

Besides choosing the hotel for the convention, there were many other things to arrange, but again, the Convention Bureau supplied me with printed lists of things to do and schedules that outlined when we should do them. We had to establish the size and number of meeting rooms we needed, choose a band for the grand ball, sort out entertainment, door prizes and guest speakers. There was more to do than we could ever have imagined, but we did it, and we did it well. Everything went smoothly, even the speech I had to give before the dinner and dance. The British consul general was our keynote speaker, and officers from the British TBPA came to Chicago. Besides making speeches, they praised our convention as the best there had ever been. Perhaps I've missed my calling, I thought, but no: having to do all that work on a regular basis would have taken the fun out of it.

During the convention planning, the meetings, the visits to hotels and such, we had to leave our children with baby-sitters or tolerant husbands. Occasionally Palmer was at home and willing to care for Wayne, but other than that, I had to rely on my friends in the apartment building. Everyone loved my little son, especially Mary and John Nicholson, who then had no children of their own. I never had to worry about him, although I'm sure, as with any child, he'd rather have had his mother at home, but it was only the occasional afternoon or evening that I had to be away during the year that led up to the convention.

One thing stands out in my mind from that convention. After I'd made my speech and introduced the keynote speaker, I sat down at the table on the platform and looked out over the sea of happy faces that were gazing up at us. All of them, like me, had been GI brides; all of them had left family and home to make a new life in the United States with their American husbands. I wondered how they had coped and what each of their stories might be. How many of them paralleled my own? I was sure each of them had suffered in one way or another, from loneliness, homesickness and alienation. For now, though, they seemed happy simply being together, sisters related by

Me on ship enjoying my first day without seasickness.

Me rubbernecking at skyscrapers in New York City.

Bob and me in the Irvines' back garden. Behind us is the porch from which we secretly believed the dog commited suicide.

A typical Sunday gathering at the Irvines'.
Left to right: Bob, me, my sister-in-law Brenda Jones, Bob's sister Roberta, Mr Irvine, Mrs Irvine and Grandma Neuhaus.

Mum and Wayne, on our first
visit home to England.

Dr Edward Crown, my
obstetrician, guardian angel
and saviour. I still believe
I owe him my life.

Bob and Wayne on vacation at Paw Paw Lake, Michigan.

A ghastly glamour shot of me taken from my modelling portfolio – aged eighteen but looking forty. When my son saw this photo many years later, he said, 'Wow, you just don't see things like that any more.' Thanks, Wayne!

Me trying to look sexy for a modelling photo shoot.

n a late-1959 visit to England. *Left to right*: my youngest brother, Chris; Chuck S. (if I'd married him I might have avoided a whole lot of trouble); me; Wayne.

GI brides, the Daughters of the British Empire (DBE) and one American friend, Mary Nicholson (*left*).

Mom Evans, one of the angels in my life. She adopted me into her family of nine and nicknamed me Number Ten.

Cowboy Wayne on Christmas Day, 1961, in Las Vegas.

Palmer and me outside City Hall, in Chicago, on our wedding day.

Palmer fooling around in front of friends, but was this a sign of things to come?

Palmer, Wayne and pregnant me, just before he left for his new job in Las Vegas.

Robin and Wayne back in Des Plaines, Illinois, after our brief stay in Las Vegas.

My adopted sister Jodi (Mom Evans's daughter) with her husband, Dominic Cortina, aka Big Dom.

Robin on her third birthday, pictured with her godparents, Mary and John Nicholson.

Left to right: Mum (on her visit to America), me holding onto Robin's ears, Spiro T. and Wayne. Taken outside my brother Peter's house in Elk Grove Village.

experience rather than blood. At that moment, I loved them all. They had become my family.

The Chicago Convention Bureau had assigned Palmer to work full time as liaison with the Non-Partisan Fund Raising Committee for the National Republican Convention to take place in Chicago in July 1960. The person he worked most closely with, and whose right-hand man he became, was Fred Gurley, chairman of the board of the Santa Fe railroad. Through Fred Gurley, Palmer was now meeting more and more famous and moneyed people, which meant more dinners and parties, all involving alcohol. The problem was that Palmer could not control his drinking and I learned that he was visiting my ex-employer, Dr H., regularly to get help. He was also spending a lot of time and money at the steam baths, trying to sober up, so that he would be physically and mentally able to attend the growing number of functions required for this major convention planning and fund raising. I didn't always know the extent of what was going on as the people he worked with did a good job of covering up for him to avoid embarrassment in political circles. There was no question at that point of replacing him: he was far too deeply involved with the convention and its organizers.

I didn't see much of him during the lead-up to the convention, but I had begun to dread him coming home. He was always drunk, and always stank of booze. Even after he had showered, the smell seeped out through his pores and he would perspire so much that his clothes were permeated with the acrid smell of sweat and alcohol. He didn't own many suits, so instead of having them cleaned between wearings, he would take them off at the dry-cleaner's and wait while they pressed them. He and his clothes made me feel sick and I could hardly bear having him near me; he often repulsed me.

'You should buy a couple of seersucker suits,' I told him. Seersucker was popular at the time: it was much cooler to wear, especially in Chicago's hot, humid weather. 'I could wash and iron them myself and we could save a lot on dry-cleaning bills.'

'Good idea,' he said. 'I'll sneak it in on my expense account.' I must have looked puzzled. 'Well, after all, it is work-related, or I'd just be wearing sweat pants, wouldn't I?' How appropriate, I thought. They don't call them sweat pants for nothing.

Finally, the convention started, one big round of parties and meetings, and not only for Palmer: sometimes my presence was required. It was one of the most exciting times of my life, being involved at such close quarters with American politics, politicians, the media and people from the entertainment world. During the convention, we had a room on the same floor as the media in the convention headquarters hotel, then known as the Pick Congress, on Michigan Avenue. The media person I remember best was Mike Wallace, who was in the next room to us – I remember how surprised I was by his pock-marked face. There were so many famous people floating around in the hallways and the hospitality rooms that it was hard not to stand and stare.

One night we had attended a huge affair in the grand ballroom of the hotel. The party, hosted by the Hawaiian delegation to the convention, was a typical Hawaiian *luau*.

Everyone was dressed in the bright colours of the tropical islands, with orchid leis around their necks, flown in especially for the occasion. I had never seen such an extravagant production, except perhaps in movies. As I was leaving the function, I stepped into the elevator, followed by Senator Thruston B. Morton, who had also just left the party after giving a speech. Senator Morton was one of America's most senior and respected politicians at the time. He greeted me and said what a nice party it had been and something to the effect that he was going to take a nap. He then took off his orchid lei and placed it around my neck as he got out of the elevator. I still have that lei pressed in my scrapbook, and for many years I delighted in telling people that I'd been 'leid' by Senator Thruston B. Morton in the elevator at the Pick Congress Hotel.

The general delegation meetings were held at the Chicago Amphitheater (McCormick Place was not yet built), and it was always packed. We had special tickets to attend the sessions and the Gurleys' chauffeur usually picked me up and drove me downtown. The limousine was also sent to collect me for a private party held in Fred Gurley's personal railroad car, which had been brought into the Chicago Stockyards for the Gurleys to entertain in. Many famous people attended the party that evening; it was all I could do to stop myself staring with my mouth wide open. I was introduced to the Davieses, who owned the *L. A. Times*; their daughter Nancy married Ronald Reagan and later became America's First Lady.

Mrs Gurley told me they were disappointed that Walt Disney had sent his apologies; apparently, he and Fred Gurley were close friends, so much so that Gurley had named one of his trains after Disney. I never could quite figure out why I was there and felt completely out of place. The Gurleys were wonderful people and very down-to-earth, but I was hopelessly embarrassed in their company on one particular occasion. Wayne, who was four or five at the time, had been invited to come downtown with us in the limousine, along with Mrs Gurley and me. Out of the blue he started calling Mrs Gurley 'Grandma'. I wanted to die, but she roared with laughter.

Later I learned that Fred Gurley had been one of those who were covering up Palmer's drinking. Apparently, it had become a mutual thing: Mr Gurley also had help from Dr H. and the steam baths during the run-up to and period of the convention. They covered for each other, the only difference being that Fred Gurley could afford it.

After the convention had nominated Richard Nixon to run against John F. Kennedy in the Presedential Election, we received a card from Nixon thanking us for our efforts on his behalf. Palmer was as mad as hell when Kennedy won that election. He thought Nixon was wonderful and continued to think that even after the Watergate scandal, which blew up years later and resulted in Nixon resigning the presidency. For some reason, even though I knew little about American politics or politicians, I never did like Nixon.

15: New Baby and Las Vegas

I began yearning for another child and was convinced that if we had one together Palmer might stop drinking. Surely, I thought, if he had a child of his own, he would grow up and be more responsible. Perhaps his parents would be nicer if I gave them a grandchild. They treated Wayne kindly but without affection. They always seemed a little uncomfortable around us, perhaps because they had spent so little time being a family in the past. I always tried to give them the benefit of the doubt, but it wasn't easy.

Our living conditions had also become an issue for me, especially when I realized that all of Palmer's workmates were living in elegant apartment buildings on Lakeshore Drive or big houses in the suburbs, while we were in the same basement apartment. I thought that if he stopped drinking and spending money foolishly, we could pay off some of our mounting debts and be able to afford a nicer apartment or house. If he was a father, things would change, I felt sure.

Every month when my period started, I would be shattered with disappointment. It wasn't easy to interest Palmer in sex – I supposed because of his drinking. He usually went to sleep far too quickly, often on the sofa, or simply couldn't perform. I begged and pleaded with him to stop drinking, for just a short while, so that I'd have a better chance of becoming pregnant, but my pleas were in vain. Occasionally he said he would try, but still he arrived home drunk each night.

I finally went to my old friend Dr Crown and asked his advice. He told me we should do a sperm count to find out if a pregnancy was possible. We already knew that I could conceive. I explained this to Palmer and, although it was embarrassing, with his co-operation I collected the semen sample in a condom, where it was secured, ready for transportation. I had to keep it warm, next to my body, and get it into the doctor's office right away. We carried it out in a very contrived way early one Saturday morning. I will never forget that trip downtown on the bus, with a semen-filled condom under my arm: I was praying all the way that it wouldn't burst.

Dr Crown inspected the sample under a microscope and invited me to look too. He pointed out that there were few sperm and they were not very active. He did say, though, that I could get pregnant. He gave me some advice on increasing the possibility of those few lazy little sperm finding their target, and told me it would help a lot if Palmer were to stop drinking, which he did not.

I won't go into detail about the acrobatics we performed to help steer those tired little swimmers in the right direction, but you couldn't do them with grace, especially if you were not in good physical condition. Often we would collapse in hysterical laughter – at least this had given us something to laugh about together. But something worked because I was soon pregnant. We were both elated, and even Palmer's parents were pleased at the prospect of becoming grandparents.

By then I had stopped working so I immediately started

on a healthy regimen of walking and exercising every day in an effort not to gain as much weight as I had in my first pregnancy. I was also hoping that it would have an effect on the size of the baby. I was not keen on giving birth to another very large one. I walked miles every day and had never felt healthier. I would also have been happier, had it not been for Palmer's drinking, which was getting worse instead of better, as I'd hoped.

For a while, we'd had a housekeeper coming in once a week to help clean and do the ironing, but now we couldn't afford that and in those days it cost only nine dollars for the day. We had become fond of our housekeeper, whose name was Mary Butler. Mary was a large jolly African American, who I think was as fond of us as we were of her. She had been unhappy that Wayne called Palmer by his first name and nagged him into calling him 'Daddy Bob'. When I told her we could no longer afford to have her, we both cried. The following week she showed up anyway. We were all still in bed and she was banging on the door but Palmer wouldn't let her in and refused to allow me to go and talk to her. He was angry that she had defied his order not to come any more but I believe she was worried about us: she knew about his drinking and had observed his crazy behaviour. It was heartbreaking hearing her calling to us, and it seemed an eternity before she finally left. I truly think she knew we needed her, and I believe she would have worked for nothing, had Palmer allowed her to come. This proved to be one of the first unreasonable control issues that was to make our future lives unbearable at times.

While I was pregnant, my friend Mary Nicholson

started taking evening classes in shorthand and typing at the nearby high school. I thought that sounded wonderful and decided it might be a good idea if I checked to see what was available for me. I found an art class that sounded interesting, and since it took place on just one evening a week, and I was spending so many evenings alone anyway, I signed up. Mary agreed to watch Wayne for me if Palmer wasn't home. I really enjoyed learning something new rather than just sitting at home wondering when Palmer would appear and in what condition he'd be. One night as I was getting ready to go to class, he arrived home and was obviously very drunk.

'Where do you think you're going?' he slurred.

'Don't you remember? I'm taking an art class at the high school,' I replied.

'No, I don't remember. You didn't tell me that so don't lie to me. You're not going anyway.'

'I've already paid for it out of my own money. I have to go. I'm in the middle of a project.' I immediately regretted mentioning my own money; I had made it secretly by sewing for people.

'You don't have money of your own. That's my money you're wasting. No wonder we're in debt.' I couldn't believe my ears when he said that. I certainly had a lot to learn about living with an alcoholic and how they twist things to shift blame.

He staggered into the bedroom and I followed him, still pleading.

'I'm not taking care of your kid while you go off gallivanting,' he spewed. 'Now leave me alone.' He flopped onto the bed. For a minute, I just stood there, watching saliva dribble out from the corner of his cruel mouth. At that moment, I hated him.

I phoned Mary and told her what had happened. She said I could bring Wayne over there if I still wanted to go to my class, so that was what I did. I wasn't going to allow that maniac to stop me having something for myself.

With Wayne safely in Mary's care, I crept back into our apartment and grabbed my handbag, but as I started towards the back door, suddenly he was there, blocking my way. He grabbed me, and dragged me away from the door towards the bedroom. There, he tried to lock me into a closet. I think he was shocked that I fought back and he loosened his grip long enough for me to break away. I ran for the back door and managed to get outside. When he realized that I had left, he came after me with an umbrella and began hitting me with it, trying to make me stop. I just kept running. I was about seven months pregnant and I couldn't believe he was doing this to me and, frankly, I didn't care if he killed me, but I was not about to give in to him. He finally left me alone and went home. I continued to the school but was in no condition to go to class and never went back. I sneaked into our apartment building and went to Mary's, where I sobbed my heart out and stayed until we were sure that Palmer was asleep. The next day he claimed not to remember what had happened.

Shortly after that incident, Palmer announced that he'd been offered a job as sales manager at the Flamingo Hotel in Las Vegas, and that he was going to accept it. What he failed to mention was that the Convention Bureau was letting him go and that he would only be working there until he had trained his replacement. He said that the Vegas hotel would pay our moving expenses and that we could stay at the hotel until we found a place to live. I was so far along in my pregnancy, and so unsure of Palmer's behaviour, that I told him he should go ahead but that I didn't want to move until after the baby was born.

In the meantime, Mary and John, who lived next door, expressed an interest in moving into our apartment when we left. After a lot of brainstorming, we came up with a plan: when our furniture was put into temporary storage, Palmer could go to Las Vegas and Mary and John would move into our apartment. Wayne and I would stay with them until after the baby arrived. Everyone thought that was a great idea. Palmer would be happy, Mary and John would be happy and I would still be under Dr Crown's care. It would also buy me time to decide if I wanted to join Palmer in Las Vegas.

One positive thing I had managed to do at that time was join a church. Wayne and I attended a nearby Lutheran church and involved ourselves in its activities. I had attended a Billy Graham event in Chicago, and had been 'saved', and I was now reading the Bible regularly and doing a home-study course provided by the Billy Graham Foundation. Palmer made fun of me, but I ignored his gibes. The church provided me with a sense of security and stability in my fractured life and I was sure it would give me the strength I needed to keep my marriage together. I had begun teaching at Sunday school and had fun creating Bible-related projects for the children in my class. I was especially touched when they brought me little presents. Sundays became very important to my sanity. The church was one place where I felt safe.

Palmer left for Las Vegas at the end of August 1961, which left Wayne and me sharing what was now Mary and John's extra bedroom. We were enjoying the relaxed atmosphere without the constant threat of Palmer's behaviour, and Mary and John enjoyed having what we jokingly called a live-in maid. I kept the apartment sparkling clean and had dinner ready for them every night when they came home from work. The peace was heavenly, and the laughter a gift. It seemed like every five minutes they'd have the camera out, taking photos of me and my giant bump, which they found hilarious.

We received regular phone calls from Las Vegas and it sounded as though things were going well out there. Palmer must have been on his best behaviour during the honeymoon phase of his new job. He told me that his bosses were pleased and impressed with his sales ability and general know-how. In fact, Palmer was a brilliant young man. He'd had a great reputation nationally and was highly thought of in the industry until his drinking ruined his career. When he was sober, he was a different person.

We began hearing of all the celebrities he was meeting, including many of the big-name stars who were headlining in the shows out there. Palmer had always been a name-dropper, often exaggerating his connections with the rich and famous, so we never really knew if he had just passed someone in the hallway or if he really was acquainted with them. He said he could hardly wait for us to get there so that we could see where he worked and meet all the important people he knew. I guess I wanted to believe him.

Again, it seemed my pregnancy would never end, and every time I saw Dr Crown for a check-up, we thought it would be the last visit before the baby arrived. Finally, before I left his office one day, the doctor gave me an injection that he said might get labour started, if the baby was ready. I went home and, sure enough, began having contractions. When they were coming regularly, Mary rushed me to the hospital. Every time we hit a bump in the road, she'd scream, thinking she might have hurt me, but the look on her face had me laughing so hard we both ended up with tears rolling down our faces.

'Oh, stop it,' I said. 'Now I've gone and wet myself!' Off we went again, and laughed all the way to the hospital.

After I'd been admitted, someone took me directly to the labour ward. There, a nurse prepped me for delivery but suddenly the contractions stopped. It had been a false alarm and eventually the doctor sent me home again. I, of course, was disappointed but Mary said she was grateful for the practice run.

'I'm sorry,' I told her.

'Don't be,' she replied, 'I've been scared to death about getting you there in time, and now, when it really happens, I'll be an old pro at playing the part of Daddy.' My pal Mary was a real trouper.

We carried on for about two more weeks, but then Dr Crown decided labour should be induced, but this time it would be in the hospital. The baby was again quite large and in the right position. Mary took me to the hospital and off we went to the labour ward. There, a nurse put me on an intravenous drug to induce labour. The contractions began almost immediately, and this time they didn't stop. Once more I was in labour for a long time but finally, in the delivery room, when Dr Crown announced that I had a healthy baby girl, I was over the moon with joy. She weighed in at nine pounds two and a half ounces, so, after all that exercising, I hadn't produced a smaller baby, but *I* was a bit smaller this time.

Robin Lee, as we named her, was born on 4 October 1961 and was the most beautiful baby: she had enormous dark eyes and a thick mop of black hair. I couldn't take my eyes off her, and when I finally closed them, I could still see her perfect face. I couldn't believe I'd been lucky enough to have a little girl, especially after I'd wished for a son as my first child. Mary made me laugh when she told me what had happened in the fathers' waiting room.

'I was a nervous wreck,' she said. 'I was pacing up and down, and someone told me I shouldn't be in there, that the room was only for fathers.'

'I am the father!' Mary had protested, in her agitated state.

We congratulated each other on the great job we had done and she left to notify Palmer. Throughout Robin's life, we have often joked about who her 'real' father was.

I soon received roses and a phone call from Robin's biological father, who cried, saying he would never drink again, that he loved me, couldn't wait to see us and couldn't live without me. In the next few days, I heard from him a lot, always with the same promises. His parents came to see the baby and they were delighted with their little granddaughter, especially because she was so much like her daddy.

We went home to Mary and John's, and for the next few days there was a stream of visitors and tons of gifts. Even the local shopkeepers sent flowers and presents, such was the excitement about our little daughter's birth. Wayne, who was now almost six, was just as excited as everyone else was about his little sister and we had to remember to make a fuss of him too. He was always such a loving little boy that no one would ever want his feelings to be hurt.

My family in England was thrilled for me because they knew how much I had wanted a girl. I wished I knew when they would get to see her; it was nearly two years since I'd been home.

I knew it was time to face the future positively so I booked our flight to Las Vegas. Palmer told me he had found and rented what he described as a luxury furnished apartment, complete with swimming pool, and until we found the right house, we were to leave our own furniture in storage. After shipping the baby gifts, we got ourselves packed up too. Then, when Robin was just ten days old, we said a tearful goodbye to Mary and John, and flew to Nevada, to start the new and wonderful life Palmer had promised us.

16: Las Vegas, City Without Clocks

When we got off the plane at McCarran Field in Las Vegas, it was like stepping into a steam bath. The heat that greeted us, even though it was evening, almost knocked me over – it was like being smothered with a hot damp blanket. I was immediately reminded of my first summer in Chicago, in 1955, when the heat had been so oppressive and I'd been so miserable. Oh, my God, I thought, if it's like this at night, what must it be like during the daytime? I couldn't dwell on that now, though, because there was too much else to think about. As we came through the gate, there was Palmer, grinning from ear to ear. He was obviously smitten with his new baby daughter and happy that we had finally arrived. By that time, he had bought a car, and drove us away to our new luxury accommodation.

In 1961, Las Vegas was not nearly as built up as it is today and we had to drive through some desert areas before we reached 'The Strip' where all the big hotels and casinos were. It was late evening so the lights were dazzling as we passed the Flamingo, Dunes, Sands hotels and many smaller properties. All of those original hotels and casinos have since disappeared, replaced with much bigger and far grander buildings. On a later visit to Las Vegas, many years later, I found that I didn't recognize the area where we had lived; in fact, I couldn't find it.

Our eyes were almost popping out of our heads as we drove down a new road that had desert on either side and pulled into the brand new Sunset Sands Apartment Complex. The buildings looked much like rows of motel units with a swimming pool between each pair. There was a small amount of grass around each pool, but other than that, it was just sand for miles around.

'Welcome to your new home,' said Palmer, as he slid open the glass patio door that took us straight into the living room.

'Is that the only door?' I asked.

'Nope, there's another just like it into the bedroom,' he replied.

'That's weird,' I said. 'Not very secure, is it?' I suppose I was a little wary after living in the big city.

'Nothing to worry about here,' he said, laughing. 'No one's going to bother us in the desert.'

Wayne was already off checking the place out. 'Where do I sleep?' he asked, and Palmer showed him a room with two double beds. 'Wow, can I have a friend to stay over?' We laughed and told him that as soon as he found a friend, he could certainly invite him to stay the night.

The apartment itself was fairly new and decent but, again, felt like a motel. There was a smallish living-dining area, a galley-style kitchen in the middle, and two large bedrooms, with a shared bathroom off a connecting hallway across the whole back of the apartment. It was a strange layout but there was a washing-machine in the kitchen, which was a great relief since we had diapers. Palmer had not used the washing-machine: it still had its Styrofoam packing inside. I discovered he had been sending all of his dirty clothes out to be laundered and ironed. Even his underwear was in the closet on hangers.

'Isn't that a bit expensive?' I asked later.

'Well, there's no dryer and I wasn't about to hang stuff out on the line,' he said. 'Besides, I didn't have an iron and wouldn't know how to use one if I did.'

Men, I thought. Mum was right. They're bloody useless.

Palmer had the next day off work so we ventured outside to explore this strange new desert world and, of course, Wayne headed for the swimming pool. 'It's too cold,' he said, shivering, with goose bumps all over him – the desert night air had chilled it. He looked disappointed. I was relaxing on a poolside lounge chair and the baby was in her buggy beside me. Palmer assured Wayne that the water would be much warmer after the sun had been beating down on it for a few hours and told him to try it again after lunch. By the time 'after lunch' came, it was too hot to be outside so he had to wait until early evening. We realized that we had to adjust our thinking and schedules to the desert temperatures.

On many occasions I ended up doing my grocery shopping at midnight since the supermarkets were open twenty-four hours a day. I was surprised by the rows of slot machines at the front of all the stores, just after the checkout lanes, and shocked to see how many people used them before leaving. I came to enjoy shopping late at night: not only was it much cooler, but that was when I was most likely to see some of the stars doing their shopping. One night, I thought I'd die of embarrassment when I almost knocked down Keely Smith – the singer, and wife of Louis Prima the band leader – with my shopping cart as we both sailed around the end of an aisle. She was startled but smiled at me. 'We really must stop meeting like this,' she said. We both laughed, but my knees were knocking. I couldn't wait to get home to tell Palmer.

Two strange weather-related incidents occurred when we lived in our new desert home. The first was a sandstorm, which almost totally removed the paint from the car – we had no garage so it was outside in the parking lot. Thank goodness, our insurance paid to have it repainted. The second was another storm, wind this time, and I had forgotten that I'd hung laundry on the line overnight. When I remembered it and went outside to retrieve it, it was gone. Now, that wasn't all bad: I'd only had some old sheets and towels out there, but lots of new sheets and towels had blown over into our yard from one of the hotels on the Strip. I decided it was poetic justice and kept them all.

Palmer couldn't wait to show us around the city and to introduce us to the people at the Flamingo Hotel, all of whom had been anxious to meet his family. The casinos were palatial, with their crystal chandeliers and all the other glitz, but the cigar and cigarette smoke made my eyes water. The sound of all the slot machines was unbelievable. It reminded me of something I used to hear on buses in England, when the conductor's little machine spat out the tickets, *ka-ching, ka-ching*. I was amazed to see how packed those places were at any time of day or night. That was when I learned that Las Vegas truly was the 'City Without Clocks', just like the title of the book by Ed Reid. There were no clocks in the casinos. Of course, the idea was that people should forget the time and how long they'd been there.

Besides the casinos and the extravagant shows, there wasn't much to see in Las Vegas. We drove up to the Hoover Dam, which was spectacular, but it gave me the heebie-jeebies. I couldn't stay there for long because, for the first time ever, I experienced some kind of phobia. It almost suffocated me. I felt closed in by all those high, cliff-like mountains. I had the baby in my arms, and when Palmer asked me to come and look over the parapet at the water below, I was petrified that I would drop Robin over the edge. I had nightmares about it afterwards.

When I studied the map of Las Vegas, I noticed there was an Indian reservation on the edge of town. I'd been disappointed when the one I'd visited in Wisconsin had turned out to be just a tourist attraction. Perhaps this is the real thing, I thought. After all, we're out in the old Wild West now. I asked Palmer to take me there and I was disconcerted to find that it was just a bunch of shacks, some not much better than chicken coops, with Native Americans living in them. It was depressing, and just one more disillusioning American experience.

'Is this really how they live?' I asked Palmer.

'Yeah,' he replied. 'They're all drunks, so what can you expect?'

Hmm, I thought. You should talk.

One of the first things I did after settling into our new home was to find a Lutheran church. After we'd attended services for several weeks, the pastor invited the congregation to come forward to accept Holy Communion. I stood in line to await my turn at the altar. When I was in front of the pastor, he stopped and looked at me, and as he began to offer the sacrament to me, he suddenly withdrew it. He leaned in close to me. 'I'm sorry but you can't receive Communion,' he whispered.

'Why?' I asked, as the heat of embarrassment rose in my face.

'You haven't transferred your membership to this church yet.'

I stood frozen to the spot for what seemed like minutes but could only have been seconds, then turned and walked out of the church. Shock and disbelief turned to rage and I began to run, tears streaming down my face. I didn't stop until I arrived home. Another rejection, I thought. I've been rejected by the bloody church. I was glad the children hadn't gone with me that day: it would have made my escape much more difficult. Palmer asked me what had happened, and when I told him, he laughed. 'That's what you get for trying to be such a goody-goody,' was all he said, which upset me even more.

The following day, the pastor came to see me. I invited him in but did not ask him to sit down.

'I'm sorry you left in such a hurry yesterday. We didn't have a chance to talk,' he said.

There was a boulder-sized lump in my throat and I wasn't sure if I could speak to him in a civil manner, but I took a deep breath and opened my mouth, surprised by my own daring. 'How dare you and your precious church stand between me and my God?' I spat. 'How dare you?'

He stammered, then tried to explain the rules of that particular branch of the Lutheran Church, which was, as

I recall, the Missouri Synod. I listened as politely as I could, and then it was my turn.

'Thank you for showing me how far your church has distanced itself from the teaching of Christ,' I told him. 'You can be sure I will not be transferring my membership to yours or any other Lutheran church.'

He told me how sorry he was to hear that and assured me that I would be welcome to attend the church as long as I understood the rule about Communion. I almost choked on that final comment.

'Does that mean you won't be able to baptize my baby either?' I asked.

'Your infant child would be exempt from the membership rule, but I will pray that you have a change of heart about your own membership.' I thanked him for his visit and showed him the door.

We ended up having Robin christened in that church because Mary and John Nicholson, who were to be her godparents, were also Lutherans, but I never again attended that so-called Christian church.

We had some interesting neighbours in the apartment complex but almost everyone worked in the casinos and slept most of the day. There was little socializing when we first moved in. A number of gorgeous showgirls lived close to us, and next to them I felt like a dowdy old frump, although I must say they didn't always look so glamorous when they first got up and wandered out to their swimming pool to work on their suntans.

We felt fortunate when a non-show-business couple with a young daughter moved in next door. They were

Don and Rosa Montgomery and their daughter's name was Robin, which was quite a coincidence. Don was a scientist who lived and worked in Los Alamos in New Mexico but was on assignment to the Nevada nuclear test sites. Rosa was the sister of Ruth Graham, the wife of evangelist Billy Graham. They were, of course, a religious family and were always thoughtful and kind to us. Their daughter Robin was a little younger than Wayne but at least he had someone close to his age to play with. I used to love hearing Rosa's stories of how she and Ruth had grown up in China with their missionary parents and about some of the funny things that had happened before her father got the hang of the Chinese language. My favourite story was about why his congregation kept giggling during his sermons. At last, someone explained to him that the Chinese word for 'pig' was similar to the word for 'Jesus' and that he often got the two mixed up by using the wrong inflection.

Despite Palmer's new job, we still seemed to be very short of money. When one of the newer neighbours asked if I would consider taking care of her child while she worked at the casino, I said I would. Stacey was about eight so now Wayne had another playmate. I hadn't initially thought to ask the mother, whose name was Marilyn, what she did for a living but when I did, she told me she was a 'gambler' and proceeded to explain what that meant.

Marilyn would go to the casinos, day or night, and start looking for a man who was alone and on a winning streak. She would then stand next to him, encouraging him and cheering him on. Many times the man would consider her to be good luck and would end up giving her some of his chips to gamble alongside him. Of course, she didn't gamble with the chips but cashed them in later. Sometimes she would end up drinking and dining with the man and perhaps he would buy her an expensive gift at one of the chic boutiques in the hotel. There were several such gambling girls; they made arrangements with the hotel boutiques to return the gifts and get perhaps half of the retail value in cash. It was quite a racket with the same items being sold many times over. I asked Marilyn if she ever went to bed with any of these men but she insisted, at least initially, that she was not a prostitute.

Later, she started staying away for longer periods. Sometimes I would have to go to her apartment to find clothes for Stacey and it looked as though a cyclone had gone through the building. There were cocktail dresses strewn everywhere and the whole place smelt of booze. I was worried that she was getting in over her head, and was increasingly concerned that she might be using drugs. She would sometimes cry uncontrollably on my shoulder, but when I tried to talk her into changing her crazy lifestyle she said she couldn't because nothing else would pay as well. In return she paid me well and always in silver dollars. Poor Stacey spent more and more time with us, and would cry for her mother. It was heartbreaking and reminded me of my lonely childhood when I was evacuated during the war and separated from my family.

It was difficult to get into the Christmas spirit, with the hot desert sun beating down every day. We put up a small tree for the children and I seem to recall that we cooked outside on the grill on Christmas Day. Somehow, Christmas just didn't seem the same out there in the desert. Wayne was happy because he got just what he wanted from Santa: a cowboy outfit. He took being a cowboy very seriously and was forever practising his draw. 'Stick 'em up, pardner,' he'd say.

We took him horseback riding at a ranch and to the National Quick Draw Contest to show him how fast he would need to draw if he wanted to be a real cowboy. Now, this cowboy business was a whole new thing for Wayne as he had previously had a Superman outfit, which he was always putting on and would leap into the room when we had company, scaring the hell out of our guests. He was funny as a little boy and, come to think of it, he still is; only the costumes have changed.

Soon after the holidays, Mary and John Nicholson came to visit us for Robin's christening. It was wonderful to see them and I realized how much I missed having them nearby. While they were with us, Palmer arranged for us all to see the show and have dinner at the Flamingo Hotel; we were to see Myron Cohen, the comedian, plus the dancing girls. Mary and I decided to splurge and have our hair done at one of the fancy salons on the Strip. Now, in the early sixties the beehive hairdo was in, so Mary and I, wanting to be trendy, asked for exactly that. It being Las Vegas, where just about everything was done to excess, we came out of that salon with the biggest hair you've ever seen.

We had a great evening out, and after we'd stumbled home across the patch of desert that separated the Strip from where we lived, Mary and I decided that our expensive coiffures were much too splendid to waste. Mary said she'd heard that if you wrapped toilet paper around your head before going to bed, it would preserve your hairdo. So, between us we used an entire roll, wrapping our enormous beehives.

The next morning when we emerged, bleary-eyed, from our bedrooms, we took one look at each other and began to laugh hysterically. After rolling about in bed all night, our carefully wrapped beehives had grown about a foot taller and skinnier, and when we finally composed ourselves enough to remove the paper, our hair looked as though it had been moulded inside a stovepipe hat. It was a terrible waste of toilet paper but the laughs we've had about that incident over the years have been worth it; I just wish we'd taken pictures.

Palmer and I played host to quite a number of his customers, most of whom were rich but pleasant company. One youngish man in particular comes to mind. Palmer brought him home for lunch one day and, in the course of conversation, he revealed that he had married the Kimberley heiress. 'I know you're not American,' he said to me, 'but are you familiar with the name?'

'Oh, yes,' I replied. 'Kimberly-Clark paper products are well known in Britain too.'

'No.' He laughed. 'I'm talking about Kimberley diamonds. You know, the Kimberley diamond mines.' Oh, Lord, I thought, and here I am, serving him a ham sandwich.

Of all the amazing things that happened while I was living in Las Vegas, one thing stands out, and it didn't involve anyone famous. I was taking the baby for a walk in her buggy one day, along the sidewalk on the Strip – in the days when you could do it safely. Coming towards me was someone who looked familiar. I thought I must be dreaming – after all, this was Las Vegas, not England. Who could I possibly know here? As we got closer, I realized it was who I'd thought it was. It was my old friend June Gradley from the South Oxhey council estate.

'June Gradley!' I almost shouted. 'What are you doing here?'

She stared back at me, clearly dazed. 'Iris Jones,' she finally managed to get out.

We hugged each other, questions pouring out of our mouths. I remembered then that my mother had told me she'd married an American but she didn't know where she lived in the States.

'My Len's still in the air force,' she explained, 'and we're stationed at Nellis Air Force base here in Vegas – but what are you doing here?'

'Well, you might say I'm stationed in Vegas too,' I said. 'I'm married for the second time and my husband works at the Flamingo Hotel.' We chatted for a while before exchanging phone numbers and addresses and promising we'd get together soon. I was over the moon to think that I would now have a normal friend in this weird place, and an old friend from England at that, another GI bride. How lucky can you get? I thought, as I walked away with a big grin on my face.

June and Len Armstrong had two young children and lived in military housing on the air force base, and I will never forget our first visit to them. They had invited us for dinner. When we got there, Robin was asleep so we laid her in the middle of their bed. She was only about three months old and not very active so we assumed she would be safe. As we sat around the table eating dinner, we suddenly heard a loud thump, followed by the sound of the baby screaming. We rushed into the bedroom and there was Robin, on the hard tiled floor. I picked her up and tried to comfort her but the screaming didn't stop. I was terrified. Len said we should take her to the base hospital to have a doctor check her over, and that was what we did, with the baby still screaming. As soon as it was our turn to be seen, she stopped crying. The doctor checked her over, found nothing detectable wrong with her but told us to come back if she seemed to be sleeping more or longer than usual. I stayed up all of that night, just watching her, but she seemed fine and the next day she showed no ill effects from her fall except a small bruise on her forehead. The guilt I suffered for leaving her alone on that bed stayed with me for a long time and after that, in similar situations, I simply created a little bed for her on the floor.

Playing host with Palmer, entertaining his customers at the hotel, was great fun as long as he didn't drink too much. I felt that although I was inexperienced I did a good job and managed to converse easily with just about anyone. Palmer told me that most people thought I was charming and loved my Englishness, whatever that meant.

The only problem was that it was difficult to acquire the necessary wardrobe for all those fancy dinner engagements. My crazy neighbour Marilyn had an abundance of evening clothes and usually came to my rescue. I borrowed dresses from her even though I often had to have them cleaned before I could wear them. Sometimes I just hung them outside for a while to get rid of the smell of smoke.

I used to love going to see and hear the entertainment in the lounges of the various hotels when we were with clients. I also remember two or three times leaving the kids with my next-door neighbour for an hour so that I could walk up to the Strip and listen to Jerry Vale, who was appearing at the Sands Hotel lounge – I was crazy about him and almost fainted when he said hello to me one evening. In those days, you could order one drink and sit there listening for as long as you liked to some of the biggest stars around. I don't think you can do that any more.

Palmer's job required him to work long hours, but I was so busy with the baby and baby-sitting that I really didn't have time to worry about what he was doing or how much he was drinking. We were still so short of money, though, that I had to take the baby to a free clinic for her inoculations. I used to feel guilty being there, along with all the poor Native American women and children. We were able to have nice evenings out because they were business-related and didn't cost us anything, but making ends meet at home was another matter. If it hadn't been for the money I earned for looking after Stacey, I wouldn't have had enough to buy groceries. The situation seemed ridiculous to me, but if I questioned Palmer about it, he always had an excuse or blamed me for being extravagant. Extravagant with what? I would ask myself. I never could figure out what was extravagant about buying diapers or baby food. The entire time we lived in Vegas, my only extravagance was that one ridiculous beehive.

In many ways, Las Vegas was the perfect metaphor for my marriage to Palmer. It was all bright lights and plenty on the surface, but underneath the glitz, and the show-off entertainment, our life and marriage were an arid desert. My children and I were like tumbleweed, blown about by the ever-changing prevailing winds, and emotionally, I was parched.

After we had been in Las Vegas for about six months, and before we'd had time to begin looking for a different place to live or get our furniture out of storage, Palmer announced that he had been offered a job back in Chicago and we were going almost immediately. I was stunned. I never understood how these things came about: I didn't know if he looked for jobs because he'd been given notice by his present employer, or if in fact they came looking for him. I just accepted it and did what I had to. What choice did I have? I certainly couldn't stay by myself in the middle of the desert with two small children.

So, once again, we were on the move. My first concern was for Stacey. That problem was soon solved: Rosa Montgomery, my friend and neighbour, promised that she would take over the child's care. Some time later, I learned that Marilyn, Stacey's mother, had disappeared for a long time. We eventually discovered that she had run off with a man who turned out to be a drug addict, and that he had abandoned her in some distant part of the country. The last I heard was that the courts had granted the Montgomerys temporary custody of Stacey, but I often wondered over the years what happened to her. I've always hated 'losing people', but my own life had become so complicated that it was often hard for me to keep my own little family intact, let alone keep track of others.

The next bad news was that since Palmer had not stayed for the minimum year at the Flamingo they would not pay for our move or the storage of our furniture. The latter had now racked up a bill of several thousand dollars. The job Palmer was going to was not paying our moving expenses either so I couldn't believe his new employer had begged him to work for them. I asked Palmer if he thought Uncle Art would help us out but he said he couldn't ask him. Apparently, unbeknown to me, he had already asked his uncle for help too many times.

We loaded everything we could into the car, added a car-top carrier and filled that, leaving just enough room for us to squeeze in. I will never forget how frightening it was going round the hairpin curves on some of the roads in the Sierra Nevada mountains. It felt as though the car was going to topple over the sheer drops at the roadsides because it was so top heavy.

That journey back to Illinois, along what is now known as Historic Route 66, took us three days – considered a fast time in 1962 – and was just one more nightmare in my life; one that would have been better forgotten were it not for two interesting things that happened along the way. One was when we stopped at a roadside café in the middle of the New Mexico desert. Armed guards, guns drawn, brought in several prisoners who were wearing typical striped uniforms. The men, chained together at the ankles, shuffled along, looking at the floor as they passed. I guessed they either were a chain gang or were being transported between prisons. They sat at a long table nearby and the whole place suddenly became silent; it felt as though everyone was holding their breath, waiting for who knew what? I glanced at Wayne and almost laughed: his eyes were as big as saucers. It was another occasion when it felt as though we had landed in a scene from a movie.

The next incident was the kindness shown to us by a poor old couple, typical hillbillies with no teeth and the sides cut out of their shoes to accommodate enormous bunions; they managed a horribly run-down motel in the Ozark mountains. It was late at night and freezing cold when we found it. When those old folks saw how exhausted we were from travelling across country with two children in that small car, they brought food and coffee to our cabin because they knew there was nowhere for us to get a meal. They were real angels and I could have kissed them. I have no idea where we were; all I know is that we had driven off the main road up into the hills. I remember thinking that someone could have murdered us in our sleep out there and no one would have known where we were or what had happened to us.

17: Chicago and Another New Job

Palmer's new job was with the O'Hare Inn, a hotel close to O'Hare Airport in Des Plaines, a north-west suburb of Chicago. While we looked for a place to rent, we stayed with Peter and Brenda, who lived in the nearby suburb of Elk Grove Village. They had three children of their own so with the four of us it was an extremely tight fit, but Wayne was happy that he had his cousins to play with and baby Robin had lots of attention from everyone. Finding somewhere to live, preferably close to where Palmer worked, became a matter of urgency.

We soon found an almost new townhouse to rent in Des Plaines; it was less than two miles from the hotel, and we quickly arranged to have our furniture taken out of storage and delivered. I have no idea how we paid the enormous bill we owed to the moving and storage company but I'm sure the money came from someone in the family; it was probably either Palmer's parents or his Uncle Art.

The house had three bedrooms and a bathroom on the second floor, then a living-dining room plus kitchen and toilet downstairs. The added bonus was a large basement with laundry room, which made a great indoor playroom. Several children lived in the complex so I didn't have to worry about Wayne being lonely. He had his first big birthday party in the basement. He and I decorated the walls with posters, hung balloons from the ceiling, and there was a long trestle table with all the snacks, treats and party favours laid out on a birthday tablecloth. He'd been so good through all the unrest of the past year that I wanted him to have a party to remember. He was allowed to invite all of his friends since there was ample space and it didn't matter how much mess they made. We finally had a place that seemed like a real home.

By now, Robin was six or seven months old and, just as her brother had been, she was a happy, good-natured baby. I always considered myself lucky to have two such contented children; they were my joy and salvation as the situation with Palmer continued to worsen.

Something exciting happened shortly after we moved to Des Plaines: Robin was 'discovered'. We were standing in line at the supermarket checkout one afternoon and I noticed that a man kept staring at us. Eventually he came up to us and remarked on what a beautiful child Robin was. He asked if I would consider letting her do some modelling. I was, of course, extremely wary, thinking he was a photographer who was simply trying to drum up business. However, when he gave me his business card, I recognized his name immediately: he was the owner of one of the biggest modelling and talent agencies in Chicago. He told me we would need to get some good photographs sent to him, and I said I'd think about it. I gave him our name and phone number but, knowing I could never afford to have professional photographs taken of my beautiful baby, promptly pushed the idea out of my mind.

Within two days of that chance meeting, I received a

phone call from the modelling agency asking me if I could bring Robin downtown to do a photo shoot for a national advertisement the next day. I told them I would need a little time to see if I could arrange transport, then phoned a friend and explained what had happened. She offered to take us so I called the agency back and said we would be there. That particular ad was for Sealy Posturepedic Mattresses and it appeared in many national publications. After that, Robin did lots of modelling jobs and we never did send any photographs to the agency. They all loved her, not only because she was such a beautiful child but also because she was so easy to work with. Wayne was usually at school when we went to the jobs, but he happened to be with us on one assignment and was asked to be in one of the photos; they were for a psychology book and we never saw them. I had hoped to keep the money Robin made in a savings account for her education but, sadly, out of necessity most of it was spent on food and to pay other bills. It wasn't a huge amount of money but I hated having to use it.

I tried hard to make some money of my own because I had real fears of my children going without, as I'd had to when I was a child. The first thing I did was baby-sitting in our townhouse complex. Then I started sewing for people as I had in the past, just simple hemming of skirts and trousers or other small tasks that could be done by hand since I had no sewing machine. The next thing I added to my repertoire was hair-cutting. At that time, I was cutting my own hair because I couldn't afford to have it done professionally and my next-door neighbour asked if I would cut her three daughters'. Before I knew it, I was cutting everyone's hair in our complex and a little stash of cash was accumulating in a box on the top shelf in the kitchen; I kept it hidden there for when I needed it and it gave me a small feeling of security. Then one day I went to get some money to buy a few things for the children, and the box was empty. The feelings I experienced at that moment of discovery are almost indescribable. I felt as though I'd been kicked in the stomach and slammed against a wall; I kept looking in the box, wondering if I was just not seeing right, but I knew what had happened. A combination of emotions swept over me like a tidal wave: hatred, disgust and disappointment were just some of what I felt for the man I had married. Palmer had found and taken all of my savings and I could just imagine the sick, smug pleasure he had felt at having outwitted me.

When Palmer came home late that night, I shoved the empty box under his nose, and he laughed. 'How could you?' I said. 'That was money I was saving for the children.'

'Liar,' he spat back at me. 'You thought you could steal money from me, didn't you, to spend on yourself?'

'It wasn't yours. It was money I made myself, doing things for people.'

'Any money coming into this house is mine. You don't have money of your own!' he shouted, and then he laughed again. 'You're pathetic, really stupid,' he said, with a sneer on his face. 'You really think you can get one over on me? No one can do that. No one's smart enough to outwit Bob Palmer, so you might as well quit trying.'

I ran outside. I didn't want him to see me crying and I was afraid of what I might say or do if I had to listen to any more of his ugly words. I wished he was dead, and I wished I could run away but, of course, I could not. I had to pull myself together, for the children's sake, but I didn't know how much more I could put up with before I went insane.

During this time, I started going to church again, at Christus Victor Lutheran church in Elk Grove Village, the suburb where my brother and his family were living. They had told me how much they enjoyed the church and its pastor so I decided to try it, in spite of my previous bad experience with the Lutheran Church.

Elk Grove Village was a new housing development and no churches had been built yet, so Christus Victor was holding services in an old farmhouse. It was wonderful to find a church that had such a good down-to-earth feel. Pastor Fisher was an unusual man and probably the closest thing to a real Christian I had ever met. The congregation consisted mostly of young couples with children, and they all worked hard at being good Christians, helping each other in every imaginable way; they were proud of what they called their missionary work within their own community.

Soon, I was teaching at the Sunday school and attending Bible studies and prayer groups, all of which gave me the peace of mind I needed to tolerate Palmer's drinking and what it was doing to our lives; the church became my sanctuary. At first, he came to church with us, which gave me hope that he was trying to change, but later he told me he had only gone in the hope that the people of the church would help him out of his financial troubles. He took me to services a few more times but then, in one of his strange exhibitions of power and control, he told me I couldn't go any more. I was devastated.

I called Pastor Fisher, told him what was happening and asked if the congregation's missionary work might extend to someone picking me up for church. It was asking a lot because we lived quite a distance from Elk Grove Village. He told me he would try to figure something out for me. Soon he was back on the telephone saying that someone had come up with a suggestion that would be far more beneficial than simply providing a taxi service. One of the men in the congregation, who worked odd hours for the airlines and often had free daytime hours, had offered to teach me to drive, using his car. I was overjoyed. We had to keep the lessons secret because Palmer would never have allowed it in case it gave me some freedom.

The lessons proceeded but until I obtained my driver's licence, I either went to a church nearby or was given lifts by some new members of our church who now lived close to us. It wasn't a problem if Palmer happened to be working on Sundays, or if he had been out late the night before and was still sleeping: we just had to leave before he had a chance to stop us.

When I got my driver's licence, I was filled with new hope. We had just one car, of course, so I could only use it if Palmer was at home. By now, I had become almost as wily as he was – he'd been a good teacher. I managed to convince him that I'd got my licence as a surprise for him so that he wouldn't always have to take me shopping and to medical appointments, and I could drive Robin to her modelling assignments after first dropping him off at work. He seemed okay with that for a while, but then came the first time he decided not to let me drive to church. I was furious. He decided he wanted to have sex instead, which was a rare occurrence. I knew from experience that this was strictly part of his game playing, his need to control me. Since the children and I were already dressed for church, I told him that was not going to happen. He went berserk.

Leaving two frightened children, he dragged me upstairs to the bedroom and tried to keep me there but I fought back. He was like a wild animal as he dug his fingernails into my flesh and kept pushing me onto the bed. Each time I fought him off and finally managed to get out of the bedroom. I ran downstairs, yelled at Wayne to take his sister to the basement, then locked myself into the bathroom. Palmer tried to break down the door, but he wasn't strong enough. Then he attempted to pry it open with a knife – I could see the tip of the blade as he tried to force the lock. At that moment, I was afraid he might stab me if he got to me, but the knife didn't work either. The next thing he did terrified me more. He poured a bottle of ammonia under the bathroom door. My eyes burned, tears streamed down my face and the fumes were choking me. I had to unlock and open the door. Thank God, I had the presence of mind to fall to the floor and pretend I'd passed out.

He left me alone then, frightened of what he had done. The hatred I felt for him at that moment was like bitter gall rising in my throat and choking me. I was afraid at the intensity of my anger and loathing. The children must have been terrified while all this was going on, but Wayne had had the good sense to carry his sister upstairs to a bedroom and lock the door instead of taking her to the basement. They stayed there until I went to them to comfort and reassure them that I was all right.

After that incident, there were a few times when I hid the car on some side street after he went to sleep at night so that I could get to wherever I might need to go the next morning. I knew he could walk to work if he had to, or take the bus. I also had extra car keys made because he would hide the keys or refuse to give them to me. I knew now how devious he could be so I began making myself think as he might in a particular situation, and always tried to keep a step ahead of him in my struggle to maintain a modicum of independence and dignity.

While we were still living in Des Plaines, Robin had her first birthday and I invited her godparents, Mary and John Nicholson, my brother and his family, Palmer's parents, and a few other close friends to join us for a little party. When it was time to feed Robin, I put her in her highchair and, since I was busy preparing food for the guests, Mary offered to feed her. As she began spooning food into the baby's mouth, Palmer's mother started calling Mary names and attacking her for taking over the care of the baby. 'You bitch!' she screamed.

Mary blanched. 'What have I done?' she asked, but the tirade continued. Mary and John gathered their belongings and left, followed shortly by our other friends. I was embarrassed for my guests but furious at this outburst of jealousy from Palmer's mother. I went upstairs, leaving him to deal with his crazy parents, and stayed there until I knew they were gone. Had I gone back downstairs while they were still there, I was afraid of what I might say to them, and of Palmer's possible reaction. Life with those unpredictable people was extremely difficult. I knew they would never act any differently towards me or any of our friends and longed for my own family, but now, with our financial situation, I wondered if I would ever see them again. I found myself praying to God for strength and an answer.

At least I had good, supportive neighbours. They provided me with companionship and a shoulder to cry on. They also paid me to do small jobs for them. A young airline pilot and his wife, who lived in the complex, asked if I would clean their townhouse. That wasn't a problem, although it was a filthy mess, until I decided to check the basement. I had wanted to look down there because a foul smell was wafting up; it was where they locked their two boxer dogs if they both happened to be out, which was usually every day.

As soon as I started down the basement stairs, I began to retch: the floor was covered with dog faeces. Desperate to make as much money as I could, I decided to tackle the monumental task. Wearing a makeshift face-mask, I began shovelling the mess into one bucket after another, carrying each load outside to a nearby vacant plot of land, and dumping it. When it was all gone, I mixed bucket after bucket of hot water and bleach, and then, barefoot, scrubbed the floor with a stiff broom. I did all this while Wayne was at school; Robin was upstairs in her portable playpen while I worked in the basement, all the time hoping that the rancid air wouldn't affect her. It took days to get that stench out of my sinuses. I imagined them as a pair of sponges that had absorbed the odours and kept them there to remind me. That young couple paid me well for all I had done for them, but I had to tell them I couldn't do it again.

I did manage to have some good laughs while I lived in the townhouse, and one thing I still laugh about involved my next-door neighbour Pat and her husband. They, too, worked for an airline and had to leave for work at an ungodly hour in the morning. That winter was particularly severe, with sub-zero temperatures for many days. Since we had no garages, we had to park our cars outside. Fearing theirs wouldn't start in the mornings, they would run a heavy-duty extension cable from the house to the car, a distance of about half a block, and connect it to an electric blanket that they wrapped around the car's engine to stop it freezing. Thankfully, it worked most of the time, and they were very proud of their ingenuity.

After we'd been in Des Plaines for eight or nine months, Palmer announced that he hated his job and was leaving the O'Hare Inn. Once again, he withheld the truth. I learned from a friend, who happened to be related to the hotel's owners, that he had been warned about his drinking, which could not be tolerated, and now he had been fired. I knew it would be more of a problem for him to find a job this time because his reputation as a drinker was beginning to catch up with him. Our future looked grimmer than ever.

Fortunately for Palmer, and for us, of course, an old friend and business associate was now in management at the brand new McCormick Place Convention Center in

Chicago, and offered him a job, which meant moving back into the city. I didn't mind going back to Chicago – in fact, I relished the idea, although the children and I would miss the new friends we had made in Des Plaines – but I hated the thought of looking for yet another apartment.

When I told Mary and John that we were leaving Des Plaines, they surprised me with the news that they were once again making a move within our old building. They were leaving the basement for an identical apartment on the second floor. This meant that our old place would be available, right when we needed it. My prayers had been answered, and I was overjoyed. In the midst of all the misery, the children and I would at least be back in our old neighbourhood with our friends around us: exactly what we needed if we were to survive this nightmare of a life.

18: Back in the Old Neighbourhood, and Al-Anon

It was wonderful to be back at 431 North Central Avenue, not only for me but also for Wayne. All of his little neighbourhood friends were still living next door and they all welcomed him, as did everyone at his old school. It was a joy to see some good come out of all the moving around.

I rejoined the Lutheran church nearby, and started attending with the children; Palmer never went with us. Soon I was teaching at the Sunday school again, which kept me focused and busy. Although I went to one or two Bible study groups and women's meetings, no one ever spoke to me. The entire congregation seemed snobbish and unfriendly. I had forgotten how this church had been the last time we'd gone there and I missed our old church in Elk Grove Village. I wished we could still go there, but it was much too far away.

During the time the children and I attended that church, I learned that there was a church-owned retreat and holiday camp for children in Lake Geneva, Wisconsin. Besides the main retreat and camp buildings, there were also cabins that Lutheran families could rent by the week. Families could make their own arrangements for meals or they could eat with the other campers in the 'mess hall'. I made enquiries and was astonished to learn how inexpensive it was to stay there for a week. I now kept some of my earnings at my next-door neighbour's house, and had enough to pay for a week, including meals.

A little worried about what Palmer would say, especially if he found out that I had money saved, I told him the church had offered us a free stay at Camp Augustana. I was sure he would tell me either that we couldn't go or that he couldn't go because of his new job, but he surprised me.

'I'll see if Jack [his boss], will let me have a week off to spend some time with the kids,' he said. Well, what a shock that was. Two days later, he told me that Jack would give him a week off if he made up the time later by working seven-day weeks at a few upcoming conventions, and he had said he would. You could have knocked me down with a feather. Then he surprised me some more.

'Why don't you see if Jeanette can go with us? She could watch the kids if we want to go out for the evening.' Jeanette was a twelve-year-old girl who lived in the next apartment building to ours. She occasionally stayed with Wayne and Robin for short periods if I had an appointment. When I asked her and her parents, they jumped at the opportunity, and I made the reservation for us to stay at the camp, for our first ever holiday together.

Camp Augustana had existed for many years and some of the buildings were tired-looking, but the lakeside setting was beautiful. When we arrived, a member of staff gave us a tour of the facilities, explained the camp rules, then took us to our cabin, which was right on the edge of the lake. Well, I didn't know whether to laugh or cry when I saw it. To say it was old and rustic would be a gross understatement, but it was adequate. There was a full-size sofa-bed in the living area, and bunk beds in a curtained-off small bedroom; Robin had to sleep in her old playpen, next to the bunks. Tacked on to the side of the cabin, a small screened-in porch was equipped with a few outdoor chairs, a table, a small sink and lots of cobwebs. Another add-on held a toilet. We had to take our showers in a communal building near the dining hall. Palmer wasn't happy, but the kids loved the adventure of it. It still amazes me that the whole week at Camp Augustana, including meals, cost me less than fifty dollars, but I'd had to work damned hard to save that small amount of money.

The first few days at the camp were great. It was a joy to see the children having so much fun together. Mealtimes with all the hordes of youngsters, who were attending music and Bible camp, were equally enjoyable. The food was good and sometimes between courses the camp counsellors led the children in song. Elbows had to be kept off the table, and anyone caught disobeying the rule, including adults, elicited a mass reaction. Once someone had called out a culprit's name, the chant would begin:

> 'Suzy, Suzy, strong and able,
> Get your elbows off the table.'

Then the offender had to stand up and run around the outer edge of the barn-like room, while everyone chanted and banged their fork handles on the tables.

> 'Round the tables you must go,
> You must go, you must go.
> Round the tables you must go,
> My fair Suzy.'

Everyone joined in and thought it was great fun, except Palmer who refused to participate; he did grin, but I'm sure he thought it beneath his dignity, especially when the children caught me on one occasion and I had to run around the hall.

Alcohol was not permitted anywhere in the camp, but Palmer had stashed beer in the car and would disappear sometimes, not saying where he was going. At first, he didn't overdo it, but later in the week, he was drinking more and became difficult. I didn't say anything because I didn't want to spoil the children's holiday, but it made me nervous, especially when he wanted to take Robin out on the water in an inflated rubber tyre.

One day, Palmer was out in a dinghy by himself and he had paddled to the middle of the lake. While he was out there a storm began to blow in, the winds became fierce and the waves suddenly had white caps. Concerned about their safety, I took the children inside the cabin, then went to see if I could spot him. Shading my eyes, I scanned the lake. For some time, I couldn't see him. As much as I hate to admit it, the thought entered my mind that perhaps he had drowned, but then he bobbed into view.

'Jeez, that was scary,' he said, once he was safely back on shore. 'For a while there, I was afraid I was going to drown.'

Hmm, I thought, and I was afraid you wouldn't.

In all, I had a great time with the children on our 'free' holiday and I dreaded going home where I knew nothing would have changed and, of course, it had not.

With Palmer's drinking getting worse all the time and his behaviour becoming increasingly unpredictable, I sought help from Al-Anon, the support group for the families of alcoholics, through the local branch of Alcoholics Anonymous. I started going to meetings whenever I could and began learning how to live with an alcoholic. I discovered that I had to react differently to his behaviour if I wanted to effect any change in the situation. On their advice, I tried ignoring his false accusations and the ugly things he said to and about me, often just walking away from him. That only served to send him into a manic rage. When I refused to argue or fight with him, he'd threaten to drag the children out of bed. To protect them, I had to put up with his vile mouth and the pushing around. He was not actually hitting me, but he'd keep poking and shoving me. Was he trying to goad me into hitting him? I don't know, but I was terrified of what the outcome might be if he became more physical.

'What's wrong with you?' I asked him one day. 'Do you really want our lives to be this way?'

'I'm not doing anything wrong. It's you that's the problem,' he snarled.

'Me? It's not me that's drinking, not me that got us into all this debt.'

'Stop nagging! There's nothing wrong with me – everything was fine until I married you! Everything was fine until you tricked me into marrying you.' He was now shouting.

'What the hell are you talking about? It was you who rushed me into marriage, and it wasn't fine, Palmer. You and your cronies were always drinking. You just didn't have responsibilities then. Don't you even care about your daughter?'

'Oh, yes, go ahead and drag the kids into it,' he yelled. 'You always use the kids when you don't have anything else to nag about.'

'Please, Palmer, please stop this,' I begged, but he just walked out.

'I'm going out for a beer,' he shouted back. 'Take it or leave it.'

Oh, God, I thought. If he only knew how much I wanted to leave. After all of those shouting matches, I began to understand why Al-Anon had advised us against reacting to our spouse's unreasonable arguments. I kept reminding myself of one of its famous sayings: 'When they're drinking, their thinking's stinking.' It made sense to me, but knowing it sure didn't help the situation.

Palmer had started 'cheque kiting'. Our financial situation had deteriorated to the extent that he was now running around cashing cheques at various banks, then depositing the money in another bank to cover cheques written on it so that they wouldn't bounce. This would begin about halfway through his pay period and went on until he received his salary to cover everything. Within a week or so, the cycle would start all over again. He would even have our friends cash cheques for him, knowing that it would take time for them to deposit his cheque and for it to clear, therefore buying him a little more time. I also found that he had been buying gift certificates with his credit cards from department stores, then purchasing a small item to get the balance back in cash. (I understand that shops no longer permit such cash returns. I believe any balance you might have simply stays on the card for future use. It would seem that shops have wised up to the cash-back practice.) There soon came a time when all of Palmer's credit cards were over their limit so he could no longer get hold of those stopgap gift certificates. His involvement in the illegal practice of cheque kiting, which continued to escalate, could have landed him in jail.

At one point, Palmer became a little less crazy and was easier to live with, but it only lasted for two or three months. I learned that Uncle Art had bailed him out again but with the ultimatum that he stopped drinking or he would never help him again. Palmer even confessed to me that, if the drinking continued, Art would disinherit him. I'm not sure if he was trying to convince himself or me that he could and would give up alcohol – after all, an estate worth at least a million dollars was surely worth the sacrifice. However, the drinking didn't stop and he was soon up to his old tricks. Soon we were in the same financial mess as before. He knew he couldn't ask his uncle for help and there was no one else to turn to so he decided it was time to call Alcoholics Anonymous. I was overjoyed.

When Palmer picked up the phone to call AA, he was crying. Here was a desperate man, finally reaching out for the kind of help he needed. I actually found myself feeling sorry for him and a little less sorry for myself with this new ray of hope and the lifeline I thought might save us.

Two men from AA arrived at the apartment. They spent a lot of time with Palmer, telling their own stories of all they had been through before they'd hit rock bottom and sought help. Those stories were scary but both men had been able to keep their families together in spite of the misery they had caused. Palmer seemed keen to stick with it: he agreed to attend meetings and call for help any time he felt the need. With this new promise from him, I was glad I had kept his drinking secret from my family; perhaps I would no longer have to deal with drunken abusive behaviour; perhaps we could begin to have a more normal life.

I hadn't told my parents what had been going on for the past couple of years for two reasons. First, I didn't want them to think that I had screwed up again, and second, I didn't want to frighten or worry them. After all, what could they have done except worry? Once, in desperation, I had called Palmer's parents to tell them about their son's behaviour, and to ask them what I should do. That had been a huge mistake, which I should have anticipated.

'You're nothing but a lying, thieving bitch,' his mother said. 'Do you think we don't know why you foreigners come to America and why you marry Americans? We know how you throw money around that doesn't belong to you. You've ruined Bobby's life and trapped him by having him give you a baby.' The pair of them took turns on the phone and the ranting went on until I had the good sense to hang up on them. Their attack left me stunned and I couldn't stop shaking. Defeated, I sank to the floor, and sat there in a daze. When I finally snapped out of it, I realized that now I had a new worry: what would Palmer do when his parents told him I had called them? They did so, and he flew into a rage that sent me running out of the house to escape him. I went to one of the neighbours and stayed there until it was safe to return, when I thought he'd be asleep.

With all that behind me, and now with new hope, I

continued to attend Al-Anon meetings and for a while it seemed that things might be getting a little better at home. The women in the group I attended told their stories of living with alcoholics and so many of the stories were familiar, many far worse than my own, including severe injuries and attempted murders. However, they seemed to be staying in their marriages because of the children or because of the strict confines of their Roman Catholic beliefs. We had two Catholic women in my group who each had thirteen children. I couldn't imagine having to deal with an alcoholic and thirteen children but I suppose they felt they had no other choice. Protecting and shielding my own two was difficult enough. Robin was still too young to understand what was going on but Wayne certainly knew. No wonder he was always so happy to go off with his own father on weekends. I didn't blame him. Often, I would gaze around the table at the faces of those brave women, and it always struck me how unhappy they looked, how drawn and tired, and how they appeared much older than their years. I wondered, if Palmer began drinking again, how long it would be before I stopped caring about my appearance, how long it would take me to look as defeated. For now, though, I was confident that Palmer's drinking days were over, even though the other women warned me about relapses. After all, a million dollars hung in the balance: why would anyone want to risk losing such a fortune? I asked myself. That was the thought I clung to and that gave me hope that things were about to get better.

My optimism was short-lived.

Palmer did not stay on the wagon for long. He was soon

drinking again, and the financial situation worsened. Apparently, he had managed to get a small amout of money from his parents, who had very little and still lived in their dreary attic apartment. I later found out that they were convinced I was sending all of Palmer's 'hard-earned money' to my family in England. I don't know if that was something he had told them, or that they couldn't believe their precious son could get himself into such a situation. Their only child could do no wrong, even though they were fully aware that there was a long history of alcoholism in the family. Palmer's father spent most of his time in a tavern, and we had all recently attended the funeral of another uncle who'd been found dead from alcoholism in a Skid Row gutter. Uncle Art paid for his brother's funeral but did not attend, such was his disgust at the abuse of alcohol.

When I asked Palmer why he had stopped going to AA meetings, he said he had only gone in the hope that they would help him out financially. It had been another of his schemes to dig himself out of the financial pit that continued to spiral downwards. He had said the same when he had stopped going to church.

What he did with his money was a mystery to me. How could anyone spend so much on drink? I wondered. But I had forgotten the visits to Dr 'Feel-good' H. and the cost of steam baths. One day when he was drunk, he told me his expense account now had tighter limits and that his boss was making him justify every penny he charged to the company; he now had to produce receipts for everything. I knew by then that it would be almost impossible for Palmer to produce receipts: he was usually too drunk to keep track of anything. He whined to me about having to use his own money to entertain customers but I no longer knew what to believe. Most of the time, I didn't believe anything he told me.

By now, I was so depressed and tense that I could neither sleep nor eat. The only relief I could find was in taking hot baths. Gradually I found myself needing to have the water hotter and hotter. It would be near scalding temperature and even then it was not hot enough so I began adding kettles of boiling water. The physical pain I felt as I lowered myself into the intense heat somehow made the emotional pain easier to bear, but when the water began to cool, the internal gut-wrenching agony rose up to choke me again. There were days when I took those baths many times but the moments of relief were brief so the number increased. In later years, when I was able to look back at the agony of those days, I came to understand why people cut themselves: it's a pathetic effort to externalize the internal pain.

When the cheque kiting became almost a full-time job, with Palmer spending entire days running around covering cheques, he told me I would have to help him.

'I can't do that,' I told him.

'You have to!' he screamed.

'I'm sorry, Palmer, I put up with a lot of things but there's no way I'm going to do anything illegal.'

He grabbed me by the hair and pulled my face up to his. 'You'll be sorry,' he hissed, through gritted teeth.

I stood my ground. 'No, this is one thing I will not do for you. I will not risk jail or deportation. You got yourself into this mess and you can get yourself out of it.' He threw me to the floor. 'If you don't stop threatening and hurting me, I'll turn you in to the police.' He stopped for a moment, but then pulled me to my feet again and began hitting me. I reached for the telephone but he grabbed it and tore it out of the wall. He over-balanced, stumbled and fell, giving me time to run out of the apartment.

I knew the children were asleep in bed and I prayed they hadn't heard this latest commotion. I didn't worry about Robin so much: I was sure that, being a baby, she wouldn't be affected, and I knew Palmer would never hurt her. Wayne, though, was a different matter. Fortunately he was smart enough to stay in his bed, hopefully with the covers pulled over his head.

It was late at night by then but I couldn't return to the apartment yet: I was too frightened of what he might do. My ribs hurt and my head felt as though it was going to burst. For a while, I just wandered the streets, but then I went to the park and sat on a bench, holding my head, rocking and quietly wailing. Inside I was screaming.

My situation was insufferable and I was in a desperate state. I didn't know what to do next so I just got up and walked some more, back and forth in the park and up and down the dark, dangerous streets of Chicago. Only one thought entered my mind, that perhaps someone would murder me and put me out of my misery. I was no more afraid of being attacked and perhaps killed on the street than I was of going home to my nightmare of a life. I honestly didn't know how long I could go on.

As I walked, I came to a church and thought I would go inside, maybe find some peace there, but all the doors were locked. Eventually I came to another. I tried the door, it opened and I went in. I walked to one of the front pews and knelt down. There I stayed, praying, for I don't know how long. Suddenly a tap on my shoulder startled me. I looked up into the face of a minister. My heart lurched. Here was someone I might be able to talk to, someone I could trust with my horrible secrets, who would offer me understanding and perhaps even a little hope. Silence stretched between us, and when I thought he was about to sit next to me, to talk to me, his words entered me like a dagger thrust into my heart: 'I'm afraid you'll have to leave now. I have to lock up the church.' I stared into his face. Had he just said what I thought he had? At first I was speechless, but then I managed to get words out.

'I'm in trouble,' I said, and the tears began to cascade down my face.

'I'm sorry,' he almost whispered, 'but you really must leave now. You're welcome to come back tomorrow.'

Numbed by what I considered cruel rejection, I got up, said nothing, and left. How much worse can it get, I wondered, when even the church turns its back on you?

I headed home. For a brief time, I had forgotten about the children but now I was worried about leaving them alone with Palmer, afraid that somehow he might have dragged them into the mire.

When I got home, he appeared to have passed out on the floor. I stepped over him and went to sleep in the children's room, locking the door behind me.

There were times when my stress level was so high and my spirit so low that I considered suicide, but those thoughts were fleeting. The love I felt for my beautiful children helped me to hang on to my sanity and stopped me doing anything so drastic; I could never have abandoned them, no matter how bad things became.

Wayne, who was now seven or eight, had begun having stomach pains. It broke my heart when the doctor diagnosed him with a childhood ulcer. Clearly, he was feeling the tension and had probably heard Palmer's tirades when we'd thought he was sleeping. I knew something had to change before someone got hurt but I didn't know where to turn. I did eventually talk to the minister of the Lutheran church I was attending, and he arranged an appointment for me to see a psychologist who worked for the church. When I was billed thirty-five dollars for my visit to him, I almost went mad. There was no way in hell I could afford it – it was a lot of money in those days. Palmer would go crazy if he saw the bill and I had no way of coming up with the payment. I took it to my minister and handed it to him.

'You know what my financial situation is. There's no way I can pay this bill, and you know that my husband can't find out about it. Please, you have to help me.'

'I'll see what I can do,' he said. In the end, all he did was arrange for me to pay it off in instalments. I was shocked and disheartened that the church had no resources to help parishioners in such cases. There certainly was no way I could pay for help at that price. Foolishly, I had thought that counselling through the church would be free but, of course, I was wrong.

19: New Neighbours and Unusual New Friends

In the spring of 1963 an older couple, Martha and Jack Evans, moved into the small basement apartment next door to ours. Martha was a kindly soul who must have been in her late seventies. She had borne nine children, been widowed, and then had married Jack, who was a bit younger than she was. Jack was a miserable old codger who went from door to door selling miscellaneous items out of a small suitcase – combs, shoelaces and sewing thread. He hated children and made no secret of it so all the neighbourhood children teased him and called him names. I'll never forget the day Wayne came running in to tell me that Jack Evans had threatened one of the boys.

'If I catch you, I'll kick your asshole up between your shoulder blades,' he had yelled. I'd heard something similar when I was a child, but knowing it had come out of Jack Evans made it seem especially funny. Occasionally, the old curmudgeon would give my daughter, Robin, a sucker, or lollipop. Robin, who was only about three at the time, began calling him 'Sucker' to the amusement of all the other children. Now, they all called him Sucker. Of course, the older children knew it meant 'idiot' and wallowed in the mischief.

Martha Evans became my surrogate mother. She knew all about my home situation and that I missed my family, so she told all of her children that they now had a new sister. They welcomed me into the family and nicknamed me Number Ten, their mother's tenth child. Martha became 'Mom' to me, and 'Grandma Evans' to Wayne and Robin. Jack, however, was still Sucker, but only behind his back.

Now I had a new angel in my life and we looked out for each other. I knew that Jack was mean to her and I assured her daughters that I would take care of her and let them know if there was ever anything I was worried about where their mother was concerned. I was included in their family gatherings and soon felt like one of them.

Mom Evans told me secretly that one of her daughters, Jodi, was married to someone high up in the 'Chicago Outfit' or 'Mob', and that she was not supposed to discuss it. She said they helped her out, just a little, financially because they knew Jack didn't bring in much money from his sales job. Jodi and I became good friends and I would often drive Mom over to see her. I learned from Jodi and another sister, Jeanne, that they all hated Jack and didn't trust him. They were pleased that their mother had someone to look out for her, and that I was right next door. And my friendship with Jodi turned out to be a godsend in ways I would never have expected.

Now that we were once again living in the city, it was easier for Palmer to take the train to work and leave the car at home. Of course, it was also easier for him to drink and not have to worry about driving. I liked having the car for shopping, visiting and keeping appointments. On one particular morning, I went out to the car to go shopping and it wasn't there. I went back into the apartment and called Palmer to see if he had taken it and forgotten to tell me, but he said he had not. I immediately called the police to report that someone had stolen our car in the night, and they came right away to take the report.

'I have to ask you, ma'am, but do you know if you're up to date with your car payments?' asked one of the officers.

'I think so, Officer, but I'm afraid my husband doesn't tell me much about that sort of thing,' I told him.

'Well, I'll just make a couple of phone calls to see what we can find out,' he said, and went outside. When he returned, I could already tell by the look on his face that it was not good news.

'Sorry to tell you this, but your car's been repossessed by the finance company and they've had it towed away. They usually do it during the night to avoid confrontations,' he explained.

'Oh, my God, I'm so sorry,' I said. 'I'm so embarrassed that I thought it was stolen. You must think I'm really stupid.' The young police officer assured me that it happened all the time and that I certainly didn't have to apologize. After they left, I crumpled. This latest assault on my dignity left me feeling as though I'd been run over by a tow truck. Now what?

I called Palmer to tell him what had happened but he didn't seem to care, I supposed because it meant he'd have one less bill to pay, but I was furious. Afraid that I'd explode if I didn't talk to someone sane, I called around the apartment building to see if anyone was at home but got no replies. Remembering that everyone else was out at work during the daytime, I went next door to cry on Mom Evans's shoulder. I hated to burden her with this new problem but I needed to tell someone.

She comforted me with a cuddle and a cup of coffee, then suggested we call Jodi to tell her what had happened and see if she had any ideas of what I could do about the situation. I didn't think for one moment that Jodi would be able to do anything about my repossessed car but Mom insisted and we called her anyway.

About an hour after that call, Jodi phoned back. She told me to go outside and check the parking lot, which I did, and there, in its rightful place, was my car. I was dumbfounded. She told me not to ask any questions and I didn't, silence being the better part of valour. Later someone told me they'd read in the newspaper that the Chicago Outfit controlled all of the towing companies in Chicago, but I never found out if that was true.

Soon after the car incident, I was attending an Al-Anon meeting, and again, as I looked around the room at all the other women, it struck me how miserable and beaten they seemed. Overcome with rage that one human being could inflict so much misery on another, I resolved that I would no longer subject myself to this reminder of Palmer's drinking by spending time with these fellow victims. I remembered one of the Al-Anon mottoes: 'Act, don't REact.' It was time for me to act.

I had started to have telephone conversations with the attorney who had handled my divorce to discover what options might be open to me: I knew I couldn't stay married to the man who was destroying my soul. I was in an extremely difficult situation because I had no money and no one to ask for help. I thought of offering my services as a live-in housekeeper, but who would have taken me on with two children?

I had tried talking to Palmer's boss, whom I knew well; I also tried to get some kind of support from his family, not his parents, of course, but they had all had enough of Palmer's shortcomings and didn't want to hear about it. Finally I broke down and told my family in England what was going on. I knew they couldn't help me financially but I desperately needed their support. I'd been reluctant to tell them about my farce of a marriage, afraid they'd be upset and embarrassed because I'd made a mess of things again, but they had to know. I needed them to be aware of what might lie ahead, but even I dreaded the thought of a second divorce. Most important of all, they needed to know of the potential danger we were in, in case something serious happened.

The next thing I knew, my father was coming over to see if he could help. He had cashed in a life insurance policy to pay for his plane ticket. I couldn't believe it. It had now been many years since I had seen my family and I was thrilled that I would soon see the only man in my life who had ever loved me with no strings attached. It was a comfort to know that I would have my father beside me; someone who I knew would be on my side.

When he arrived, we had a grand reunion. It had been a long time since I had seen him and I was afraid he might look old, but he hadn't aged one bit. If anything, he was more handsome than ever. He and I had many long talks, both practical and philosophical, and he was a big hit with all of our friends. Even Palmer took to him and behaved himself when we were together. Dad asked me if I was sure that Palmer had a drinking problem because he hadn't seen any signs of it. I tried to explain how devious he could be and told him not to be fooled by the face he had put on for him but, sadly, Dad didn't seem convinced.

My father had his first exposure to the life of the rich and famous when I received an invitation to bring him to my adopted sister Jeanne's wedding. Palmer had not been invited but we covered that by saying how nice it would be if Dad could take his place. Jeanne had been divorced for years but was now marrying a fairly well-off businessman. I guessed it would be a swank wedding, and I was right. The reception, held at a famous restaurant in downtown Chicago, was like a movie. I spent most of the time pointing out well-known people, and my father was wide-eyed. I don't think he ever stopped talking about that wedding, which he told everyone was a Mafia wedding although, of course, it was not. There were a number of Chicago Outfit people there because of family connections, but Jeanne's new husband, Jesse, had no other relationship with them that I knew of.

My dear father, who was in America to help me, had now been completely hoodwinked by Palmer's bullshit. Palmer had become a master con artist and could charm the bees out of the trees when he had to. He started taking my father all over Chicago with him, using his special contacts and considerable influence to impress him. He arranged personal tours of McCormick Place and the museums, and Dad saw things that the public normally is not privileged to see. He was wined and dined at all the luxury hotels, and introduced to many of Palmer's VIP associates. Dad was wallowing in the luxury and attention and it was clear that he had forgotten why he had come to

Chicago. I loved having him with us but he had defeated the purpose of his visit by drinking with Palmer. I'm not sure if he ever had a talk with Palmer about what had been going on, but if he did, Palmer forgot it.

After my father went back to England, Palmer pushed me again to help with the cheque kiting. Just as before, I refused, and he realized that hitting me would not intimidate me into doing his bidding. Now he found a new way to get to me. It was the final straw. He went to the children's bedroom where they were sleeping, dragged them out of bed and started telling them that I was a terrible person who didn't want to help get food for them or take care of them. Wayne and Robin were crying and looking pleadingly at me. I felt like a volcano that was ready to erupt, but I knew I had to remain calm for their sakes. I wanted to kill Palmer but, using every ounce of self-control I could muster, I stayed cool and agreed to do what he wanted if he let them go.

He allowed me to put them back to bed and I managed to calm them down, telling them that Daddy was just playing a silly game. I went to him then and told him to come into the kitchen where the children wouldn't be able to hear anything.

There, I stuck my finger into his face and said, 'If you ever do anything like that again, anything that might affect my children, I only have to make one phone call, and you will be maimed or dead.' I added that he'd better start looking over his shoulder, because someone might be watching him. I'd heard that line in a movie and it seemed the right thing to say at the time, even though I was quaking in my shoes.

He shoved my finger away and laughed. Then he started to hit me. I screamed and went on screaming, which was why one of my neighbours called the police.

When they arrived, Palmer was so belligerent that, instead of just talking to him, they handcuffed him and took him to jail. I was afraid that he would say something to them about the threat I'd made but I think even he was smart enough to know that he shouldn't risk bringing it up. He stayed in jail overnight, but in the morning they released him. He came home grinning, as though nothing had happened, took a shower and went to work.

The abuse was becoming more frequent and the drinking was worsening. I found out that he was getting off the train a couple of stations before ours so that he could stop for another drink, then try to walk it off before he got home. I hadn't been aware of his feeble efforts to hide the truth. He would come home reeking of alcohol and sweat, making himself more and more repulsive to me with each passing day. The only thing helping me now was the tranquillizers my doctor had prescribed for me. I still had suicidal thoughts, but I knew I would never act on them. Wayne would have been all right because his father was a good man, but I could never have left Robin in Palmer's care.

The next time he was especially violent to me I managed to get out of the front door, went to my neighbour's apartment and called the police myself. Palmer knew what I was going to do so, thinking he was smarter than everyone else, he was pretending to be asleep in bed when the police arrived. I couldn't believe it but, fortunately, the police didn't either. Again, he became extremely belligerent to the officers, and again, they hauled him off to jail.

Within hours, he was back, and when I refused to let him in, he tried to break down the back door. I opened it after he'd promised to behave himself. He was laughing at how easy it had been to get someone to bail him out, sneering and saying that no one could ever get the better of 'the great Robert Palmer', as he now often referred to himself. I was stunned to learn that one of our friends in the building had paid the bail money, and could never figure out what that particular person found funny about Palmer's dangerous behaviour.

The next day I went to the police to swear out a restraining order against Palmer. All it meant was that if he hit me again he could go to jail, and not just for one night, but then the police officer told me the awful truth. 'In all honesty, ma'am, a restraining order is useless until after the act is committed,' he continued. 'In my experience it's often too late by then. I've seen women end up dead. I don't mean to scare you, but you'd be better off getting as far away from that lunatic as you can.' I knew he was telling the truth from the many magazine and newspaper articles I had read. If I let this go on much longer, I might become a statistic, and I was not about to let that happen. There had to be something I could do, but what?

I talked to my lawyer friend again about a divorce, but he said there was no way he could take the case because he knew it would be a mess; also, his partners would never agree to take on such a contiguous case. I talked to a number of other attorneys and one or two of them said they would take it on, but they wanted a huge retainer fee, which was out of the question. I'd had the promise of a little help from friends, but not nearly enough to pay the enormous amount required to handle such a nightmare divorce.

To add to my confusion, a couple of my friends were telling me once more that they thought Palmer was a latent homosexual, pointing out his effeminate gestures and his walk. I still didn't think it was true. From what I had read about alcoholics, I believed that his unusual gait and gestures could have been from poor co-ordination, caused by heavy consumption of alcohol. He had told me early in our relationship that he was very choosy and that I was the only woman he had ever had sex with, except for one ugly incident he'd bragged about. He and a friend had got drunk enough to have sex with some elderly teachers they'd met in the bar of a hotel where they were attending a convention. He thought it was funny, and roared with laughter about how grateful the 'old gals' had been. The story disgusted me, and I wondered how I could have forgotten such cruel behaviour. I once asked him about the Jewish girl he'd claimed to have been engaged to, but he told me they had never had sex because they had been too scared.

The situation was making me ill. I couldn't eat or sleep and often couldn't stop crying. I lost weight that I could ill afford to lose and I had gone back to taking scalding hot baths every few hours. Now worried about my mental state, there was just one more thing I could try. I made an appointment to see my old friend Dr Edward Crown.

When Dr Crown saw the state I was in, he leaned back in his chair and asked me to tell him everything. I must have rambled and cried for ages, and he listened patiently as I poured out all that had been happening over the past few years. When he thought I had finished, he calmly leaned forward, picked up the telephone and dialled a number he obviously knew by heart. He spoke briefly to someone and then hung up. I hadn't heard what he'd said to the other person, as he was an extremely soft-spoken man; it was often difficult to hear him when he was speaking directly to me. He wrote a name and number on a piece of paper and handed it to me, telling me to call this person as soon as possible. He said the man was an attorney who would take care of me, and that I shouldn't worry about anything, except looking after the children and myself. Before I left his office, he pulled me into his arms, the way a loving parent might, and gave me the kind of hug that tells you someone cares about you very much. I looked up into his face and realized we both had tears in our eyes. I had just experienced a goodness that I had almost forgotten existed.

I called Roy Golson, the attorney, and made an appointment to see him. I told no one what I was doing. I didn't feel I could trust anyone to keep it from Palmer. He seemed to have an uncanny way of finding things out but this was one thing I could not afford to have sabotaged.

Mr Golson listened to the story of my life with Palmer and rolled his eyes. He knew we were in for an uphill battle and I don't think he was at all happy about handling the case. I never did find out the connection between him and Dr Crown but it must have been a strong one to make him agree to open such a can of worms.

20: Another Divorce and the Aftermath

The first thing that Attorney Golson did after taking on my divorce case was to secure a court order to get Palmer out of our apartment. It was essentially an eviction notice, and if he did not leave, he would be in contempt of court and subject to arrest. Mr Golson and the judge advised me to stay away for a while to avoid any possible repercussions once the shock hit him. The children and I went to my brother's house for a few days.

On receiving the court order, Palmer instructed an attorney to fight it. His attorney, who happened to be one of his drinking partners, had no idea of the magnitude of the circumstances involved, or of Palmer's previous arrests. Apparently, it took him little time to tell Palmer that he must obey the court, that he had no recourse. And so the battle began, and a battle it was.

Palmer moved out and I had no idea where he was staying. He constantly harassed me with phone calls, and even though I had my phone number changed to an unlisted one, he soon had it. I complained to the telephone company, and again changed my number, but within a day, he had the new one and the ranting calls started again. He would laugh and tell me repeatedly that I was wasting my time, reminding me that he had connections everywhere, even in the phone company. That was when he started stalking me. He seemed to know every move I made, everywhere I went, and with whom. He took great pleasure in calling me and giving me a run-down of my activities. He was also calling our friends, trying to turn them against me and spreading untrue rumours about me. I wasn't worried about that because everyone knew they were untrue. Fortunately, he did not find out about the friends who had Mob connections or I'm sure he would have tried doing something to discredit me in that regard. Perhaps he did know but was clever enough not to mess with those people. I often wondered what might have happened if he had tried to make trouble for me in my innocent friendship with them. I suspect they would not have tolerated his behaviour and I'm sure just a warning from them or their attorneys would have frightened him into silence but, thank God, that never happened.

Mr Golson kept me posted of all the happenings and more than once told me how lucky I was that Dr Crown was a friend because he would never have taken my case if he had felt he had a choice in the matter. Apparently Palmer was now busy trying to dig up dirt on Mr Golson, who was constantly receiving calls and letters from him, warning that he would not stop until he got him disbarred. He did, in fact, file a perjury claim against Mr Golson, but the court threw it out.

When the divorce case finally got to court, we went before Judge Fred Slater, who was an African American. That added to Palmer's anger, as he was extremely prejudiced. Having a black judge, I know, was the ultimate insult to him. Repeatedly, the case was held up by Palmer's delaying tactics, one of them being an effort to get the judge kicked off the bench. He accused me, my witnesses, my lawyer and the judge of perjury, filing charges against us all. He also filed a petition demanding a change of venue, claiming that Judge Slater was biased, but in the end, he not only ran out of lawyer friends, who were all sick of him, but angered the judge almost to the point of being counter-sued. I don't know how he managed to stay out of jail throughout the whole fiasco but at last I was granted the divorce, full custody of Robin and child support payments. Palmer received a warning from the court that he could lose his visitation rights with his daughter if he displayed any drunken or abusive behaviour anywhere near us.

While all of this had been going on, I had placed an ad in the newspaper for a roommate to share the apartment and expenses. I thought the children and I could share one bedroom and we could let the other. The only serious response I got was from a woman with two children who convinced me that we could make it work by putting two sets of bunk beds in the children's bedroom and that she and I could share the other. I met her and the children and they seemed pleasant enough. Deborah had a good job at the Chicago Rehabilitation Hospital but, having recently lost her husband to cancer, was in a temporary financial bind because of all the medical bills. She begged me to give it a try. She claimed to be a gourmet cook and offered to make all of our meals; she also said how much she loved housekeeping and that she would be happy to take on that responsibility as well. I thought this was too good to be true and arranged for them to move in. Before I'd met Deborah I'd asked her if she had a lot of furniture as I didn't have room for very much.

'Not really,' she said. 'After my husband died, I sold everything. But I do have a record player and a stand-alone bar.'

'Wow, you sound like a portable party,' I told her. 'I can certainly make space for that.'

I was finally free of a situation that I'd thought would never end. Palmer was ordered to pay all court costs while I waited anxiously for the bill from my attorney, but it never came. I don't know if Dr Crown paid it, or if Mr Golson had taken my case as a favour to him. I could only give thanks daily and wonder why someone had been so kind to me. Today, when I think about Dr Crown, tears well in my eyes and my heart is full; I owe so much to him and I still tell people about the angel who saved me.

The whole process of getting Palmer out of my life seemed to take years but it was only a few months, and all that time there had been a growing fear that it was not over. The secret I had been keeping, and hoping was not true, was that I might be pregnant. I thought back to the last time Palmer and I had had sex, if you could call it that. He had attacked and viciously raped me. I thought of his low sperm count and how difficult it had been for me to get pregnant with Robin. I couldn't be pregnant, I told myself, but the queasiness I was experiencing each morning worried me. Holding on to the hope that it was just nerves, I finally confided in a friend.

'Of course you're not pregnant. After all the stress you've been under, I'm not surprised you feel sick. Don't forget that you've had to take medicine before for your nervous stomach,' she assured me. I'm not sure that either of us believed what she said, but neither could we bear the thought that that one last night of drunken abuse could end up with a baby.

To put my mind at rest, I went to my family doctor and had a pregnancy test. Waiting for the result was a nightmare but getting the news that the test was positive was the cruellest blow of all. Hadn't I suffered enough? If Palmer found out he would be back in my life and I would never be able to get him out of it. Once more, I thought about killing myself but again I realized that I could never do that to my children or my family. In desperation, I called Dr Crown to see if he or anyone he knew would perform an abortion but he told me that that was the one thing he couldn't help me with and sadly wished me luck. And so began the next painful episode in my mess of a life.

I began checking with everyone I thought I could trust to see if they knew of anyone who had ever had an abortion or if they knew anyone or anything that might lead to finding someone. There was no way I could have the baby. I tried scalding hot baths and douches, I took massive doses of laxatives. All any of it ever did was make me sick. I did get one lead on someone who might help and went to see an elderly doctor who had an office in an old Polish neighbourhood of Chicago. She spoke in broken English and seemed nervous. When she learned how far along my pregnancy was, she said she would not be able to help me. She had been my last hope. After leaving her office, I sat in my car for what seemed hours, bawling my eyes out, all the time thinking, Why me, God, why me?

The thought entered my mind that we should go to England, but how could I ever get enough money to pay for three airfares? What would my family say anyway, about taking in a family of three, or what would be four? The situation was impossible. Then, when I was at the lowest point of my despair, I received a phone call from a close friend. She told me she had talked to someone she worked with who had taken his girlfriend, on more than one occasion, to have unwanted pregnancies terminated. She had the phone number of the doctor, plus special instructions for calling him, and I prayed that this would not be another brick wall.

The call had to be made from a public telephone. Then he would call back, perhaps after checking the number, all of which I thought was odd but I suppose in the days of illegal abortion they had to be careful. When I talked to the man, he told me I needed to have three hundred dollars in cash and that I had to phone him again on the day of the procedure from a different public phone. Then I would be given an address. It was a great relief to learn I could bring someone with me as I had heard that I might have to go alone to cut down the risk to the abortionist of exposure. My friend agreed to accompany me.

I borrowed the three hundred dollars from friends and the big day finally arrived. Paralysed with fear we set off for the mystery rendezvous. I felt like a low-life criminal. I kept thinking this must be a nightmare and hoping I would soon wake up. The previous night, I had lain in bed thinking and wondering. How had I arrived at this terrible point in my life? Wasn't it only yesterday I had boarded a ship with my GI husband, headed for a new and wonderful life in America? What had gone wrong? Was I being punished for something?

We made the call from a public telephone, as directed, and received the address of the clinic. It was in a slum area on the south side of Chicago; we knew the area to be one of the so-called black ghettos. My teeth were chattering and I was trembling with fear, but glad that I wasn't alone. We found the address, which was a large commercial-type building. We'd been told it was a clinic but there was no sign outside to indicate such. Filled with dread, we pushed open the door and went in. There was a hand-lettered sign on a bulletin board in the hallway, which read, 'Health Center'. The building was old, dark and dirty inside, with paint peeling off the walls. The entrance-hall floor was marble, and a flight of marble stairs with wrought-iron railings and banisters led up to a second floor, which disappeared into the darkness. I remember wondering why there were no lights on.

As we stood there looking around, an upstairs light flicked on and a nice-looking man of about forty called to us. 'Please come up,' he said. 'I'll be ready for you soon.'

'Here we go,' said my companion. 'Just hang on for a little while longer.'

I managed a weak smile but I was shaking uncontrollably as we climbed the long, curved stairway. If she hadn't been holding my arm tightly, I'm sure I would have either run away or collapsed.

The young man ushered us into a small office, invited us to sit down and introduced himself as the doctor. I glanced around, hoping to see some evidence of his professional status but there was none. At that juncture, I knew I was at the point of no return and had accepted my fate.

'Do you have the money?' he asked.

I rummaged in my handbag, produced the envelope containing the fee and handed it to him.

'Please excuse me for a moment,' he said, and left the room.

'He's gone to count the money,' my friend whispered.

'Probably,' I said.

'Oh, shit, what if he doesn't come back? What if we've been ripped off?' she said.

Before I could respond, he reappeared. Phew, I thought.

He sat behind his desk and explained, 'I use two different methods for the terminations I perform, but I need to examine you before I know which method will be best for you. The first would be what is called a D and C. That's where we dilate the cervix slightly and use an instrument to scrape the inside of the uterus. The other way, if your pregnancy is too far advanced, is to pack the uterus with an irritant, which then causes you to have a miscarriage. Either way is completely safe, but the latter takes longer to come to completion.'

It all sounded terrible and confusing to me, but I said nothing and just nodded my understanding.

He told my friend to wait in his office then took me into an examination room, told me to take off my pants and lie on the table. Again, as much to take my mind off what was happening as anything, I scanned the walls for medical diplomas and saw none. There was no covering on the worn, cracked-leather examination table. He did not give me a gown to put on, or cover me with a sheet, and it was freezing cold. With a gloved hand, he shoved my legs apart and examined me.

'Hmm,' he muttered. 'You're much further along than I'd hoped.' My heart lurched and I was afraid he was going to tell me that he couldn't help me, but he did not. He sat me up and explained the only method available to us at this point was the packing he had described earlier.

'Do you still want to go ahead?' he asked. I nodded, yes, and lay down again, still shaking.

'Take deep breaths and try to relax,' he said, but I could not.

He began by dilating the cervix, using a series of gradually larger instruments. He had warned me that there would be pain but I had not anticipated how excruciating it would be. He gave me a wad of bandage to bite down on so that I would make no noise. Tears streamed down my face into my ears and I was screaming into the sodden wad in my mouth. At last, when the cervix was open enough, he started inserting what felt like yards of what I hoped was sterile gauze bandage. As he worked, he explained that this would set up an irritation that would cause a miscarriage. He reiterated that this had been the only option left open to me. When I thought I could take the pain no longer, he said he had finished. He removed the instruments, and then, leaving a length of the bandage taped to the inside of my thigh, he told me I could get up. When I tried to stand, everything went black. I felt myself sway and knew I was going to pass out. He grabbed me by the arm and steered me into a chair, where I sat, cradling my stomach, while he gave me instructions for what to do after I got home.

He explained that I should start having contractions in about twelve hours. When that happened, and when I was sure they were strong and regular, I should gently begin pulling the gauze bandage out, but definitely no sooner. He said it would be bloody and to do it over the toilet, adding that the miscarriage would occur shortly after that and then it would be all over.

He walked me back into his office and I heard myself groan as the world spun and a blanket of black wafted over me. Hanging on to the edge of his desk, I willed myself to remain conscious, then sat on the closest chair.

'Here,' he said. 'Drink this straight down. It will steady your nerves and raise your blood pressure.' He handed me a shot of whiskey.

I took one sip, but the smell of it made me heave, and I vomited all over his filthy carpet.

Just then, my friend came back into the office; she had been outside smoking. She looked at me with sad eyes, and put her arms around me. Self-loathing choked me and I was filled with disgust at what I'd just been subjected to. I was also disgusted at the law that drove women to such extreme and dangerous procedures. I was shaking violently from head to foot and heard the doctor tell my friend that I was probably in shock.

'Come on, let's get you home,' she said, as she led me out into the hall and down the stairs. I almost laughed when I heard the door slammed and locked behind us.

'They want to make sure we don't try to come back for a refund,' I told my friend, but neither of us was laughing. I wondered if that man had really been a doctor, but at that point I didn't care. I couldn't wait to get away from the awful place. All I wanted was the security of my own bed.

When we got home, my friend made me a cup of tea, made sure I was comfortable, and then had to leave. Exhausted, I climbed into bed, pulled the covers over my head and finally went to sleep. When I woke up, I had no idea what the time was: it was dark and the house was silent, and I wondered where my roommate, Deborah, was. She should have been home by now. Wayne and Robin had gone to spend the weekend with their grandparents and my roommate had promised she would help with them when they came home the following day if I was not feeling well. I got up and went to the kitchen where I found a note from Deborah saying that she and her children would be away for a few days so she couldn't help, after all. So, there I was, alone. I would just have to deal with it.

A few hours passed before I started having minor contractions. All of this time I'd been feeling like a stuffed turkey: there was tremendous pressure inside me from the packing that the doctor had inserted. Every time I went to the toilet, I expected to see something, but I really didn't know what to expect. I paced up and down in the apartment with the hours seeming to drag by, but at last the contractions became more regular and intense. When I was sure they were coming at regular intervals, and more than the prescribed twelve hours had passed, I went into the bathroom to begin pulling out the bandage.

The whole thing was surreal. I slowly removed the yards of gauze, thinking and fearing that I could pull my insides out if I wasn't careful. I could feel large blood clots coming out with the bandage, my head was spinning and I was heaving with nausea, but I knew I had to stay conscious and strong. I decided to have a bath with water as hot as I could bear, and lay there in the numbing heat, crying, but I knew I had to stay active for the contractions to continue.

As time went by the pain continued and I was bleeding heavily. Every once in a while I would feel intense pressure and would sit on the toilet to pass large blood clots, all the time thinking that one might be the actual foetus. I was too petrified to look. Sometimes the pain would cause me to double over but that made me strangely happy because I knew I was in the midst of a miscarriage and it would soon be just a memory.

After a couple of days, the bleeding was still heavy and I was soaking dozens of pads. I was no longer having contractions but was still in excruciating pain. I hadn't known exactly what to expect so I thought this was normal, but eventually, with growing concern, I called the doctor at the clinic. He said it sounded as though I might not have finished aborting yet and I should give it a while longer. In the back of my mind, I kept thinking of how long I had been in labour with my two children and that this was probably no different. Dr Crown had always said that my babies never wanted to leave me, and although I only ever thought of this pregnancy as an unwanted foetus resulting from rape, and never as an actual baby, I understood that the process might be the same, so I waited.

For the rest of that week I was barely able to function and take care of the children. I was still in pain and bleeding, and each day it had been harder to put on a happy face. The following weekend the children were off again for their weekend visits and I was relieved as I was feeling tired and in need of rest. I believe it was late on a Saturday evening, after I had taken a nap, that I got out of bed, found I'd been lying in a pool of blood and fainted. When I came to, I was so weak that I could hardly move but I knew I needed help. I managed to get to the telephone and called all my closest friends in the apartment building but no one was at home. In desperation I thought of the only other friend who lived close by and that was Pete Huber. He was an old friend of Palmer's but now totally disapproved of him and his treatment of me and the children; he often phoned to see how we were getting along. Pete lived just a few blocks away so I called him.

Pete was a bashful and homely bachelor who, when he wasn't playing golf or travelling for his job, could usually be found at home. He was a wonderful person and I always felt sad that he was alone. He would have made someone a great husband although he always seemed somewhat ill at ease and shy with women. He probably wouldn't have been much of a father: he always said he couldn't stand children, but I thought that was just tough-guy talk.

When Pete answered his phone, I was so relieved that I started to sob. 'Pete, can you please come over? I need you.' He slammed down the phone and was at my door in minutes. I had to crawl to the door to let him in.

'What the hell's going on?' he asked.

'Can't explain,' I said. 'Please take me to Cook County Hospital, Pete. I need help.' I had no medical insurance so I had to go to the free county facility. Without a word, Pete wrapped a coat around me, then got me into his car, where I must have passed out because I don't remember the rest of that journey.

When I came to, I was at the hospital, lying on a gurney, and a nurse was wheeling me into the emergency room. Things moved fast and it all became a bit of a blur, but soon someone hooked me up to an IV and the nurse told me I was being admitted. It was only then that I focused on her nametag and realized I was in West Suburban Hospital, not the free Cook County Hospital. At that point, I didn't have the strength to question it.

Later, when Pete came back to visit me, he told me there was no way he could leave me at Cook County Hospital with what he called 'all those animals'. I also learned that he had guaranteed payment of my hospital bill. When I protested, he told me frankly that he had more money than he knew what to do with and it was about time he did something useful with some of it. He sat beside me and apologized for the way Palmer had been treating me, as though he felt an element of responsibility. He said he wished he'd had the courage to do something to help me before but he hadn't known how. He and Palmer had been friends for years but he couldn't forgive him for what he had done to me and the kids.

After an examination and some tests it was determined that I was still pregnant but that the foetus was dead; I needed a surgical abortion.

'Have you ever had a miscarriage before?' a doctor asked me.

'No, never,' I told him. There was never any indication that they suspected I'd had an abortion.

'You need to have blood transfusions before we can

247

take you for surgery,' a nurse explained. 'You'll need about five pints. Do you have family or friends who would donate blood? If you can get donors, your hospital bill will be greatly reduced,' she added.

'I'll see what I can do,' I told her, but as I didn't want anyone to know what was going on, how could I ask them to give blood?

'You might also need more blood later,' she said, but by then, pain medication took over. I began to feel woozy and, at last, comfortable.

While I was receiving the transfusions, I asked the hospital social worker to phone my church and tell the pastor I needed to talk to him. I wanted him to issue a request for blood donors. I knew how expensive blood was and if we could get the blood replaced it would be less of a burden for my dear friend Pete. The pastor did not visit me but sent word that he had put out the plea, both at the Sunday services and in the church bulletin. I waited for news of donors, but not one person came. That was when I decided to leave the church. After my experience in Las Vegas, and now this, I was convinced that it was the last place I was ever going to find any actual Christians.

As I was receiving the third pint of blood, I started itching all over and my palate swelled to meet my tongue, much as it had when I'd had that allergic reaction to ragweed pollen some years ago. This, though, was far worse – I could hardly breathe. Suddenly the place was alive with bells ringing and lights flashing: I was having a severe allergic reaction to the transfusion. Someone stopped it and now doctors came running from all directions. I received massive antihistamine injections, which alleviated the situation. Soon after that fiasco, my blood count was rechecked and it was determined that it was safe to take me to surgery. I could have cried out of sheer happiness and relief.

When I woke up after the surgery, I was back in my room, which was in the maternity department, and I felt fine. A nurse told me I would not be having the rest of the blood transfusions, but that I'd probably receive iron injections to get my blood count up to normal. My family physician, Dr Leroy Besic, whom the hospital had called in, told me that if I hadn't received help when I did, I could have died because of the amount of blood I'd lost.

'All's well that ends well,' I told him. I was still a bit silly from the drugs they'd given me.

Having told the hospital switchboard that I wanted no calls, I was surprised when the phone rang. Cautiously, I picked it up and was horrified to discover it was Palmer, the one person I hadn't wanted to hear from. Apparently, he had told the switchboard that he was my husband.

'What are you doing in the maternity department?' he demanded. 'Have you got yourself knocked up?'

'Don't be ridiculous,' I told him. 'I'm here because it was the only available room.' That seemed to satisfy him.

'What are you in there for?' he barked.

'Not that it's any of your business any more, but I was having some female problems and had to have a D and C.'

'Where are the kids? Who's taking care of them?'

'They're at my brother's and they're fine,' I told him.

My roommate had let me down again, her promise to watch the kids forgotten. My good friend and neighbour Mary Nicholson was there when the children had come home from their weekend visits. Since Palmer was under orders not to come to my apartment, he had watched Robin walk to the door, and was unaware who had let her in – a good thing because he hated Mary and would have caused a scene; he still accused her of perjury in our divorce case, and brought it up at every opportunity. Anyway, Mary had phoned my brother and sister-in-law, told them I was in hospital for a D and C, and asked if she could bring the kids there for a few days, so that was what had happened.

When I came home from the hospital, I was still feeling very weak but it was as though the weight of the world had been lifted from my shoulders. I could now look for a job and, with my child-support payments and Deborah's rent, I would be able to make it. However, just when the future was beginning to look a little brighter, Deborah announced that she was leaving. 'I've been offered a fantastic position with much higher pay,' she rattled on, 'but the job is in Michigan and I have to move right away.'

I can't say I was sorry to see her go but the timing was lousy. Deborah had not turned out to be the wonder woman she had promised. She frequently stayed away from home, sometimes for several days at a time, but she did pay me well to take care of her two children. She did not exhibit good personal hygiene and one of my naughty neighbour friends had taken to calling her 'Nellie Rotten Crotch' because of her body odour. Her idea of preparing gourmet meals had turned out to be a joke. She once promised the kids a special treat if they cleaned up their room. It turned out to be cereal for dinner instead of a real meal, which I thought not only odd but mean. Deborah often had flowers delivered to her and I believed her stories of rich suitors, but after she moved out, I found out some surprising things about her.

My friend Mary and I had the job of clearing out the bags of belongings she had left in our basement storage unit. We were astounded to find that she was using a fictitious name, and there was evidence of other names she had used. We also discovered that her husband had not died of cancer but had divorced her; the papers were there to prove it. There were dozens of unpaid bills from various other US states, and we thought it pathetic when we also found the bills for the flowers she had been sending to herself. She had moved out in a hurry, and had left such a lot of her belongings that we suspected she was in some new trouble. I always felt sorry for her two children and often wondered what might have happened to them.

I had decided to wait until I felt stronger before looking for a job but with each passing day I felt worse and was growing weaker. I couldn't eat and was frequently nauseated, so I made an appointment to see Dr Besic. 'Do you know that I always refer to you as Dr Be Sick?' I'd told him on a previous visit.

He'd laughed. 'Well,' he said, 'my sister in California is also a doctor, and she had a K legally added to Besic. She thought she'd have the last laugh.' Weird, I thought, the things you find out on any given day.

When I walked into his office this time, he took one look at me and shook his head.

'No wonder you're feeling ill, you're seriously jaundiced,' he said. 'I'm surprised you haven't noticed. Here, look in this mirror.'

I was astonished at what I saw in the bright light of his office. The lighting in my apartment was not the best, but I had been leaving the overhead lights off because brightness had begun to bother my eyes. 'Oh, my God,' I said. 'I look like a canary. What's happened to me?'

Dr Besic knew, of course, about my recent hospital stay and I had told him about the abortion. He explained that apparently I had contracted hepatitis either from the abortion itself or from the blood transfusions. He assured me that I would be all right if I had plenty of bed rest and a good healthy diet (I learned many years later that he should have told me to avoid alcohol entirely), but all I could think about was what might go wrong next.

Wayne was at school and Robin was two and a half when all this was happening. I figured I could get Wayne off to school in the mornings, then lie on the couch while Robin played and sleep when she took her nap. Later, when Wayne came home from school, he could watch Robin for a while so that I could get dinner ready, and I would go to bed when they did. Somehow, we were going to get through this.

Pete Huber had been calling from wherever he happened to be in the country to check on us every couple of days. He seemed genuinely concerned. He knew I was still ill, but I assured him that we had it all sorted out and promised I would be getting plenty of rest. Then, a few days later, a special-delivery letter arrived from him. I couldn't imagine what he was sending, and when I opened the envelope, I almost died of shock. It contained airline tickets for the children and me to go to England for a month, plus some extra money for expenses. The letter with it had me sobbing my heart out. He said that since he had no family of his own he would consider it a privilege to be part of ours, even if only for a little while. He said he would be on the road for the next few months, covering the golf tournament circuit, and he would see us when we got back to Chicago. I didn't have a phone number where I could call him and I just stared at the plane tickets, crying like a baby.

I tried to find out where Pete was from his brother, Joe, but he didn't know how to contact him either. I suspect Joe wondered what I wanted with his brother, but he didn't ask and I didn't tell.

I'm sure my family wondered where the money had come from for the trip but I simply told them it had come from a special guardian angel. I hadn't told anyone in my family about all that had happened, not while it was happening or afterwards. Why burden my parents with the worry? What could they have done? I hadn't told my brother and his wife in America either because, with their small children and problems of their own, they certainly didn't need to hear about mine. They had bought my stereo set from me and the money from that had helped tide us over, and I had also cashed in a couple of Wayne's savings bonds so that we could keep going. It had been just enough to help make ends meet until I could find a job.

We went to England, which was just what I needed to rebuild my strength. My mother simply thought I was run-down and did her best to see that I got plenty of rest and good food. The children had a great time and we loved being with my family; I could happily have stayed there for ever, but that was out of the question. Again, it was hard for me to return to America. I was frightened of having to face it alone, but I knew it would have caused an international incident if I had stayed in England. I felt that I'd received another chance at life, and I owed it to the friends who had so kindly helped me when I had most needed them. I had to go back and give it my best shot.

21: Strange Encounters, and Life after Palmer

Back in America, I had just started looking for a job and was temporarily baby-sitting and sewing again when I received a phone call from one of my adopted sisters, Mom Evans's daughter Jeanne. Jeanne worked for a large restaurant in Chicago but she also had another business on the side. It wasn't really a model agency, but she provided demonstrators and hostesses for conventions and trade shows. She knew I needed work and said she had the contract to provide girls to work in registration and in the exhibitors' booths at the National Restaurant Association Trade Show at McCormick Place Convention Center. She said the assignment would last for seven days but the pay would be excellent, and she would provide the clothes we were to wear.

After returning from England, I was in much better physical condition. I had regained some of the weight I'd lost and my curves were back. A healthy colour had returned to my cheeks, which was wonderful after the yellow of hepatitis, so I felt confident and told her I would see about getting a baby-sitter. If I could make the necessary arrangements, I would love to work for her.

I soon arranged for Robin to attend good old Gay Time Nursery School temporarily, and Wayne would go to Mom Evans when he got out of school. I called Jeanne back to say we were all set. She asked if I knew of anyone else who might be interested, as she still needed people, so I called Bobby McCarthy; she said she'd like to do it too. At that point, I had forgotten that Palmer worked for McCormick Place but it was huge and, with a bit of luck, I might not run into him.

Bobby and I met and went together to have our dresses fitted; they were pink gingham, 'all-American-girl'-type outfits, with multicoloured gingham frills around the hem. Bobby and I were greatly relieved that we didn't have to wear French maids' uniforms, which might have been the case since this trade show was all to do with food service. We also had to wear high-heeled pink pumps and, if I say so myself, we looked smashing. Selected to work for Continental Coffee Company, we would be serving coffee and cookies throughout the day, and handing out information to the thousands of visitors.

Working at McCormick Place for just one week was difficult: I had to take two trains and a bus to get there, and I had to be there by eight a.m. It was a good thing the pay was generous or it might not have been worth the effort. The journey wasn't too bad in the morning, but coming home that first night, I thought my feet were going to fall off; they were steaming when I finally took off my shoes. Stupidly I had forgotten to take comfortable ones to travel in. Believe me, I didn't forget them the next day.

The Continental Coffee salesmen were pleasant and polite, and treated Bobby and me well. We didn't have a lot of time for kidding around as we were busy all the time but we did have plenty of laughs. One man kept watching me and hovered around, asking if I needed anything. He was especially kind and thoughtful and even brought us both lunch. Bobby kept telling me to watch out as someone seemed to have his eye on me, and it became obvious that he was interested. The man in question was Spiro T. and he was a Greek American. After a while, the other salesmen were teasing him about me. Spiro had known Jeanne for years from calling at her restaurant, so he just told them he knew me through her because she was my adopted sister.

On the second day, Spiro started talking more to me, asking me about myself, and about where I lived. When I told him that I had to take two trains and a bus to get to and from McCormick Place, he offered to drive me home that night. Of course, I accepted his offer. When he dropped me off outside my apartment building, he asked hesitantly if I would like a ride to work in the morning. I jumped at the opportunity, thanking him for his kindness, and off he went, saying he would see me at six thirty in the morning.

For the rest of the restaurant show, Spiro picked me up and brought me home every day. He started calling me 'Princess'. He couldn't do enough for me and I have to admit that I enjoyed having someone fawn over me. He was like a little boy with a crush. On the last day of the show as he dropped me off at home, he asked if he could call me some time to see how I was doing, and I agreed.

I had hardly stepped inside the apartment door when the phone rang.

'Hi, Princess,' he said, sounding nervous. 'I'm just calling to see how you're doing, like you said I could, but can I take you out for dinner tonight?' The silly man, after dropping me off, had gone to the nearest public phone to call me.

'Aw, thanks for the invitation, but I'm exhausted and still have to feed the children,' I told him, 'but call me again some time and I'll see what I can arrange.'

'Some time will be soon,' he said. 'I've hardly slept since the first day I saw you and I was afraid I might never see you again.'

Floored by this sudden outpouring, I didn't know what to say so I thanked him and said I'd look forward to hearing from him. I had just heaved a sigh of relief that I hadn't run into Palmer at McCormick Place, and now I was buoyed up by having someone pay such kind attention to me.

Jeanne phoned me soon afterwards to tell me she had heard about Spiro's infatuation with me. She warned me to be careful because he was married. I told her I knew he was and that I didn't intend to get involved with him, and at the time, I meant it. Later, when I told my friend Mary about it, she said that maybe dating married men was the way to go, as it sure would keep me from making any more foolish mistakes. I had vowed never to marry again and thought perhaps she was right, but I never dreamed that shortly after that conversation, I would begin a long and beautiful affair with a married man.

Some time after the Continental Coffee assignment, I took the children with me to visit my friend Bobby, who lived in a small rented house on Chicago's south side; I wanted to tell her how my crazy relationship with Spiro was progressing, and to catch up on all of her news. While our children played together, Bobby told me that her ex-husband, Jim, who was now a sign painter, was a hopeless drunk, and she had no idea how she'd put up with his behaviour for as long as she had. 'Any money he earned from painting signs was spent before he got home. We were in debt up to our ears, and all he did was laugh about it. Everything was always a big joke to Jim,' she said. Her story was all too familiar to me but I had no idea that she, too, had been going through some of the same things that I had; she'd never talked about it much before.

As we were chatting, there was a pounding on the back door immediately followed by Jim barging in; he had a friend with him.

'We've done some salvage work at one of the old theatres they were tearing down in Chicago,' he told us. 'We've brought home two beautiful slabs of marble.'

'Home?' questioned Bobby. 'Did you forget you no longer live here?'

'Well, I thought since I contribute to the rent, you might let me store a couple of things here.'

'Oh, yes, you do *occasionally* contribute to the rent,' Bobby said. 'Where do you plan to store it, Jim? You already have tons of stuff here. When do you guys plan on removing or selling some of it? You did tell me that was your plan.'

'For now, we're taking it up into the attic. It won't be in your way there,' he said, and off he and his mate went.

We sat there, listening to all the huffing and puffing as they struggled to carry the heavy slabs of marble up the attic stairs. Suddenly there was an ominous creaking, followed by a loud crack. We ran into the next room to see where the sound had come from and when we looked up, there was a huge hole in the ceiling, with a prosthetic wooden leg sticking through it. From up in the attic we could hear hysterical laughter followed by Hans, Jim's friend, shouting, 'Well, don't just stand there, Jim, you idiot! Help me pull my goddamn leg outta here.'

When the two of them finally came back downstairs, after extricating Hans's somewhat damaged leg, we all laughed until tears rolled down our faces. I'd noticed that Hans walked with a limp but had no idea he had a wooden leg. From what I had witnessed and stories I had heard, Jim and Hans would have made a great comedy team.

'See what I mean?' Bobby said, after the two men left on another expedition. 'Everything is a big joke, and I mean everything. He's always had big plans to sell this stuff he drags in, but he and Hans only really enjoy getting it, not selling it. It's just a big game to them. I always told Jim he should have married Hans.'

After we'd had a cup of tea, we continued chatting and Bobby disclosed some of the problems she'd encountered since coming to America; things she had never shared with me before. She was yet to make a visit home, and hardly ever heard from her family.

'Enough about misery,' she said. 'Let's try to forget all that.' Then, as if to lighten the mood, she told me about an incident that occurred while she and Jim were still married.

'I'd been so angry with him about his drinking, I hadn't talked to him for days, and when he'd tried to have sex with me, I'd refused. I told him to go screw himself. Well,' she continued, 'one night, I was in bed reading when I heard him come home. I could tell he was drunk by the sound of his fumbling and stumbling, so I turned off the reading light and pretended I was asleep. I heard him come into the room, and then heard him rummaging in the bedroom closet. Then, the closet light clicked on and he called out to me, "Yoo-hoo, take a look at this, Bobby." I sat up and looked to see what was so important, and there he stood with a big grin on his face. He was stark naked, had a hard-on, and he'd painted a sign that said, "It pays to advertise," and hung it on his willy. What are you going to do with someone like that, Iris? I couldn't stop laughing, and that was how he always thought he could get out of everything.'

'I see what you mean, Bobby. In a way you're lucky he made you laugh instead of cry, like my ex. I guess that's what you get for marrying a cartoon artist.'

Over the years, Bobby and I had had many such conversations about our marital and other problems, but at least she was lucky enough to have in-laws who supported her. They knew their son was a deadbeat and had taken over his responsibility for the children by helping Bobby whenever they could; I envied her.

In the meantime, Palmer was still harassing me with phone calls and I realized it did no good to change my phone number because he always found out what the new one was. I heard that he was still trying to dig up dirt about me, and about anyone that had contact with me. He caused a great deal of embarrassment and annoyance to some of my friends and neighbours, often calling in a drunken state late at night. Even our poor old building janitor and his wife told me he had called, trying to bribe them. He wanted them to watch what I was doing and report to him if I had any male visitors, or if they found liquor bottles in the trash. I thought that was ironic coming from him. His behaviour was increasingly sick and unpredictable, and even though there was still a court order against him doing any of these things it didn't seem to faze him. Everyone involved knew what was going on and was trying to ignore him. It wasn't easy.

Occasionally, even though my relationship with Spiro was growing stronger, I still had dinner with Palmer's old golfing friend, Pete Huber, if he happened to be in town; he once took me to the Masters Golf Tournament when it was being played in the area and that was very exciting. We had become good friends and, knowing that, Palmer no longer had anything to do with him. He had tried unsuccessfully to get information about me out of Pete but there wasn't anything to tell. He was jealous of our friendship and accused Pete of having sexual relations with me, which he had not, and he viciously attacked his old friend as a traitor. Pete and I were fond of each other, true, but our relationship was always purely platonic.

I also had regular telephone conversations with Chuck M., an old lawyer friend from my first marriage, and would sometimes meet him for lunch if I happened to be in downtown Chicago. Chuck was doing well for himself, as he was now a full partner in the prominent law firm he had worked for since qualification. He was an Irish Catholic, married, with four or five children, but had always kept in touch with me. He was sympathetic to what was going on in my life and could always make me laugh with his dry sense of humour.

I'll never forget the first time Chuck asked me out for dinner (yes, another married man). I had always been a little nervous when we'd had lunch together as I had seen him as being a bit out of my league. Raised in England where the class system was so prevalent, I still saw professional people as 'above my station'. I did, however, agree to have dinner with him that night and engaged the help of my friend Mary in putting together an appropriate outfit for my big evening out.

So there I was, all decked out in Mary's basic little-black-dress, Mary's pearls, Mary's black coat with the mink collar, Mary's long black leather gloves and Mary's evening bag. At the last minute when I got a run in my stocking, I even had to borrow a pair of nylons from her. We still laugh about my famous date, when the only things I was wearing of my own were my underwear and a pair of second-hand shoes, but that wasn't the funniest thing about that evening.

Painstakingly, I got myself ready to go out. Then, protected by an apron, I prepared the children's dinner and waited for Mrs Stella, our janitor's wife, to come around to baby-sit for the evening.

'You look pretty, Mommy,' said Robin.

'Why are you wearing Auntie Mary's dress?' asked Wayne. 'And isn't that Auntie Mary's coat?'

I told them I was going to meet someone important, and that seemed to satisfy them as they both grinned at me. By now, I was a nervous wreck. Everything went like clockwork, however, and as Mrs Stella came in at the back door, the front-door bell rang. He was here. I kissed the children goodbye, threw on my beautiful borrowed mink-trimmed coat and flew out of the front door.

Chuck and I were both nervous, he because I'm positive he had never been on a date with another woman, and me because I was going out for dinner with a married man of class. Like a blithering idiot, I blurted out that I was so nervous that 'my bone was as dry as a throat', and when we realized what I had said, we both relaxed into fits of laughter.

'I know the feeling,' he was finally able to say.

We drove out to the suburbs, to a fancy and well-known restaurant called Richard's Lilac Lodge. I had heard that some of Chicago's mobsters hung out there, not that I would have recognized any of them. After our car had been valet-parked, we entered the grand chandeliered lobby and stopped to take off our coats. As the coat-check girl helped me off with my lovely borrowed coat, Chuck's eyes became as big as saucers.

'What the hell is that?' he said, almost choking on his words. I looked down, and the world suddenly went into slow motion. I stood there, paralysed. I had forgotten to take off my coverall floral apron. I wanted the floor to open up and swallow me. Then, clutching my coat back around me, I dived into the nearby ladies' room, locked myself inside a cubicle and sat there wondering if I would ever be able to show my face again.

I decided the best and only thing I could do was face the music. I rolled the apron up as tightly as possible and stuffed it into my dinky borrowed handbag, I wasn't about to throw a perfectly good apron into the trash, and went bravely out to face a bewildered Chuck, who was waiting for an explanation.

'Jeez, I thought you were wearing a floral nightgown,'

he said, and laughed until tears rolled down his very red face. I honestly don't know how we ate our dinner that night, but it definitely helped to have a couple of drinks first.

Almost forty years later, I can still see that apron, with its frills and flowers. That night it must have looked every bit as big and looming as a pink elephant. As a good friend of mine said after hearing that story, 'God does speak to us in strange ways.' I'm sure that was a reference to the fact that I'd been out with a married man.

Another thing that happened during my early dating days after my divorce from Palmer was the attempt by my Outfit-related friends at fixing me up with someone in 'the family'. I'm sure it was their way of trying to bring me into it; they wanted me to be safe and protected the way they all were. Anyway, they set me up on a blind date with 'Mike the Bear', who was to pick me up and take me out for dinner. Well, the name alone scared the hell out of me, and when I met him, I knew why he had acquired that nickname. He was the hairiest man I'd ever met. He was a nice-looking, dark-haired Italian, but if you've ever seen a movie about the Mob, you've seen this man. Had he been an actor, he most definitely would have been typecast as a gangster. He even drove a big black Cadillac with tinted windows.

We had a pleasant enough evening out, but he wasn't my type and I probably wasn't his. I don't think he had ever read a book, he had no idea what was going on in the world and obviously couldn't have cared less. He wanted to see me again but I told him I was dating someone else and that I thought it was getting serious. I said he could call me but I think he got the message. When I told my adopted sister Jodi that it wasn't going to work, she laughed and said she hadn't really thought it would, but he had been the only single man she knew in her husband's circle and thought it was worth a try. She also told me they had warned him to be on his best behaviour. Somehow, I could never quite see myself going out with, or married to, someone called Mike the Bear. Of course, if I had hooked up with him, I doubt Palmer would have bothered me again – ever!

I was now working full time for Catholic Charities Legal Aid Department in downtown Chicago. As an intake worker, I screened all potential clients for eligibility before they saw one of our team of lawyers, each of whom specialized in a different facet of the law. It was interesting, hearing the stories of people's legal problems. Most of the lawyers were either fresh out of law school or probably not particularly ambitious. They must have been paid fairly well but probably not as well as they would have been if they had been successful in their own right. I imagine working for Legal Aid at least guaranteed a regular income.

One of the clients was a paranoid schizophrenic. It was always difficult filling out the intake papers since we all knew that her perceived problems were part of her condition. She reported being followed by the CIA, spied on and physically tortured by aliens from outer space, poisoned by her neighbours, and stalked and sexually abused by Howard K. Smith, a well-known television reporter. My fellow workers had not warned me about this client, and the first time she was on my caseload, they all just sat there, watching my face. I'm sure, had I been a cartoon, there would have been giant question marks sticking out above my head.

My favourite client was the blind ninety-one-year-old African American gentleman who was being sued in a paternity case. Shaking his head sadly, he told me, in all seriousness, 'Honey, I's wishin' it was me, but da truth bein', I ain't had me no lovin' since I be eighty-three or theyabouts.' I made sympathetic noises but had a difficult time keeping a professional straight face.

Another job I took on to earn a little extra money was selling Sarah Coventry jewellery at home demonstration parties. I had my doubts about this from the very beginning as some of their sales gimmicks cracked me up and I wasn't sure I'd cope with using the company's sophomoric sales methods. One rule was that we had to wear the jewellery but only one earring because someone would eventually mention it. 'Excuse me, but did you know you only have one earring on?' Your rehearsed response was to be something like, 'Oh, I'm so glad you noticed, and isn't Sarah Coventry jewellery beautiful? Let me tell you about it, blah blah blah.' I knew immediately that I could never have pulled that off without laughing. Another thing in our demonstration routine was the wearing of one long black glove over which to drape necklaces and bracelets, as I described the magnificence of each piece. I tried that at my first demonstration, organized by my dear friend Mary, for all our mutual friends and neighbours. Mary, wonderful host that she was and still is, made the fatal mistake of serving wine, which yours truly also enjoyed. Within minutes, we were all falling about, laughing so hard that the tears were rolling down our faces and I ended up just laying the jewellery on the table and telling everyone, 'Have a look at it, girls, and just let me know if you want to order any of this stuff.' I honestly cannot remember if I sold anything that night but we had one heck of a good time.

My adopted sister Jodi organized my next jewellery party for some of the Outfit wives. Now that was a real joke. Every one of those women was drop-dead gorgeous and dripping with jewellery of the real kind. I'm sure they came because no less a person than Dominic Cortina's wife had invited them and, of course, she had done it to help me. Once again, there was food and cocktails and we were all having a grand old time until Jodi spoke.

'Haven't we forgotten something?' she asked.

'Oh, my Gahd, we're supposed to be buying this stuff,' I heard, from one rather tipsy woman.

So, for my second jewellery demonstration, I simply told them all the funny things I had been trained to do to sell this stuff. They found my descriptions highly entertaining and more than one told me it was just a little bit bizarre. Then I told them that, out of respect for their intelligence, I would simply lay my wares on the table, along with the order forms, and they could carry on partying. We had a fun time and I made some money that night but wondered what those women would do with the junk jewellery they had ordered. Later, I apologized to Jodi for putting her through such a fiasco.

'Are you kidding?' she said. 'All the girls told me they couldn't remember having such a good laugh, and they hope we can do it again some time.'

'Over my dead body,' said I.

I did one or two more jewellery parties after that but I couldn't be serious about it. Besides, all that partying was wearing me out!

22: The Safety of Married Men

For now, I was perfectly happy dating married men. It sounds awful, I know, but I had to avoid making any more mistakes. I was beginning to realize that, in my need for love, I was vulnerable and had to be aware of my own susceptibility; I had to be ever vigilant, had to avoid my heart ruling my head. I had already made too many mistakes. I was still young and had plenty of time to enjoy life without risking my children's or my own health and happiness. I knew I must never expose my children to such turmoil again.

I was seeing more and more of Spiro T. No man had ever treated me the way he did, with what I can only call gentle adoration. He called me his princess and that was exactly how he made me feel. He knew I had just come through a terrible phase of my life and was determined to make it up to me. At first it bothered me that he was married but he had convinced me that his marriage was in name only and that his wife and he lived almost completely separate lives. Of course, that was what I wanted to believe.

Spiro talked a lot about his mother, who was first-generation Greek, and often brought me Greek food that she had prepared. He also told me about his daughter, an only child whom he adored. 'I want so much for you and Sally to meet,' he told me, and added, 'when the time is right.'

'I'll look forward to that day, no matter when it is,' I assured him.

When Christmas came he overwhelmed the children and me with gifts. He made sure we had everything we wanted or needed. I cried when I saw everything he'd put under the tree on that Christmas Eve, threw my arms around him and cried some more. 'I don't know what to say, Spiro. It's all too much. You really are our special angel,' I blubbered. He assured me that it had given him great pleasure to help make our Christmas special. Then I gave him his present. I had knitted him a golf cardigan, and covers with numbers on for his clubs.

Now it was his turn to cry. 'That's the nicest thing anyone has ever done for me,' he said, through his tears. 'I don't know what I've done to deserve finding you.' I echoed his words, adding that I was only sorry he couldn't be with us the next day to see the kids open their presents.

He wasn't able to see us on Christmas Day because he was going to be with his family, as was their tradition. That was fine by me as we usually spent Christmas with my brother Peter and his family. Spiro had explained that his wife was Jewish and didn't celebrate Christmas, so he had always kept his Greek family's traditions alive by spending the day with his mother and brothers.

We saw each other almost every day or evening, and even when he said he couldn't come for one reason or another, he often surprised me by showing up. When he wasn't there, I received regular phone calls from him so he could tell me that he missed me. He was never possessive or overbearing, just attentive and caring. The children loved 'Mr T.', as they called him, and he was always bringing little treats for them too. Sometimes if he had to make an emergency service call, out in the suburbs on a weekend, he would call, tell us to get ready and take us with him. He'd drop us off at a motel with a pool so that the kids could play and swim until he came to pick us up. He was always trying to think of nice things to do for us, and different ways to surprise us. I had come to adore him just as much as he seemed to adore me, but there was never talk of anything permanent on either side. At that point, we were both comfortable with our situation, just the way it was; for me, it was safe.

Spiro was a wonderful lover and he taught me things I had never experienced in either of my two marriages. My first husband had little sexual experience, and neither did Palmer, who had had little interest in the activity, unless it came in the form of a brutal attack. It was Spiro who introduced me to oral sex. The first time it happened was a near disaster. Spiro and I had been out for dinner and had had a few glasses of wine. The children were away overnight and we were both feeling amorous. Spiro knew I was still somewhat bashful in the sex department but, aware that I was a little tipsy, he told me to relax and let him pleasure me, whatever that meant. I was apprehensive but gave in to his coaxing and lay back on the bed, letting him undress me. He then proceeded to do what I thought was the unthinkable. At that moment, I made the big mistake of looking at him, down there. In our moment of hot passion, he had forgotten to take off his horn-rimmed glasses, and from that angle, he looked exactly like Groucho Marx. I totally lost it and burst out laughing.

'What's so funny?' he asked, as he repositioned and smoothed himself out.

'I can't tell you yet,' I managed to get out, before rolling over and covering myself to hide my embarrassment. 'I'm sorry, I'm too ashamed of myself.'

Poor Spiro, he was alternately embarrassed and hurt over that incident and, sadly, that was the end of our lovemaking that night. I did eventually tell him what had happened, but he was not amused; I believe that was the only time I ever upset him. To this day, whenever I think of that episode, or see a picture of moustachioed Groucho Marx, I still laugh. What can I say? I've always had a weird sense of humour topped off with a vivid imagination.

There was one other funny, or perhaps I should say peculiar, thing about Spiro. He had six toes on each foot. I was so glad he'd told me ahead of time about this little abnormality because he loved to have his feet rubbed. Had I come across that sixth toe with no warning, I might have been visibly freaked out and hurt his feelings again!

During that period, I received a phone call from my mother, and what she told me completely floored me. Mum had never called me before and I thought at first that she was ringing to tell me that someone had died, but that was not the case. She told me that my father had left her for another woman. He was still president of the Watford Christian Spiritualist Church and he had run off with the church secretary. My poor mother was in a terrible state, but told me she was managing to hang on, with the support of my two younger brothers who were both still living at home.

'I know there's nothing you can do, Iris, but I thought you should know what's happened,' she said.

'My God, is he completely insane? What the hell does he think he's doing? What the hell does he think you're going to do?' I yelled.

'I was afraid to tell you. I knew you'd be upset. I don't know what's going to happen – I just can't think,' she told me, and I could tell she was crying.

'Don't cry, Mum, the bastard's not worth it.'

'Don't call him that, Iris. It's her fault, not his,' she said. Of course she would defend him, I thought. She always has. And of course she was crying: he was the only one she'd ever cried for. But that was all in the past. The question was, what could we do about anything right now?

'Do you think you'd like to come over and stay with me for a while, Mum? I think we should figure out how to get you here. It would do you good to be away from there for a while. Please, Mum, it would help me too if we can arrange it.' She said she would think about it, and then, almost immediately, agreed to come.

After I'd hung up, I just sat there, dazed by what I had heard. I couldn't believe what my dad had done, and at that moment, I hated him.

In a state of shock, I called my brother Peter at work and told him I needed to see him right away. Yes, my reaction was extreme, but it was as though I'd heard that my father had died. That was how devastated I was. No, I hadn't had a happy childhood. No, I'd never felt loved or that I came from a particularly happy family, but, in spite of its many faults, my family had been my anchor, the only constant in my life. I needed to know I still had that family and that they'd always be there for me, always my refuge. Hearing that my family was suddenly no longer the cohesive unit I wanted and needed it to be had shaken me to my very core.

I'm sure my brother couldn't imagine what the problem was as I hardly ever called him. He came straight from work, though, and the minute he walked through the door, I broke down in tears. He kept asking me what was wrong, what had happened, but I couldn't get the words out of my mouth.

'Let me make us a cup of tea first,' was all I could say. It was performing the old English ritual that finally settled me enough to tell him about Mum's phone call and the details of what had happened.

Peter was livid. 'That bastard, that bastard,' he kept saying.

'Mum and I talked about her coming over here for a while,' I told him. 'I think she needs to get away.'

'The sooner the better,' he agreed.

The next day, I heard that Peter had called Dad at the boarding house where he was staying, and that they'd had a terrible row. Dad had become enraged when Peter referred to the lady-friend as a 'broad'. Our father's defence of her further angered my brother and me, especially knowing that he had never defended our mother or given her support; it all seemed so damned unfair and selfish. What did he expect Mum to do? How could she manage on her own? Had he thought of that?

It took me a while to realize the irony of my extreme

reaction to Dad's abandonment of my mother: I was dating a married man but, of course, to me that was different. It's strange how children, no matter their age, never see their parents as just ordinary people. It would seem that we always expect them to be exclusively our unselfish parents with no weaknesses or needs of their own.

My mother, with our help, was able to arrange a cheap trip to America on a charter flight through the Transatlantic Brides and Parents Association (TBPA). In spite of the reason for the visit, I was excited that she was coming as she had never been to America before and normally would never have gone anywhere without my father.

When Spiro learned of Mum's impending visit, he immediately started a little savings account so that we could spoil her and give her a good time. He knew I would never take money from him so he said the account was strictly for my mother. He was always surprising me with his thoughtfulness and I truly think he was just as excited as I was about her visit.

Mum stayed for about two months, splitting her time evenly between my brother and me. We took her everywhere and all of our friends spoiled her too. I'll never forget her happiness when Peter surprised her by taking her to see Liberace, who was appearing in Chicago at the time; she needed a little joy in her life. One night after we had been out for dinner with Spiro, she realized she had lost her watch during the evening. The next day she had a beautiful new one, courtesy of Spiro; she was completely smitten with him, as was I.

When she and I were having a tearful discussion about Dad, Mum called his lady-friend a whore and blamed her for the whole thing. She wouldn't believe it was Dad's fault, even with his long history as a philandering womanizer. I pointed out to her that she was in effect calling me a whore, too, since she knew Spiro was married. Good old loyal Mum stopped for a minute – you could almost hear the wheels turning in her brain. 'Well, that's different, Iris,' she protested, 'completely different.' Well, perhaps it was somewhat different since Spiro was still living with his wife. However, the fact remained that I was the other woman. I wasn't a whore, but I was his mistress. Mum adored Spiro and would never have heard a disparaging word against him.

While Mum was staying with me, my adopted sister Jodi invited us to her house for lunch one day. At the time, Jodi and Dominic lived in a beautiful house in River Forest, a suburb renowned for the many underworld figures who lived there. My dear mum was nervous about being in such a grand home as she was still living in a council house and had never been inside such a palatial residence. Jodi had prepared a delicious lunch for us and later her sister Jeanne joined us. As we were eating, Jodi's husband, Dominic, walked in, looking as though he had just stepped from the pages of a gentleman's magazine. He had on a beautiful silk suit and, as always, he was meticulously groomed, right down to his manicured fingernails. Dominic was what you would call a big man, a handsome Italian, who struck a commanding figure, but the Dominic I knew was a gentle giant, and always a true gentleman.

After Jodi had introduced him to my mother, he kissed her cheek and welcomed her to his home. He then proceeded to cook himself lunch. Mum was stunned. My father had never prepared his own lunch and here was this rich big-shot so-called gangster (funnily enough, I never did think of Dominic in that way) cooking his own food. He told Jodi he was expecting someone for a game of cards and asked her to send him into the den when he arrived. A little later his visitor arrived and Jodi introduced him to us as Sam. After he had disappeared behind closed doors, Jodi quietly told me who he was and it was a name readily recognized. She didn't have to say another word because he was one of the most infamous underworld figures of his day. His name was in the newspapers too often for it not to be recognized. I didn't explain all this to Mum until later when we were at home.

'Blimey,' she said. 'D'you mean to tell me I just had lunch with a gangster? You'd never know it to look at him, would you? He seemed like such a lovely bloke.'

'He is, Mum,' I assured her. 'He is a lovely bloke.'

The Mob affiliation was never discussed, nor would it have been suspected, as the people I knew were all involved in legitimate businesses. A name might be mentioned, as in the case of Sam, but there was never any hint of impropriety. There was never a swear word used or permitted in the house, the children were raised strictly, were extremely well mannered, and the family attended the local Catholic church regularly.

Not too long after my mother and I had had lunch with her, Jodi called me, warning me not to be surprised to see Dominic's name in the newspaper, in connection with a big headline story. She sounded upset but didn't elaborate; she simply wanted me to be prepared and she asked me to make light of it if her mother seemed unduly concerned.

The newspaper headlines were about the indictment of a large number of Chicago Outfit figures, including Dominic, on charges of racketeering and illegal gambling. I don't recall how long the case dragged on but Dominic served time in federal prison in Minnesota and Jodi moved there for a while to be near him. When he came out of jail, Dominic was ill with kidney disease, which Jodi said they'd been unable to get proper treatment for while he was in prison. When they eventually returned to the Chicago area, he made a good recovery and they were soon living in an even more sumptuous house in Oak Brook, another of Chicago's rich suburbs.

There were many times when I envied the way 'the family' took care of its own, especially when one was in jail or ill. Jodi and the children never had to worry about anything except their separation from Dominic and the valuable years that were lost.

When the time came for my mother to return to England, we all felt she was as ready as she would ever be. She was now anxious to get home to my brothers, Robert and Chris, and we thought she'd be better able to face life without Dad. It broke my heart to see her get back on the plane, knowing what she would face when she arrived at home. I wished I could have gone with her, to help her through the pain, but I promised her I would come soon. I was determined to teach her how to live without suffering the mental anguish brought on by Dad's abandonment. He had already caused her too much agony over the years. I had to make her see him for what he was, and help her understand that, in all likelihood, he would never change. She simply had to let him go, and get on with her life without him. In my heart, though, I knew I was hoping for the impossible.

With Mum now gone and my relationship with Spiro still strong, everything seemed to be going well, but then I got a bit of a shock. One evening when I was at home alone, except for the children who were in bed, the front-door bell rang. It was late and I couldn't imagine who it might be, unless one of my neighbours had forgotten their lobby key. I went to the door and there stood a woman I had never seen before.

'Are you Iris?' she asked.

'Yes, I am,' I said. 'Can I help you?'

'I don't know,' she said, her voice quivering. 'I'm Mrs T.'

Wham! I felt as though I'd been hit over the head with a sledgehammer. In a state of total shock, I invited her to come in and sit down. I was quaking and she was visibly shaking.

She proceeded to tell me that she had found out about her husband's affair with me through phone calls she had been receiving from a man named Robert Palmer who had told her that he was my husband. He was now constantly harassing her with calls to the family home and had even talked to their children, telling them about their father's affair, causing terrible emotional trauma. He was also calling her husband at his restaurant and had threatened to kill him. She said her husband had adamantly denied having an affair and had assured her that he had never heard of me. He had reported the threatening phone calls to the police but she still thought it was just an act to cover up the affair.

Suddenly this whole situation did not sound right. I

knew that Spiro only had one child and this Mrs T. had mentioned children in the plural. Spiro did not own a restaurant.

'What is the name of your restaurant?' I asked her.

'The Lamplighter, on Madison Avenue,' she said.

'I go there a lot,' I told her. 'It's my favourite restaurant.'

The Lamplighter was a lovely little romantic place, not far from where I lived; all my friends went there. Suddenly something clicked in my mind. 'What is your husband's name?' I asked.

'Spyros,' she said.

Oh, my God, I thought. Palmer's made a huge mistake. Palmer, 'the stalker', in doing his detective work had found out the name of my favourite restaurant. Somehow, he had learned the identity of the man I was seeing. He had then discovered the name of the Lamplighter's owner, which was similar. It was too much of a coincidence not to be the same person. He had incorrectly deduced that he finally had the goods on both of us.

When I explained it to the poor woman sitting on my couch, I thought she was going to kiss me. I told her all about Palmer, how sick he was, and encouraged her to have her husband press charges against him but I don't know if he ever did. She hugged me before she left and thanked me for helping to straighten out what she had thought was the end of her marriage. Later, I called her husband and apologized for all that he and his family had been subjected to. He was nice about it but, obviously, he'd been terribly shaken by the whole experience. Spiro and I thought it best to stop frequenting the Lamplighter as a courtesy to those poor people who had been the innocent victims of my ex-husband's warped mind.

I thought that the real Spiro would want out of our relationship when he found out what kind of a situation could erupt without warning, but he never once even hinted at it. I suppose that was why I tended to believe that his marriage was as he had told me, in name only, and that they would part as soon as their daughter left home. It suited me the way it was since I had no desire for a permanent relationship with anyone at that time in my life. Seemingly, insurmountable battles had been fought and won and the lessons I had learned along the way had made me stronger and more confident.

I still had the occasional lunch or dinner with Pete Huber and Chuck M. and was grateful for their continued friendship; they both knew of my relationship with Spiro and had advised me to be careful. How comforting it was to know that I had such good friends and that they genuinely cared about me. Yes, I was still living in my basement apartment but I had a decent job, my friends around me, my children were happy, and we had everything we needed, right there in our familiar neighbourhood.

It had now been approximately ten years since I had come to America as a sixteen-year-old GI bride, but it seemed a lifetime since I had stepped off that ship in New York; sometimes it felt like several lifetimes. I still missed my family and my country and lived for my next trip 'home'. I now knew dozens of other former GI brides and we supported each other in different ways; life in America had finally become easier for most of us. Many of us were now American citizens, but if anyone ever heard us talk, they'd know that in our hearts we would always be British. We had made our home in America but I can't think of anyone who didn't still refer to Britain as home.

Spiro had entered my life when it was at its lowest ebb. He had helped to make me healthy, strong and confident again; he made me feel beautiful and cherished. He showed genuine concern and affection for my children and they had grown fond of him. What more could I want? We were happy with the way things were, and when the time was right, I knew we would be together for ever. Now, filled with optimism, I was confident that this man would never hurt, betray or disappoint me. My future looked bright, and I was no longer afraid of anything.

This GI bride, just one of more than a hundred thousand, had come a long way, both geographically and metaphorically; I didn't know what Fate had in store for me, but at that crossroads of my life, my children and I were happy, safe and secure, and I was ready for anything the world might throw at me.

Epilogue

I cannot leave my story without a few words about what happened to some of the people who featured strongly in this part of my life story.

Bob Irvine, my first love and husband, married several more times, but after his last marriage ended, he lived alone for many years. We always remained friends and I sent him a card on what would have been our fiftieth wedding anniversary; he got a big kick out of that. I think I always loved him in a special way.

Bob Palmer, my second husband, never remarried. He lived with his parents until they died and then continued living alone, supported by the state. He never stopped drinking and subsequently developed serious health problems; he ended up on dialysis and in a wheelchair. He continued to harass me for many years, but he had given me my beautiful daughter, Robin, the best thing he did in his sad and troubled life.

As for my relationship with my parents, my visits with them remained the anchor for my often-troubled life; I always lived for that next trip home. My father never changed: he continued his flirtatious ways, much to the embarrassment of the family. Mum's words still ring in my ears, 'There's no fool like an old fool,' but she never stopped being jealous.

Pete Huber and I lost touch after he moved to another

state. I wondered why I stopped hearing from him, and when I located and spoke to his brother Joe, he told me that Pete had died of leukaemia. I was deeply saddened to lose such a friend, and I will never forget his kindness to my children and me. Pete, with Dr Edward Crown, renewed my faith in humanity. They saved my life.

I am still in touch with Jodi Cortina and her daughter Vicki, who now live in Florida. Dominic, who was nicknamed Big Dom, The Hat and Large, died in 1999 of cancer at the age of seventy-four. His attorney, John C. Tucker (one of America's top criminal lawyers), wrote in his book *Trial and Error* of Dominic and his business partner Donald 'The Wizard of Odds' Angelini: 'We soon discovered that Donald and Dominic were delightful company and men of impeccable honesty and candor in their dealings with us. That was also their reputation with their betting clients, their employees, and even the FBI agents who had spent many years trying to catch and convict them.' Another comment I read, which made me grin, said: 'Cortina never was associated with the violent faction of organized crime. In fact, he and Angelini were known for not strong-arming clients but instead for treating them politely. In some cases, prosecutors said, the duo even suggested that their clients give up gambling for their own well-being.' Dominic was well respected and liked by all who knew him; he was indeed a gentle man.

Barbara, or Bobby, McCarthy, my very first GI bride friend, struggled to raise her two daughters following her divorce, but eventually remarried and became Mrs Stuart Oliver. We lost touch after she moved to California, but I was glad that she and her girls were happy and cared for. I later learned that she had remained an officer with the Transatlantic Brides and Parents (TBPA) until she died suddenly and tragically of a brain aneurysm.

Spiro T. and I continued our beautiful love affair until . . . Well, that's another story.

For now, let me leave you with my dear friend Woody Barlow, who wrote: 'I am still dealing with myself. I look forward to future moments of joy and grief – they seem to blend together over time in moments that give weight to reflection and oddly disconnected thoughts.' Thanks for allowing me to quote you, Woody; it seems to say it all for me as I arrive at yet another crossroads in my life. I don't know where the next road will take me, but I look forward, with optimism, to the ongoing journey.

Acknowledgements

To everyone who contributed and gave permission for me to share pieces of their stories and lives in *The GI Bride*: June Gradley Armstrong, Shirley Ashburn, Jodi Cortina, Vicki Annecca, Mary Nicholson, Cindy Ballmaier, my son Wayne Irvine, and my daughter Robin Palmer. To Valerie Bettag for providing a forum for local writers to share and improve their writing skills at the Sidmouth Writing Circle. To Alison Kerruish and Margaret Pilkington for their continued friendship and encouragement. To my editor Daniel Bunyard, for his patience, support, suggestions and encouragement; ditto to my dear friend Roger Stanley for his excellent feedback and suggestions. To my treasured writing friend Woody Barlow, who tells me he'd rather be pecked to death by a chicken than check every punctuation mark in a manuscript. Last, but by no means least, to my wonderful life partner, Ralph Brooks, who not only provides loving support and encouragement but also brings me cups of tea when I need them the most. Ralph, I finally picked a winner!

IRIS JONES SIMANTEL

FAR FROM THE EAST END

From the dirty streets of the East End to the Welsh countryside, will little evacuee Iris ever find somewhere to belong?

Born in 1938 under threat of looming war, Iris spent her early years playing in the rubble of bombed buildings in Dagenham by day and cowering in a dusty shelter at night. But the hardships of poverty and the dreaded Blitz could not match the pain she felt at her parents' indifference. She prayed that just once her mother would hold her when the bombs rained down. But loneliness only intensified when she was evacuated.

Finding the nurturing home she had always dreamt of in her adopted Welsh parents, she wonders what, when she returns to London after the war, will be waiting for her. Will she ever be able to love her philandering father, depressive mother and an angry, bullying brother? Will her family even survive? Or will she have to look farther afield for the affection she so longs for?

'A mesmerizing life story told by an extraordinary 74-year-old with an incredible zest for life' This is Exeter

'A natural and authentic voice, employing comedy, pathos and disarming honesty to depict a hotchpotch of family members' Saga Magazine

JEFF PEARCE

A POCKETFUL OF HOLES AND DREAMS

The poor boy who made his fortune . . . not just once but twice.

Little Jeff Pearce grew up in a post-war Liverpool slum. His father lived the life of an affluent gentleman whilst his mother was forced to steal bread to feed her starving children. Life was tough and from the moment Jeff could walk he learned to go door to door, begging rags from the rich, which he sold down the markets. Leaving school at the age of fourteen, he embarked on an extraordinary journey, and found himself, before the age of thirty, a millionaire.

Then, after a cruel twist of fate left him penniless, he, his wife and children were forced out of their beautiful home.

With nothing but holes in his pockets, Jeff had no alternative but to go back down the markets and start all over again. Did he still have what it took? Could he really get back everything he had lost?

A Pocketful of Holes and Dreams is the heartwarming true story of a little boy who had nothing but gained everything and proof that, sometimes, rags can be turned into riches . . .

CHRISTINE MARION FRASER

BLUE ABOVE THE CHIMNEYS

The wild childhood of a Glasgow tenement urchin

Born during the Second World War in Glasgow, Christine Fraser was her mother's eighth child. Growing up with her siblings in a tiny flat, learning to avoid her hardworking, hard-drinking one-eyed father, making a menace of herself in the streets along with the other urchins, Christine lived an impoverished life but never once cared. Until she was struck down by a terrible illness.

Suddenly, her wild days of childhood were over. A long spell in hospital completely changed her life. Now she found herself dependent on others for so many of her needs. And on top of that her mother and father died.

Yet Christine was always resourceful and never once looked down. She knew that always there, if you looked hard enough, was some blue up above the chimneys.

MOLLY WEIR

SHOES WERE FOR SUNDAY

'Poverty is a very exacting teacher and I had been taught well'

The post-war urban jungle of the Glasgow tenements was the setting for Molly Weir's childhood. From sharing a pull-out bed in her mother's tiny kitchen to running in terror from the fever van, it was an upbringing that was cemented in hardship. Hunger, cold and sickness was an everyday reality and complaining was not an option.

Despite the crippling poverty, there was a vivacity to the tenements that kept spirits high. Whether Molly was brushing the hair of her wizened neighbour Mrs MacKay, running to Jimmy's chip shop for a ha'penny of crimps or dancing at the annual fair, there wasn't a moment to spare for self-pity. Molly never let it get her down as she and the other urchins knew how to make do with nothing.

And at the centre of her world was her fearsome but loving Grannie, whose tough, independent spirit taught Molly to rise above her pitiful surroundings and achieve her dreams.

He just wanted a decent book to read ...

Not too much to ask, is it? It was in 1935 when Allen Lane, Managing Director of Bodley Head Publishers, stood on a platform at Exeter railway station looking for something good to read on his journey back to London. His choice was limited to popular magazines and poor-quality paperbacks – the same choice faced every day by the vast majority of readers, few of whom could afford hardbacks. Lane's disappointment and subsequent anger at the range of books generally available led him to found a company – and change the world. ·

'We believed in the existence in this country of a vast reading public for intelligent books at a low price, and staked everything on it'
Sir Allen Lane, 1902–1970, founder of Penguin Books

The quality paperback had arrived – and not just in bookshops. Lane was adamant that his Penguins should appear in chain stores and tobacconists, and should cost no more than a packet of cigarettes.

Reading habits (and cigarette prices) have changed since 1935, but Penguin still believes in publishing the best books for everybody to enjoy. We still believe that good design costs no more than bad design, and we still believe that quality books published passionately and responsibly make the world a better place.

So wherever you see the little bird – whether it's on a piece of prize-winning literary fiction or a celebrity autobiography, political tour de force or historical masterpiece, a serial-killer thriller, reference book, world classic or a piece of pure escapism – you can bet that it represents the very best that the genre has to offer.

Whatever you like to read – trust Penguin.